Insights to Performance Excellence 1998

Insights to Performance Excellence 1998

An Inside Look at the 1998 Baldrige Award Criteria

Mark L. Blazey

ASQ Quality Press
Milwaukee, Wisconsin

Insights to Performance Excellence 1998: An Inside Look at the 1998 Baldrige Award Criteria
Mark L. Blazey

Library of Congress Cataloging-in-Publication Data
Blazey, Mark L.
    Insights to performance excellence, 1998 : an inside look at the
1998 Baldrige Award criteria / Mark L. Blazey.
      p.   cm.
    Rev. ed. of: Insights to performance excellence, 1997.
    Includes index.
    ISBN 0–87389–380–8 (alk. paper)
    1. Total quality management—Awards—United States.
2. Benchmarking (Management)—United States.   3. Malcolm Baldrige
National Quality Award.   I. Blazey, Mark L.   Insights to
performance excellence, 1997. II. Title.
HD62.15.B58   1998   98-12442
658.5′62′07973—dc21   CIP

10 9 8 7 6 5 4 3 2 1

ISBN 0-87389-380-8

Acquisitions Editor: Roger Holloway
Project Editor: Jeanne W. Bohn

ASQ Mission: To facilitate continuous improvement and increase customer satisfaction by identifying, communicating, and promoting the use of quality principles, concepts, and technologies; and thereby be recognized throughout the world as the leading authority on, and champion for, quality.

Attention: Schools and Corporations
ASQ Quality Press books, audiotapes, videotapes, and software are available at quantity discounts with bulk purchases for business, educational, or instructional use. For information, please contact ASQ Quality Press at 800-248-1946, or write to ASQ Quality Press, P.O. Box 3005, Milwaukee, WI 53201-3005.

For a free copy of the ASQ Quality Press Publications Catalog, including ASQ membership information, call 800-248-1946.

Printed in the United States of America

 Printed on acid-free paper

American Society for Quality

Quality Press
611 East Wisconsin Avenue
Milwaukee, Wisconsin 53202

This book is dedicated to the memory of my father,
who taught me the value of continuous improvement,
and to my family, who provide support for the continuous search for quality: my mother, Ann Marrer Blazey;
my brothers Scott, Brian, and Brent; my children
Elizabeth and Mark; and most of all, my lifelong
partner and loving wife Karen.

Contents

Preface

A substantial portion of my recent professional life has been spent helping people become quality award examiners. These people come from all types of organizations and from all levels within those organizations. Participants include corporate quality directors, state organization chiefs, small business owners, heads of hospitals, and school superintendents, to name a few. This book was originally developed for them. It was used as a teaching text to guide their decisions and deliberations as they provided feedback to organizations that documented their continuous improvement efforts using Baldrige Award-type management systems. Many examiners who used this text asked me to publish it in a stand-alone format. They wanted to use it to help their own organizations, customers, and suppliers guide and assess their continuous improvement efforts.

These two groups of readers—examiners of quality systems and leaders of high performing organizations—can gain a competitive edge by understanding not only the parts of a high performance management system, but how these parts connect and align. My goal for this book is that readers will understand fully what each area of the quality system means for organizations and find the synergy within the seven major parts of the system: leadership, strategic planning, customer and market focus, information and analysis, human resource focus, process management, and business results.

Corporate and education leaders have reported that this book has been valuable as a step-by-step approach to help identify and put in place continuous improvement systems. As this progresses, improvement efforts in one area will lead to improvements in other areas. This process is similar to experiences we have all encountered as we carry out home improvement: Improve one area, and many other areas needing improvement become apparent. This book will help identify areas that need immediate improvement as well as areas that are less urgent but, nevertheless, vitally linked to overall improvement.

Acknowledgments

Curt Reimann, Harry Hertz, and the dedicated staff of the Malcolm Baldrige National Quality Award office have provided long-standing support and guidance in promoting quality excellence. I also appreciate the typing assistance and proofreading of Stephanie Adams. The book would not be possible in a timely fashion without the design and layout expertise, dedication, and commitment of Enterprise Design and Publishing, and the substantive contributions of valued friends and customers Russell Buyse of R. Buyse & Associates, Inc., Mary Gamble of Hellmuth, Obata, and Kassabaum (HOK) architects, Karen Davison of Quantum Performance Group, Inc., Jeff Martin of Business Systems Solutions, Maryann Brennan, John A. Pieno Jr., and Dione Geiger of the Florida Sterling Council, Mike Brown of Amoco, John Lawrence of Xerox Business Services, Ed Hare and April Mitchell of Air Products and Chemicals, George Bureau and Dan MacIntosh of Appleton Papers, Inc., Debra Danziger-Barron of Northern Trust Co., Jim Shipley of the Pinellas County Schools, Karen Hoffman of Baxter Healthcare Corporation, George Hoyt of AMP, Inc., Tom Kubiak of Honeywell, Inc., Beverly Centini of the Pennsylvania Quality Leadership Awards, Pat Billings of the Minnesota Quality Award, Wendy Brennan of First Union National Bank, Gerald Brown and Anne O'Brien of the Vermont Quality Award, and Wendy Staeger of the National Council for Performance Excellence. The chapter on site visits is used with permission of Quantum Performance Group, Inc. The core values, criteria, selected glossary terms, and background information in this book are drawn from the *Malcolm Baldrige National Quality Award 1998 Criteria for Performance Excellence.* Portions of the Organizational Assessment Survey are used with permission from the National Council for Performance Excellence.

—*Mark Blazey*

Introduction

The *Malcolm Baldrige National Quality Award 1998 Criteria for Performance Excellence* and scoring guidelines are powerful assessment instruments that help leaders identify organizational strengths and key areas for improvement. The primary task of leaders is then to use the information to achieve higher levels of performance.

Building an effective management system capable of driving performance improvement is an ongoing challenge because of the intricate web of complex relationships among management, labor, customers, stakeholders, partners, and suppliers. The best organizations have a management system that improves its work processes continually. They measure every key facet of business activity and closely monitor organizational performance. Leaders of these organizations set high expectations, value employees and their input, communicate clear directions, and align the work of everyone to achieve organizational goals and optimize performance.

Unfortunately, because of the complexity of modern management systems, the criteria used to examine them are also complex and difficult to understand. *Insights to Performance Excellence 1998* helps performance excellence examiners and organization improvement practitioners clearly understand the 1998 Baldrige performance excellence criteria and the linkages and relationships between the items.

Five types of information are provided in this book for each of the 20 items that comprise the criteria.
- **The actual language of each item, including notes.**
- **A *plain English* explanation of the essence of the item** with some suggestions about meeting key requirements.
- **A summary of the requirements of the item in flowchart form.** The flowcharts capture the essence of each item and isolate the requirements of each item to help organizations focus on the key points the item is assessing. Note that most boxes in the flowcharts contain an item reference in brackets [ ]. This indicates that the criteria require the action. If there is no item reference in brackets, it means the action is suggested but not required. Occasionally a reference to "[scoring guidelines]" is included in a box. This means that, according to the scoring guidelines, the requirement to evaluate and refine a process is required to score above the 50 percent level.

- **The key linkages between each item and the other items.** The major or primary linkages are designated using a solid arrow (———►). The secondary linkages are designated using a dashed arrow (- - - - ►).
- **Examples of effective practices that some organizations have developed and followed.** These samples present some ideas about how to meet requirements. Examiners should not take these sample effective practices and convert them into requirements for organizations they are examining.

Several changes have been made to this 1998 edition.
- A few significant changes in this edition were required by changes in the Baldrige criteria. Changes have been made in the flow diagrams and the linkages between the items.
- An explanation of the changes in the criteria between 1997 and 1998 is provided in this edition.
- Primary and secondary linkages between the items have been defined.
- The first section of the book has been expanded to include a broader rationale for using the Baldrige criteria to improve organization performance, as well as more lessons learned from using the criteria.
- A new section has been added to guide organizations through a streamlined self-assessment process.

Taken together, *Insights to Performance Excellence 1998* will strengthen your understanding of the criteria and provide insight on analyzing your organization, improving performance, and applying for the award.

Insights to Performance Excellence

This section provides information for leaders who are transforming their organizations to achieve performance excellence. This section
- Presents a business case for using the Baldrige criteria to improve organizational performance.
- Describes the core values that drive organizational change to high levels of performance and underlie the Baldrige criteria.
- Provides practical insights and lessons learned—ideas on transition strategies to put high performance systems in place and promote organizational learning. This section emphasizes themes driven by the 1998 criteria and core values. It also includes suggestions about how to start down the path to systematic organizational improvement, as well as lessons learned from those who chose paths that led nowhere or proved futile despite their best efforts.

The Business Case for Using the Baldrige Performance Excellence Criteria

The journey of change an organization embarks upon when it embraces the basic values of high performing organizations promises to be marked by storms and perils. All leaders know that change is tough. Because they know they will be asked and perhaps tempted to turn back many times, they appreciate improvement examples from organizations that are ahead of them on the journey. These are organizations that have held the course despite rough waters and internal attempts at mutiny.

This section of the book describes some public and private sector organizations that have gained ground and made rapid strides forward on their journeys. It then identifies the core values that have guided these organizations to achieve high levels of performance excellence.

These high performing organizations outrun their competition by delivering ever-increasing value to stakeholders through an unwavering focus on customers and improved organizational capabilities. Examples of improved capabilities have occurred in all sectors of the economy, not just the private sector. These results range from time and cost savings to customer retention and loyalty.
- Government agencies have registered impressive improvements. The Air Force Material Command, winner of the President's Quality

Award, modified repair procedures resulting in savings of $10,000,000 per year. Rework on landing gear maintenance went from 90 percent to 0 percent in one year. In four years they saved nearly $2,000,000,000 by involving contractors in identifying systems changes to save money.

- Xerox Business Services (XBS), a 1997 Baldrige winner, provides document services throughout the world. XBS increased revenues more than 30 percent annually, growing into a $2 billion business in less than five years.

- ADAC Laboratories of California, a 1996 Baldrige Award winner, designs, manufactures, markets and supports products for health care customers. Customer retention increased from 70 to 90 percent during the past five years. Since 1990, average cycle time declined from 56 hours to 17 hours and revenue tripled.

- For the past two years, Trident Precision Manufacturing, another 1996 Baldrige Award winner, has experienced zero defects in its custom products. Trident's quality rating for its major customers (based on customer reports) is higher than 99.8 percent.

- Wainwright Industries, a 1994 Baldrige winner, cut the time for making one of its principal extruded products from 8.75 days to 15 minutes, and reduced defect rates tenfold.

- Cadillac, a 1990 winner, reduced the time for die changes in its stamping plant from eight hours to four minutes by redesigning the entire process.

- Corning Telecommunications Products Division, a 1995 Baldrige Award winner, has become the world market leader and the low-cost provider, and has earned the highest customer satisfaction ratings in the industry by far.

- In five years, Solectron Corporation, a 1991 and 1997 Baldrige winner, experienced a sales increase from $130 million to $3.7 billion, representing a 2,800 percent improvement. Net profits soared more than tenfold. Market share doubled since 1992. The stock price went up sixty fold since 1989.

- At Federal Express, a 1989 Baldrige winner, cost per package was cut by more than 40 percent.

- At Motorola, a 1988 winner, production of a new pager begins within moments of a new customer placing an order, and the new pager is ready to ship within one hour.

- Globe Metallurgical, Inc., a 1988 Baldrige winner, experienced a 60 percent increase in revenues and a 40 percent increase in profits since 1992.

- Ames Rubber Corporation, a 1993 Baldrige winner, achieved a 99.9 percent quality and on-time delivery status through sharing quality techniques with suppliers.

- AT&T Consumer Communications, a 1994 Baldrige winner, listened to its customers and received its largest customer response ever in a short time frame to its "True" marketing program.
- AT&T Transmission Sales Business Unit, a 1992 winner, achieved a tenfold improvement in equipment quality and a 50 percent reduction in cycle time that saved $400 million over six years.

Similar findings are appearing throughout the world as organizations use the Baldrige performance excellence criteria to manage their businesses.

As expected, organizations demonstrating these performance results also do better on the stock market—a lot better! According to an October 18, 1993 Business Week study, the three publicly traded, whole company Baldrige Award winners outperformed the Standard & Poor's 500 from the time of their winning through September 30, 1993, by 8.6 to 1.

The Baldrige Award office in the U.S. Department of Commerce found similar results in recent studies.

- They "invested" a hypothetical sum of money in each of the publicly-traded whole companies that won the Baldrige Award since 1988. They tracked the investment from the first business day of the month following the announcement of the Baldrige winners' award (or the date they began trading publically), to December 1, 1997. Adjustments were made for stock splits. The results, released in February 1998 at the 10th Quest for Excellence Conference, showed that the publicly traded Baldrige-winning companies outperformed the S&P 500 by a 2.7 to 1 margin, achieving a 394.5 percent return on investment compared to 146.9 percent for the S&P 500.
- The Baldrige Award office also tracked a similar investment for the 52 publicly traded applicants that received Baldrige Award site visits. As a group, they outperformed the S&P 500 by approximately 80 percent, achieving a 216.0 percent return compared to 118.7 percent for the S&P 500.

The Core Values to Achieve Performance Excellence

Today, approximately 40 states and a dozen countries worldwide use the Baldrige criteria to identify performance excellence in businesses, schools, health care facilities, and government agencies. These organizations find that the performance excellence criteria help guide them through difficult management decisions on their endless journeys. Their actions and policies are driven by a consistent set of core values.

The Baldrige performance excellence criteria are built on a powerful set of common values that characterize high performing organizations. This section identifies the 11 core values that underlie the criteria. These values bind an organization together and yield high performance. High performing organizations deliver ever-increasing value to stakeholders by improving organizational capabilities.

These core values are critical for successful organizations of any size and in any sector—from small mom-and-pop shops to hospitals, government agencies, public utilities, schools, and businesses.

By adopting these values, organizations can optimize their performance. As competition gets tougher, nothing less than optimization will do. No organization will be immune from the ravages of poor quality, suboptimization, and failing to satisfy customers.

The first value is a passion for **customer-driven quality.** Without this, little else matters. Customers are the final judges of how well the organization did its job, and what they say counts. It is their perception of the service and product that will determine whether they remain loyal or constantly seek better providers.
  • Organization personnel must systematically listen to customers and act quickly on what they say.
  • Dissatisfied customers must be heeded most closely, for they often deliver the most valuable information.
  • If only satisfied and loyal customers (those who continue to do business with us no matter what) are paid attention, the organization will be led astray. The most successful organizations keep an eye on customers who are not satisfied and work to understand their preferences and meet their demands.

The most potent value is **continuous improvement and learning.** High performing organizations are learning organizations—they create a culture of seeking to evaluate and improve everything they do. They strive to get better at getting better.
  • A culture of continuous improvement is essential to maintaining and sustaining true competitive advantage.
  • Without systematic improvement and ongoing learning, organizations will ultimately face extinction.
  • With systematic continuous improvement, time becomes a powerful ally. As time passes, the organization grows stronger and smarter.

Management by fact is the cornerstone value for effective planning, operational decision making at all levels, employee involvement, and leadership.

- Everyone makes decisions every day. However, without data, the basis for decision making is intuition—gut feel.
- Most drivers decide when to fill their fuel tanks based on data from the fuel gauge and get very uncomfortable if the gauge is broken. Yet people routinely make decisions of enormous consequence about customers, strategies, goals, and employees with little or no data. This is a recipe for disaster, not one designed to ensure optimization.

Organizations must invest in their people to ensure they have the skills for today and for the future. This core value has broadened from employee participation and development to **valuing employees.** In high performing organizations, the people who do the work of the organization should make most of the decisions about how the work is done. However, a significant barrier exists that limits employee decision making—access to data and poor data-based decision-making skills.

- Leaders are unwilling to let subordinates make decisions based on intuition—they reserve that type of decision for themselves.
- Therefore, access to data and developing skills to manage by fact is a prerequisite for optimizing employee contributions to the organization's success.
- Organizations cannot effectively push decision making down to the level where most of the work is done unless those doing the work have access to the necessary data and are skilled at making fact-based decisions.

Fast response is a value usually driven by customer requirements and the desire to improve operating efficiency and lower costs.

- Except for a few pleasurable experiences, everyone wants things faster.
- Organizations that develop the capacity to respond faster by eliminating activities and tasks that do not add value, find that productivity increases, costs go down, and customers are more loyal.
- Analyzing and improving work processes enables organizations to perform better, faster, and cheaper.
- To improve work processes, organizations need to focus on improving design quality and preventing problems. The cost of preventing problems and building quality into products and services is significantly less than the cost of taking corrective action later.
- It is critical to emphasize capturing learning from other design projects.
- Use information concerning customer preference, competitors products, cost and pricing, marketplace profiles, and research and development (R&D) to optimize the process from the start.
- Public responsibility issues and factors including environmental demands must be included in the design stage.

To remain competitive, every organization must be guided by a common set of **measurable goals** and **a long-range view of the future.**
- These measurable goals, which emerge from the strategic planning process, serve to align the work of everyone in the organization.
- Measurable goals allow everyone to know where they are going and when they deviate from their path.
- Without measurable goals, everyone still works hard, but they go in different directions—suboptimizing the success of the organization.

Achieving long-range goals is increasingly difficult without internal and external **partnership development.**
- Internal partnership agreements with workers, including labor unions and other units as appropriate, must be created and strengthened.
- External alliances and strategic partnerships are key to enhancing overall capabilities quickly. Such partnerships characterize high performing organizations that think strategically about maximizing performance for their customers.

Every high-performing organization practices good **corporate responsibility and citizenship.**
- Organizations must determine and anticipate any adverse effects to the public of their products, services, and operations. Failure to do so can undermine public trust and distract workers, and also adversely affect the bottom line. This is true of both private and public organizations.
- Safety and legal requirements need to be met beyond mere compliance.

A **results focus** helps organizations communicate requirements, monitor actual performance, make adjustments in priorities, and reallocate resources. Without a results focus, organizations can become fixated on processes and lose sight of the important factors for success.

Every system, strategy, and method for achieving excellence must be guided by effective **leadership.**
- Effective leaders convey a strong sense of urgency to counter the natural resistance to change that can prevent the organization from taking the steps that these core values for success demand.
- Such leaders serve as enthusiastic role models, reinforcing and communicating the core values by their words and actions. Words alone are not enough.

There are always better ways to do things. Our challenge is to find them, but we are not likely to find them alone. We must create an environment—a work climate where better ways will be sought out, recognized, and put in place by everyone.

Practical Insights

Connections and Linkages

A popular children's activity, connect the dots, helps them understand that, when properly connected, apparently random dots create a meaningful picture. In many ways, the 7 categories, 20 items, and 29 areas to address in the Baldrige criteria are like the dots that must be connected to reveal a meaningful picture. With no paths to make the web, or join the dots, human resource development and use are not related to strategic planning; information and analysis are isolated from process management; and overall improvement efforts are disjointed, fragmented, and do not yield robust results. This book describes the *linkages* for and between each item. The exciting part about having them identified is you can look for these linkages in your own organization and, if they don't exist, start building them.

Transition Strategies

Putting high performance management systems in place is a major commitment that will not happen quickly. At the beginning, you will need a transition strategy to get you across the bridge from management by opinion or intuition to more data-driven management. The next part of this section describes one approach that has worked for many organizations in various sectors: creating a performance improvement council.

Performance Improvement Council

Identify a top-level executive leadership group of 6 to 10 members. Each member over that number will seem to double the complexity of issues and make decision making much more cumbersome. The executive leadership group could send a message to the entire organization by naming the group the performance improvement council—reinforcing the importance of continuous performance improvement to the future success of the organization.

The performance improvement council should be the primary policy-making body for the organization. It should spawn other performance improvement councils at lower levels to share practices and policies with every employee in the organization as well as to involve customers and suppliers. The structure permeates the organization as members of the performance improvement council become area leaders for major improvement efforts and sponsors for several process or continuous improvement task teams throughout the organization. The council structure, networked and cascaded fully, can effectively align the work and optimize performance at all levels and across all functions.

Council Membership

Selecting members for the performance improvement council should be done carefully. Each member should be essential for the success of the operation, and together they must be sufficient for success. The most important member is the senior leader of the organization or work unit. This person must participate actively, demonstrating the kind of leadership that all should emulate. Of particular importance is a commitment to consensus building as the modus operandi for the council. This tool, a core of performance improvement programs, is often overlooked by leadership. Other council members selected should have leadership responsibility for broad areas of the organization such as human resources, operations planning, customers, and data systems.

Performance Improvement Council Learning and Planning

The performance improvement council should be extremely knowledgeable about high performance management systems. If not, as is often the case, performance improvement council members should be among the first in the organization to learn about continuous improvement tools and processes.

To be effective, every member of the council (and every member in the organization) must understand the Baldrige criteria because the criteria describe the components of the entire management system. Participation in examiner training has proved to be the very best way to understand the complexities of the system needed to achieve performance excellence. Any additional training beyond this should be carried out in the context of planning—that is, learn tools and use them to plan the performance improvement implementation, practices, and policies.

The performance improvement council should
- Develop an integrated, continuous improvement strategic performance improvement and business plan.
- Create the web (communication plan and infrastructure) to transmit performance improvement policies throughout the organization.
- Define the roles of employees, including new recognition and reward structures to cause needed behavioral changes.
- Develop a master training and development plan. Involve team representatives in planning so they can learn skills close to when they are needed. Define what is provided to whom, and when and how success will be measured.
- Launch improvement projects that will produce both short- and long-term successes. Improvement projects should be clearly defined by the performance improvement council and driven by the strategic plan. Typical improvement projects include important human resource processes such as career development, performance measurement, and diversity, as well as improving operational products and services in the line areas.
- Develop a plan to communicate the progress and successes of the organization. Through this approach, the need for performance improvement processes is consistently communicated to all employees. Barriers to optimum performance are weakened and eliminated.

The Critical Skills

A uniform message, set of skills or core competencies, and constancy of purpose are critical to success. Core training should provide all employees with the knowledge and skills on which to build a learning organization that continually gets better. Such training typically includes team building, leadership skills, consensus building, communications, and effective meeting management. These are necessary for effective teams to become involved in solving critical problems.

Another important core skill involves using a common process to define customer requirements accurately, determining the ability to meet those requirements, measure success, and determine the extent to which customers—internal and external—are satisfied. When a problem arises, employees must be able to define the problem correctly, isolate the root causes, generate and select the best solution to eliminate the root causes, and implement the best solution.

It is also important to be able to understand data and make decisions based on facts, not merely intuition or feelings. Therefore, familiarity with tools to analyze work processes and performance data is important. With these tools, work processes can be analyzed and vastly improved. Reducing unnecessary steps in work processes, increasing process consistency, reducing variability, and reducing cycle time are powerful ways to improve quality and reduce cost simultaneously.

Courses in techniques to acquire comparison and benchmarking data, work process improvement and reengineering, supplier partnerships and certification, role modeling for leaders' strategic planning, and customer satisfaction and loyalty will help managers and employees expand their optimization and high performance thrust across the entire organization.

Lessons Learned

Twenty years ago the fierce global competition that inspired the quality movement in the United States was felt primarily by major manufacturers. Today, all sectors are under intense pressure to "be the best or be history." The demand for performance excellence reaches all corners of the economy, from manufacturing and service industries to professional services, education, health care, public utilities, and government. All of these segments have contributed valuable lessons to the quality movement and have played an important part in our recovery from the economic slump caused by poor service and products of the 1970s. Relying on the Baldrige model, we will share some of the insights and lessons learned from leaders of high performing organizations.

Leadership

Great Leaders Are Great Communicators Who Lead by Example

One characteristic of a high performance organization is outstanding performance results. How does an organization achieve such results? How does it become world-class? While no scientific studies have been able to document a single road that leads to such success, we have found unanimous agreement on the critical and fundamental role of leadership. There is not one example of an organization or unit within an organization that achieves profound improvement without the personal and active involvement of its top leadership. Top leaders in these organizations create a powerful vision that focuses and energizes the work force. Everyone is pulling together toward the same goals. Frequently, an inspired vision is the catalyst that overcomes the organizational status quo.

Great leaders are great communicators. They identify clear objectives and a game plan so the organization succeeds in its mission. They assign accountability, ensure that employees have the tools and skills required, and create a work climate where transfer of learning occurs. They reward teamwork and data-driven improvement. While practicing what they preach they serve as role models for continuous improvement, consensus building, fact-based decision making, and push authority and accountability to the lowest possible levels.

One lesson from great leaders is to minimize the use of the word *quality*. Too often, when skilled, hard-working, dedicated employees are told by leaders, "We are going to start a quality effort," they conclude that their leaders believe they have not been working hard enough. The work force hears an unintended message, "We have to do this because we are not good." They frequently retort with, "We already do quality work!" Registered professionals (engineers, chemists, psychologists, physicians, teachers) often exacerbate the communication problem by arguing that they, not customers, are the only ones is a position to know and define "quality." These messages confuse the work force. Unfortunately, the use of the word *quality* can create an unintended barrier of mistrust and negativism that leaders must overcome before even starting on the road to performance excellence.

As an alternative, we advise leaders to create a work climate that enables employees to develop and use their full potential, to improve continually the way they work—to seek higher performance levels and reduce activities that do not add value or optimize performance. Most employees readily agree that there is always room for improvement.

The use of the word *quality* can also open leadership to challenges as to what definition of quality the organization should use. This leads to our second lesson learned.

Leaders will have to overcome two organizational tendencies—to reject any quality model or theory "not invented here" and to think that there are many equally valid models. Quality differs from a decision tree or problem-solving model where there are many acceptable alternatives. The Baldrige model— and the many national, state, and organization assessment systems based on it—is accepted worldwide as the standard for defining performance excellence in organizations worldwide. Its criteria provide validated, leading-edge practices for managing an organization. A decade of extraordinary business results shown by Baldrige Award winners and numerous state-level, Baldrige Award-based winners have helped convince those willing to learn and listen.

To be effective, leaders must understand the Baldrige model and communicate to the work force and leadership system their intention to use that model for assessment and improvement. Without clear leadership commitment to achieving the requirements of the comprehensive Baldrige model, resources may be spent chasing facts, narrow focuses, and isolated strategies such as reengineering, quality circles, and ISO 9000 certification, to name a few. Without clear leadership there will be many "hikers" walking around but no marked trails for them to follow. Once leaders understand the system and realize that it is their responsibility to share the knowledge and mark the trails clearly, performance optimization is attainable. This brings us to our third leadership lesson learned.

A significant portion of senior leaders' time—as much as 60 percent to 80 percent—should be spent in visible Baldrige-related leadership activities such as goal setting, planning, reviewing performance, recognizing and rewarding high performance, and spending time understanding and communicating with customers and suppliers, not micro-managing subordinates' work. The senior leaders' perspective in goal setting, planning, and reviewing performance must look at the inside from the outside. Looking at the organization through the critical eyes of external customers, suppliers, and other stakeholders is a vital perspective.

The primary role of the effective senior leader is not to manage internal operations, but rather to be visionary and focus the organization on satisfying customers through an effective leadership system. Leaders must role model the tools of consensus building and decision making as the organization focuses on its vision, mission, and strategic direction to keep customers loyal.

Falling back on command-and-control behavior will be self-defeating. The leadership system will suffer from crossed wires and mixed messages. Commandments such as "I want this mission rolled out by the end of the second quarter" fall into the self-defeating, major mistake category.

Using the consensus approach to focus the organization on its mission and vision will take longer, of course. However, this is similar to taking more time during the product design phase to ensure that problems are prevented later. The additional time is necessary for organizational learning, support, and buy-in, particularly around two areas—integrating global marketplace realities and better understanding the competitive environment. The resulting vision will have more depth. The leadership system will be stronger. Finally, the deployment of the vision and focus will take a shorter time because of the buy-in and support created during the process.

L is for Listen

Successful leaders know the power in listening to their people—those they rely on to achieve their goals. One vital link to the pulse of the organization is employee feedback. To know whether what you have said has been heard, ask for feedback and then listen carefully. To know whether what you have outlined as a plan makes sense or has gaping faults, ask for feedback and then listen. Your leadership system, cannot improve without your listening and acting on employee feedback and in fact, your goals and action plans cannot be improved without it. In fact, the 1998 Baldrige criteria [Item 1.1a(2)] specifically examines the extent to which leaders use employee feedback in assessing and improving the leadership system.

Manage and Drive Change

Business leaders can count on relentless, rapid change being part of the business world. The rate of change confronting business today is far faster than that driven by the Industrial Revolution. Skills driven by the Industrial Revolution carried our parents through a 40-year work cycle. Today, our children are told to expect five career (not job) changes during their work life. Human knowledge now doubles every 5 to 7 years, instead of the 40 years it took in the 1930s.

There are several lessons for leaders today. Change may not occur on the schedule they set for it. It is often faster or too uneven to predict at all. Also, change driven by leaders is often resisted by those most successful—they have difficulty seeing the need to change. Take for example, a school district that scheduled a quality improvement workshop for its middle school faculty. The day before the training, the district leadership received a letter protesting the workshop on the grounds it was not needed. The letter was signed by the 20 best teachers in the school. To the credit of the school district leadership, they held the workshop anyway, and the truly outstanding teachers saw the value in continuous improvement.

Leaders who hold the values of high performance will need to drive change to make the necessary improvements. Embracing the concepts of organizational learning (not just individual) will facilitate change in the organization.

Leaders will need organizational learning as an ally as they manage change and drive it through the organization.

Strategic Planning

Deploy Through People Not Paper

Strategic Planning is Performance Improvement Planning, Deployment, and Implementation. The organization's strategic plan is also its quality—business, human resources—performance improvement plan. Easily enough said, but trying to get agreement on exactly what strategic planning is will result in an interesting variety of ideas. Therefore, the planning process should begin by ensuring that all contributors agree on terminology. Otherwise the strategic plan may in fact be incomplete—a marketing plan, a budget plan, or a financial business plan, depending on who is leading the team.

Developing separate plans for each aspect of business success is counterproductive. It guarantees a nonintegrated and short-lived systematic performance improvement effort. Therefore, leaders should concentrate on the few critical improvement goals in the strategic plan necessary for organizational success, such as improving customer loyalty and reducing errors or cycle time. The well-developed strategic plan also
* Documents the financial impact of achieving these few goals
* Details actions to support the goals
* Discusses the competitive environment that drives the goals

One highly successful organization simplified this document to a single electronic page, to which senior leaders referred each month by computer during performance results reviews.

The most critical lesson learned when it comes to strategic plans is that there can be no rest until it is certain every person in the organization knows the strategic plan and can describe how he or she contributes to achieving the plan's goals and objectives. Remember the hiking analogy: *Don't let hikers onto the trails until they all know where they are going, what they have to do to get there, and how to measure progress so that they know they are going in the right direction and maintaining satisfactory progress.* The same basic principles apply to running a high performance organization.

A standard technique used by examiners is to meet with the chief executive officer to gain an understanding of the personal vision and plan for the organization. The examiner then interviews the receptionist and many others at all levels, asking them to explain the organization's vision and plan and their role in achieving the plan. In high performance organizations, the examiner gets a consistent story from people at all levels. Additionally, the examiner gets a sense that the vision and plan are real and attainable. Deployment of the strategy happens through people, not paper.

In any case,
- Ensure that the strategic plan does not merely rest in a prominent position on the bookshelves of top managers.
- Ensure that it is used to drive and guide actions and is understood by all.

If these actions are not taken, work will not be aligned. People may work hard, but are likely to pull in many directions. This scenario leads to nonproductive pet projects and programs competing for time and other resources. It is critical to get everyone in the work force pulling in the same direction.

Customer and Market Focus

Customers Expect Solutions to Problems They Don't Know They Have

The high-performing organization systematically determines its customers' short-term and long-term service and product requirements. It does this based on information from former as well as current and potential customers. It builds relationships with customers and continuously obtains information, using it to improve its service and products and understand better customer preferences. The smart organization determines the drivers of satisfaction and loyalty of its customers, compares itself to its competitors, and continuously strives to improve its satisfaction and loyalty levels.

As the organization becomes more and more systematic and effective in determining customer needs, it learns that there is high variation in customer needs. The more sophisticated the measurement system, the more variation will become apparent. It is particularly important that organizations focus on this vital process and make it a top priority that their customers have access to people to make known their requirements and their preferences. How else can modern organizations ensure they are building relationships with their customers—after all, few of us have store front windows on Main Street where our customers come and chat regularly.

One specific lesson learned comes from voice mail—a big step forward in convenience and efficiency can be a big step backward in customer relationship building if used poorly. For example, a major international financial institution put their highest priority customers on a new voice mail system. Customers were never informed about the system and one day called their special line to find rock music and a three tiered voice mail system instead of their personal financial account manager. This is a good example of a step in the wrong direction—customers were never asked about their requirements and preferences and the organization heard about it quickly in the form of lost accounts and angry, frustrated customers.

Another important first lesson is to segment customers according to their needs and preferences and do what is necessary to build strong, positive relationships with them. More and more customers are looking for service providers to define their unique needs for them and respond to those unique needs. In short, customers are expecting solutions to problems that they, the customers, have not yet realized.

Organizations that make it easy for customers to complain are in a good position to hear about problems early so that they can fix them and plan ahead to prevent them. If organizations handle customer complaints effectively at the first point of contact, customer loyalty and satisfaction will increase. When organizations do not make it easy for customers to complain, when finally given the chance to provide feedback, they will not bother to complain; they simply will no longer do business with these organizations.

As the customer-focused organization matures, it will likely evolve around customer types. This evolution leads to restructuring that is guided by shared organizational values. The speed with which this restructuring occurs varies according to marketplace conditions and the organization's ability to change. Today we see more restructuring that eliminates parochial, regional centers in favor of creating customer service groups that meet customer requirements around the world using up-to-date technologies.

The next lesson has to do with educating the organization's leadership in the fundamentals of customer loyalty and customer satisfaction research models before beginning to collect customer satisfaction data. Failure to do this may affect the usefulness of the data as a strategic tool. At the very least, it will make the development of data collection instruments a long, misunderstood effort, creating rework and unnecessary cost.

Do not expect everyone to welcome customer feedback—many fear accountability. Time and time again, the organizations most resistant to surveying customers, conducting focus groups, and making it easy for customers to complain are the same organizations that do not have everyday contact handling systems, response time standards, or trained and empowered frontline employees to serve customers and deal with their concerns promptly. Frontline employees who are not ready to acknowledge customer concerns are not capable of assuming responsibility to solve customer problems.

No single feedback tool is intended to stand alone. A mail-based survey does not take the place of personal interviews. Focus groups do not replace surveys. The high performance organization uses multiple listening posts and trains frontline employees to collect customer feedback and improve those listening posts. In the high performance organization, for example, even an accounts receivable system is viewed as a listening post.

Do not lose sight of the fact that the best customer feedback method, whether it be a survey, focus group, or one-on-one interview, is only a tool.
- Make sure the data gathered are actionable.
- Aggregate the data from all sources to permit complete analyses.
- Use the data to improve strategic planning and operating processes.

Finally, be aware that customers are not interested in your problems. They merely want products or services delivered as promised. They become loyal when consistent value is provided that sets you above all others. Merely meeting their basic expectations brands you as marginal. To be valued you must consistently delight and exceed the customers' expectations.

Information and Analysis

Data-Driven Management and Avoiding Contephobia

The high performance organization collects, manages, and analyzes data and information to drive excellence and improve its overall performance. Said another way, information is used to drive actions. Using data and information as strategic weapons, effective leaders compare their organization constantly to competitors, similar service providers, and world-class organizations.

While people tend to think of data and measurement as objective and hard, there is often a softer by-product of measurement. That by-product is the basic human emotion of fear. This perspective on data and measurement leads to the first lesson learned about information and analysis. Human fear must be recognized and managed in order to practice data-driven management.

This fear can be found in two types of people. The first are those who have a simple fear of numbers—those who hated mathematics in school and probably stretch their quantitative capabilities to balance their checkbook. These individuals are lost in numerical data discussions. When asked to measure or when presented with data, they can become fearful, angry, and resistant. Their reactions can actually undermine improvement efforts.

The second type of individual, who understands numbers, realizes that numbers can impose higher levels of accountability. The fear of accountability, *contephobia* (from fourteenth-century Latin *to count*, modified by the French *to account*), is based on the fear of real performance failure that numbers might reveal or, more often, an overall fear of the unknown that will drive important decisions. Power structures can and do shift when decisions are data-driven.

Fearful individuals can undermine effective data-driven management systems. In managing this fear, leaders must believe and communicate through their behavior that a number is not inherently right or wrong. It is important for leaders at all levels to demonstrate that system and process improvement, not individuals, are the focus of performance improvement.

A mature, high performance organization will collect data on competitors and similar providers and benchmark itself against world-class leaders. Some individuals may not be capable of seeing the benefit of using this process performance information. This type of data is known as benchmarking data. The focus is on identifying, learning from, and adopting best practices or methods from similar processes, regardless of industry or product similarity. Adopting the best practices of other organizations has driven quantum leap improvements and provided great opportunities for breakthrough improvements.

Lesson number two, therefore, is that an organization that has difficulty comparing itself with dissimilar organizations is not ready to benchmark and is not likely to be able to optimize its own performance as a result.

The third lesson in this area relates to not being a DRIP. This refers to a tendency to collect so much data (which contributes to contephobia) that the organization becomes underline{d}ata underline{r}ich and underline{i}nformation underline{p}oor. This is wrong. Avoid wasting capital resources and stretch the resources available for managing improvement by asking this question: "Will these data help make improvements for our customers, key financials, employees, or top result areas?" If the answer is no, do not waste time collecting, analyzing, and trying to use the data.

Human Resource Focus

Human Resource (Not the Department)

Personnel departments have been renamed in many organizations, often to "human resources." This name change often draws attention to the fact that people are valuable resources of the organization, not just commodities to be hired and fired and filed. Now, however, the leap made by successful organizations is that human resources need to be part of every strategic and operational decision of the organization. This focus goes far beyond the department of human resources. In high-performing organizations, employees are treated like any valuable asset of the organization—investment and development are critical to optimize the asset. Human resources should be perceived as internal customers, and a vital part of the supply chain that eventually serve an external customer.

One of the valuable lessons learned in this regard is not to let an out-of-date or territorial "personnel or human resources department" use archaic rules to stop your performance improvement program. Although many human resources professionals are among the brave pioneers in high performance organizations, others have tried to keep compensation and promotions tied to "seat time" rather than performance. This outdated approach will definitely stop progress in its tracks.

Another area human resources may try to influence is training and development, where they may insist on tying course offerings to their traditional schedule rather than "just in time learning," and content to tradition (we've always offered this and its been quite a hit), rather than pressing organizational needs of the future.

The Big Challenge Is Trust

The high-performing organization values its employees and demonstrates this by enabling people to develop and realize their full potential while providing them incentives to do so. The organization that is focused on human resource excellence maintains a climate that builds trust. Trust is essential for employee participation, engagement, personal and professional growth, and high organizational performance.

The first human resource lesson is perhaps the most critical one. That is, revise—overhaul, if necessary—recognition, compensation, promotion, and feedback systems to support high performance work systems. If leaders personally demonstrate all the correct leadership behaviors, yet continue to recognize and reward "fire fighting" performance, offer pay and bonuses tied only to traditional bottom-line results, and promote individuals who do not represent high-performance role models—those leaders will find their improvement effort is short-lived. The leadership system with all its webs and intricate circuits will short out due to mixed signals.

Promotion, compensation, recognition, and reward must be tied to the achievement of key business results, including customer satisfaction, innovation, and performance improvement. The promotion/compensation tool is a powerful tool in aligning, or misaligning, the work of the organization.

A second human resource lesson learned relates to training and development. Training is not a panacea or a goal in itself. The organization's direction and goals must support training, and training must support organization priorities. Its human resources are the competitive edge of a high performing organization. Training must be part of an overall business strategy. If not, money and resources are probably better spent on a memorable holiday party.

Timing is critical. Broad-based work force skill training should not come first. Many organizations rush out and train their entire work force only to find themselves having to retrain months or years later. Key participants should be involved in planning skill training so that important skills are delivered just in time for them to use in their assignments.

Continuous skill development requires management support to reinforce and strengthen skills on the job. Leadership development at all levels of the organization needs to be built into employee development. New technology has increased training flexibility so that all knowledge does not have to be transferred in a classroom setting. Consider many options when planning how best to update skills. After initial skill building occurs, high-performing organizations emphasize organizational learning where employees take charge of their own learning, using training courses as only one avenue for skill upgrading. Transferring learning to other parts of the organization or projects is a valuable organizational learning strategy and reinforcement technique. Training must be offered when an application exists to use and reinforce the skill. Otherwise, most of what is learned will be forgotten. The effectiveness of training must be assessed based on the impact on the job, not merely the likability of the instructor or the clarity of course materials.

Employee surveys are often used to measure employee satisfaction and improve employee satisfaction. Surveys are especially useful to identify key issues that should be discussed in open employee forums. Such forums are truly useful if they clarify perceptions, provide more in-depth understanding of employee concerns, and open the communication channels with leaders. Organizations have success in improving employee satisfaction by conducting routine employee satisfaction surveys, meeting with employees to plan improvements, and tying improvements in satisfaction ratings to managers' compensation.

Two final human resource excellence lessons have to do with engaging and involving employees in decisions about their work. Involving employees in decision making without the right skills or a sense of direction produces chaos, not high performance.

- First, leaders who empower employees before communicating and testing that a sense of direction has been fully understood will find that they are managing chaos.
- Second, not everyone wants to be empowered, and to do so represents a barrier to high performance. While there may be individuals who truly seek to avoid responsibility for making improvements, claiming "that's management's job," these individuals do not last long in a high-performing organization. They begin to stick out like a lone bird in the winter. Team members who want the organization to thrive and survive do not permit such people to influence (or even remain on) their team.

The bigger reason for individuals failing to "take the empowerment and run with it" is management's mixed messages. In short, management must convince employees that they (managers) really believe that employees know their own processes best and can improve them. Consistent leadership is required to help employees overcome legitimate, long-standing fear of traditional management practices used so often in the past to control and punish.

Remember, aligning compensation and reward systems to reinforce performance plans and core values is one of the most critical things to enhance organizational performance; however, getting employees to believe their leaders really trust them to improve their own processes is difficult.

Process Management

Listen to Process Owners and Keep Them Involved

Process management involves the continuous improvement of processes required to meet customer requirements and deliver quality products and services. Virtually every high-performance organization identifies key processes and manages them to ensure that customer requirements are met consistently and performance is continuously improved.

The first lesson learned has to do with the visibility of processes. Many processes are highly visible such as serving a meal or purchasing. However, when a process is hard to observe, such as course design or customer response, as so many are in the service sector, it cannot be assumed that everyone will see the organization as a collection of processes. The simple exercise of drawing a process flow diagram with people involved in an invisible process can be a struggle, but also a valuable revelation. With no vantage point from which to see work as a process, many people never think of themselves as engaged in a process. Some even deny it. The fact that all work—visible and invisible—is part of a process must be understood throughout the organization before employees can begin to manage and improve key processes.

Once this is understood, a second process management lesson comes to light. Process owners are the best ones, but not the only ones, to improve their processes. They must be part of process improvement teams. These teams are often made up of carefully selected cross-discipline, cross-functional, multi-level people who bring fresh insight to the examination of a process. Do not lose sight of the process owner—the person with expert knowledge of the process who should be accountable for long-term improvement to it. To try to ensure that all of its process improvement teams were cross-functional and multilevel, one organization enlisted volunteers to join process improvement teams. Using this democratic but misguided process, a marketing process improvement team ended up with no marketing expertise among its members. Instead, a group of frustrated support and technical staff members, who knew nothing about marketing, wasted time and money mapping and redesigning a process doomed to fail.

The third process management lesson learned involves an issue mentioned earlier. When focusing too closely on internal process data, there is a tendency to lose sight of external requirements. Organizations often succeed at making their processes better, faster, and (maybe) cheaper for them, but not necessarily to the benefit of their customers. When analyzing internal process data, someone must stubbornly play the role of advocate for the external customers' perspective. Ensure that the data will help make improvements for customers, key financials, employees, or top result areas. Avoid wasting resources on process improvements that do not benefit customers, employees, or the key performance of your organization.

A fourth lesson involves design processes, an important but often neglected part of process management. The best organizations have learned that improvements made early in the process, beginning with design, save more time and money than those made farther "downstream." To identify how design processes can be improved it is necessary to include ongoing evaluation and improvement cycles.

Business Results

Encourage Activities That Lead to Desired Business Results

Results fall into five broad categories.
- Customer satisfaction
- Financial and market
- Human resource
- Supplier and partner
- Organization-specific, such as product and service quality and internal operational and support performance

Customer satisfaction is a critical and ongoing result that every successful organization or work unit within an organization must achieve. Systems must exist to make sure that the data from customer satisfaction and dissatisfaction are used at all levels to plan and make improvements. Remember that when customers are asked their opinion, an expectation is created in their minds that the information will be used to make improvements that benefit them.

Some organizations have found it beneficial to have their customers analyze some of their business results with the idea of learning from them as well as building and strengthening relationships. This may or may not be appropriate for your organization but many successful ones have shared results with key customer groups at a level appropriate for their specific organization.

Financial and market performance is a key to survival. Organizations that make improvements that do not ultimately improve financial performance are wasting resources and growing weaker financially. This is true for both private sector (for profit) and public sector (not-for-profit, education, government) organizations. It is important to avoid over-reliance on financial results. Financial results are the lagging indicators of organization performance. Leaders who focus primarily on financials often overlook or cannot respond quickly to changing business needs. Focusing on finances to run the business—to the exclusion of leading indicators such as operational performance and employee satisfaction—is like driving your car by looking only in the rear view mirror. You can not avoid pot holes and turns in the road.

Human resource performance results provide early alert to problems that may threaten success. Absenteeism, turnover, accidents, low morale, grievances, and poor skills or ineffective training suboptimize organizational effectiveness. By monitoring performance in these areas, leaders can adjust quickly and prevent little problems from overwhelming the organization.

Supplier quality performance can significantly affect organizational operating effectiveness and customer satisfaction. To the extent an organization depends on suppliers, it must ensure that supplier performance improves—otherwise it must absorb (or pass on to customers) supplier waste, errors, inefficiency, and rework. An organization that tolerates poor supplier performance places its own business at risk.

Organization-specific product and service quality results provide useful information on key measures of the product or service itself. This information allows an organization to predict whether customers are likely to be satisfied—usually without asking them. For example, one of the nation's most successful and fastest-growing coffee shops knows from its customers that a good cup of coffee is hot, has a good taste, not too bitter, and has a rich aroma.

The measures for these product characteristics are temperature, pH (acidity), and the time lapsed between brewing and serving. With these measures, they can predict whether their customers are likely to be satisfied with the coffee before they serve it. One important lesson in this area is to select measures that correlate with, and predict, customer preference, satisfaction, and loyalty.

Organization-specific operational and service results pertain to measures of internal effectiveness that may not be of immediate interest to customers, such as cycle time (how long it takes to brew a pot of coffee), waste (how many pots you have to pour out because the coffee sat too long), and payroll accuracy (which may upset the affected workers). Ultimately, improving internal work process efficiency can result in reduced cost, rework, waste, scrap, and other factors that affect the bottom line, whether profit-driven or budget-driven. As a result, customers are indirectly affected. To stay in business, to remain competitive, or to meet increased performance demands with fewer resources, the organization will be required to improve processes that enhance operational and support service results.

Award Criteria Framework

The Baldrige performance excellence criteria contain three basic elements.
- Strategy and action plans—the context for aligning work and achieving performance excellence
- System—consisting of the driver triad and work core, producing business results
- Information and analysis—the brain center of high-performing organizations

Figure 1 depicts the entire system. Figures 2, 3, and 4 break out the major components of the system.

Strategy and Action Plans

Strategy and action plans are the set of organization-level requirements, derived from short- and long-term strategic planning, that must be done well for the organization's strategy to succeed. Strategy and action plans set the context for action in high-performing organizations and provide the vehicle through which leaders drive the organization to achieve success. Strategy and action plans guide overall resource decisions and drive the alignment of measures for all work units to ensure customer satisfaction and market success.

Strategy and action plans are represented in the framework as an umbrella that covers the organization's entire work system.

Criteria for Performance Excellence—Systems Framework

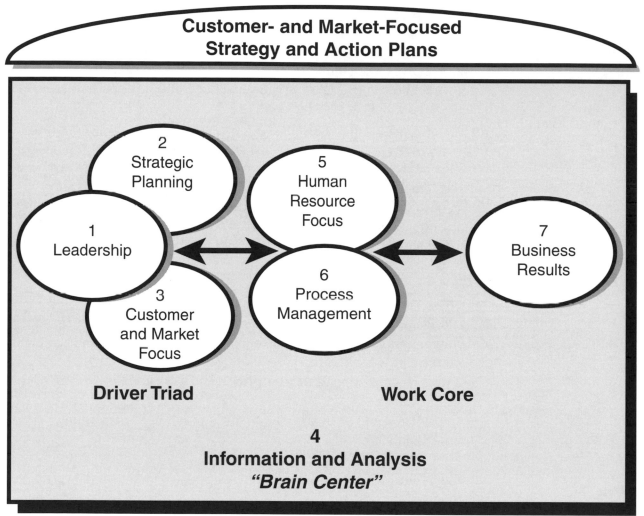

Figure 1

System

The *system* is comprised of two core activities that produce key business results.

- The driver triad
- The work core

The business results are a composite of customer, financial, and nonfinancial performance results, including human resource development and public responsibility.

The Driver Triad

As Figure 2 indicates, the *driver triad* consists of three categories.
- Leadership
- Strategic Planning
- Customer and Market Focus

The processes that make up these categories require leaders to set direction and expectations for the organization to meet customer and market requirements (Category 1). Customer and market focus (Category 3) processes produce the information that leaders use to determine what current and potential customers want. Strategic planning (Category 2) and goal setting provide the vehicle for determining the short- and long-term strategies for success as well as communicating and aligning the work of the organization. Leaders use this information to set direction and goals, monitor progress, make resource decisions, and take corrective action when progress does not proceed according to plan.

Driver Triad

Figure 2

The Work Core

The work core, as the name suggests, describes the processes through which the core work of the organization takes place. As Figure 3 indicates, the work core consists of human resource focus (Category 5) and process management (Category 6), which produce the business results (Category 7).

These categories recognize that the people of an organization are responsible for doing the work. To achieve performance excellence, these people must possess the right skills and must be allowed to work in an environment that promotes initiative and self-direction. The work processes provide the structure for continuous learning and improvement to optimize performance.

Business results reflect the organization's actual performance in terms critical for success. These include customer satisfaction, financial and market performance, human resource performance, supplier performance, and internal operating effectiveness.

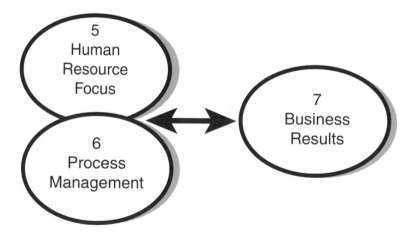

Work Core

Figure 3

Information and Analysis

Figure 4 depicts how information and analysis (Category 4) is the foundation for the entire management system. Information and analysis is the "brain center" of the management system. It is the platform on which the entire system operates. Information and analysis processes are critical to the effective management of the organization and to a fact-based system for improving organizational performance and competitiveness.

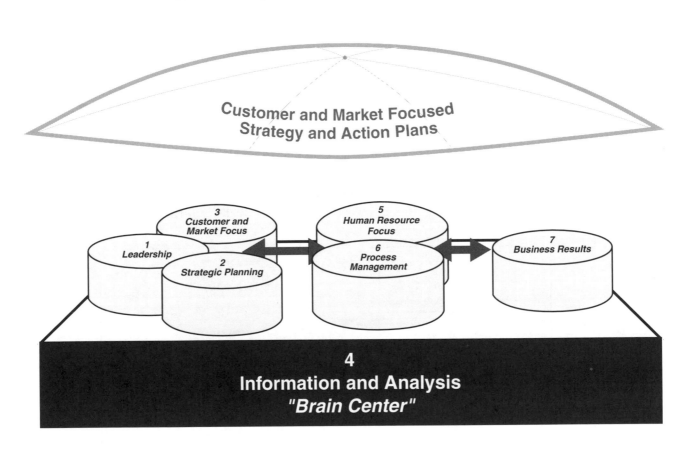

Figure 4

Award Criteria Organization

The seven criteria categories are subdivided into items and areas to address. Figure 5 demonstrates the organization of Category 1.

Items

There are 20 items, each focusing on a major requirement. Item titles and point values are on page 31.

Areas to Address

Items consist of one or more areas to address (areas). Information is submitted by applicants in response to the specific requirements of these areas. There are 29 Areas to address.

Subparts

There are 63 subparts. Areas consist of one or more subparts, where numbers are shown in parentheses. A response should be made to each subpart.

Notes

In 1998 the notes have been expanded to 51 from the 1997 total of 45 to provide a better explanation of the item requirements and identify some of the more obvious linkages. **Notes do not add requirements.** Examiners may not use the explanations in the notes as if they were criteria requirements.

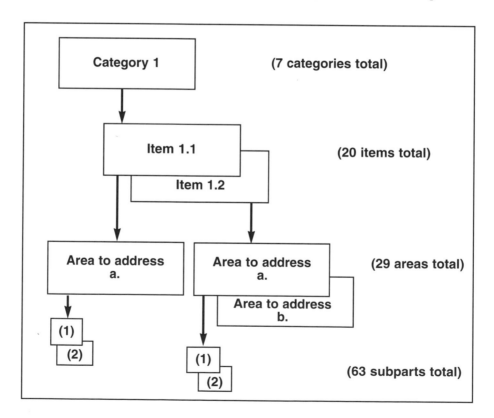

Figure 5

Baldrige Award Categories and Point Values

Examination Categories/Items		Maximum Points
1 Leadership	**(110 points)**	
1.1 Leadership System		80
1.2 Company Responsibility and Citizenship		30
2 Strategic Planning	**(80 points)**	
2.1 Strategy Development Process		40
2.2 Company Strategy		40
3 Customer and Market Focus	**(80 points)**	
3.1 Customer and Market Knowledge		40
3.2 Customer Satisfaction and Relationship Enhancement		40
4 Information and Analysis	**(80 points)**	
4.1 Selection and Use of Information and Data		25
4.2 Selection and Use of Comparative Information and Data		15
4.3 Analysis and Review of Company Performance		40
5 Human Resource Focus	**(100 points)**	
5.1 Work Systems		40
5.2 Employee Education, Training, and Development		30
5.3 Employee Well-Being and Satisfaction		30
6 Process Management	**(100 points)**	
6.1 Management of Product and Service Processes		60
6.2 Management of Support Processes		20
6.3 Management of Supplier and Partnering Processes		20
7 Business Results	**(450 points)**	
7.1 Customer Satisfaction Results		125
7.2 Financial and Market Results		125
7.3 Human Resource Results		50
7.4 Supplier and Partner Results		25
7.5 Company-Specific Results		125
Total Points		**1000**

Key Characteristics—1998 Performance Excellence Criteria

The criteria focus on business results and the processes required to achieve them. Business results are a composite of the following:
- Customer satisfaction and retention
- Financial and marketplace performance
- Product and service performance
- Productivity, operational effectiveness, and responsiveness
- Human resource performance and development
- Supplier performance and development
- Public responsibility and good citizenship

These results areas cover overall organization performance, including financial performance. The results areas also recognize the importance of suppliers and of community and national well-being. The use of a composite of indicators helps to ensure that strategies are balanced—that they do not inappropriately trade off among important stakeholders or objectives or between short- and long-term goals.

The criteria allow wide latitude in how requirements are met. Accordingly, the criteria do not prescribe
- Specific tools, techniques, technologies, systems, measures, or starting points; that organizations should or should not have departments for quality, planning, or other functions
- How the organization or business units within the organization should be organized

Processes to achieve performance excellence are very likely to change as needs and strategies evolve. Hence, the criteria themselves are regularly evaluated as part of annual performance reviews to ensure that they continue to distinguish high-performing organizations from all others.

The criteria do not prescribe specific approaches or methods, because
- Organizations are encouraged to develop and demonstrate creative, adaptive, and flexible approaches for meeting basic requirements. Nonprescriptive requirements are intended to foster incremental and major (breakthrough) improvement as well as basic change.
- Selection of tools, techniques, systems, and organizations usually depends on many factors such as business size, business type, the organization's stage of development, and employee capabilities and responsibilities.

- Focusing on common requirements within an organization, rather than on common procedures, fosters better understanding, communication, sharing, and alignment, while supporting creativity and diversity in approaches.

The criteria support a systems approach to organization-wide goal alignment. The systems approach to goal alignment is embedded in the integrated structure of the criteria and the results-oriented, cause-effect linkages among the criteria parts.

The measures in the criteria tie directly to customer value and to overall performance that relate to key internal and external requirements of the organization. Measures serve both as a communications tool and a basis for deploying consistent overall performance requirements. Such alignment ensures consistency of purpose while at the same time supporting speed, innovation, and decentralized decision making.

Learning Cycles and Continuous Improvement

In high-performing organizations, action-oriented learning takes place through feedback between processes and results facilitated by learning or continuous improvement cycles. The learning cycles have four, clearly defined and well-established stages.
1. Plan—planning, including design of processes, selection of measures, and deployment of requirements
2. Do—execute plans
3. Check—assess progress, taking into account internal and external results
4. Act—revise plans based on assessment findings, learning, new inputs, and new requirements

Goal-Based Diagnosis

The criteria and the scoring guidelines make up the diagnostic assessment system. The criteria, as discussed previously, are a set of 20 results-oriented items. The scoring guidelines spell out the assessment dimensions—approach, deployment, and results—and the key factors used to assess against each dimension. An assessment provides a profile of strengths and areas for improvement to help organizations identify areas that, if addressed, will move the organization ahead. As a result, this diagnostic assessment is a useful management tool that goes beyond traditional performance reviews.

1 Leadership—110 Points

The **Leadership** category examines the company's leadership system and senior leaders' personal leadership. It examines how senior leaders and the leadership system address values, company directions, performance expectations, a focus on customers and other stakeholders, learning, and innovation. Also examined is how the company addresses its societal responsibilities and provides support to key communities.

Leadership is the focal point within the criteria for addressing how the senior leaders guide the company in setting directions and seeking future opportunities. Organizations should give primary attention to how the senior leaders create a leadership system based upon clear values and high performance expectations that addresses the needs of all stakeholders. Values typically include the following core values for performance excellence: focus on customers, continuous improvement and learning, employee participation and development, management by fact, design quality and prevention, partnership development, fast response, long-range view of the future, and a results focus. The category also includes the company's responsibilities to the public and how the company practices good citizenship.

1.1 Leadership System (80 Points)
Approach/Deployment Scoring

Describe the company's leadership system and how senior leaders guide the company in setting directions and in developing and sustaining effective leadership throughout the organization.

In your response, address the following Area:

a. Leadership System

Describe the company's leadership system, how senior leaders provide effective leadership, and how this leadership is exercised throughout the company, taking into account the needs and expectations of all key stakeholders. Include:

(1) a description of the company's leadership system and how it operates. Include how it addresses values, performance expectations, a focus on customers and other stakeholders, learning, and innovation; and

(2) how senior leaders:
- set and communicate company directions and seek future opportunities for the company, taking into account all key stakeholders;
- communicate and reinforce values, performance expectations, a focus on customers and other stakeholders, learning, and innovation;
- participate in and use the results of performance reviews; and
- evaluate and improve the leadership system, including how they use their review of the company's performance and employee feedback in the evaluation.

Note:

Company performance reviews are addressed in Item 4.3. Responses to 1.1a(2) should therefore focus on the senior leaders' roles in and uses of the review of overall company performance, not on the details of the review.

This item addresses how the organization's senior leaders set directions and build and sustain a leadership system conducive to high performance, individual development, initiative, organizational learning, and innovation. The item asks how leadership takes into account all key stakeholders—customers, employees, suppliers, partners, stockholders, the public, and the community.

The item calls for information on the major aspects of leadership—creating values and expectations; setting directions; projecting a strong customer focus; encouraging innovation; developing and maintaining an effective leadership system; and effectively communicating values, directions, expectations, and a strong customer focus.

- Values and expectations should take into account the needs and expectations of key stakeholders.
- Setting directions includes creating future opportunities for the organization and its stakeholders.
- An effective leadership system promotes continuous learning, not only to improve overall performance, but also to involve all employees in the ongoing challenge to enhance customer value. To be successful, leadership must ensure that the organization captures and shares learnings.
- Leadership's communications are critical to company success. Effective communication includes ongoing demonstration that stated values, directions, and expectations are indeed the basis for the organization's key decisions and actions. Communications need to include performance objectives and measures that provide a sharp focus as well as help alignment of organization units and work processes.

This item includes the senior leaders' role in reviewing the leadership system, using employee feedback and reviewing overall company performance. This aspect of leadership is crucial, because reviews help to build consistency behind goals and allocation of resources. High performance organizations are flexible and responsive—changing easily to adapt to new needs and opportunities. Through their roles in developing strategy and reviewing organization performance, senior leaders develop leadership systems and create an organization capable of adapting to changing opportunities and requirements.

Finally, an effective leadership system is focused on continuously learning to improve overall performance, creating work processes that support efficient and effective accomplishment of performance objectives, and enhancing customer focus.

- Continuous learning requires processes to evaluate and refine leadership effectiveness (including personal effectiveness) and the full range of work processes *systematically*.
- Evaluations of the organization's leadership, which are essential to improve the leadership system, should include assessments of leaders by employees (such as an upward evaluation) and might also involve assessments by peers, direct reports, a board of directors, or other employees (typical factors in a 360-degree evaluation).

1.1 Leadership System

How senior leaders guide the organization in setting direction and developing and sustaining an effective leadership throughout the organization

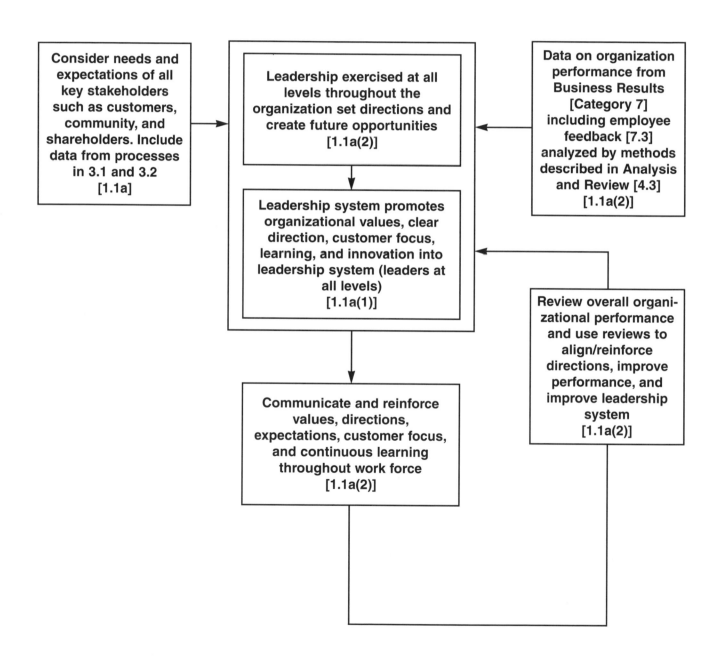

1.1 Leadership System Item Linkages

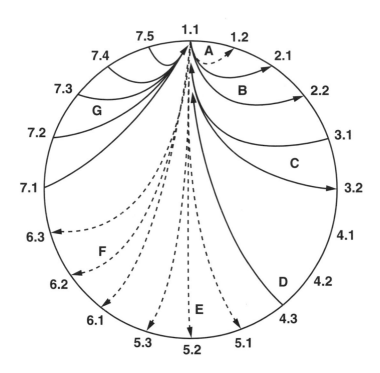

	Nature of Relationship
A	Leaders at all levels [1.1] must role model and support corporate responsibility and practice good citizenship [1.2].
B	Leaders [1.1] participate in the strategic planning process [2.1] and ensure that plans are deployed at all levels throughout the organization and used to align work [2.2a]. Leaders [1.1] also approve the goals and measurements set forth in the plan [2.2b]. They are responsible for using comparative data to set stretch goals.
C	Leaders [1.1] use information from customers [3.1 and 3.2] to set direction and create opportunity for the organization. Leaders [1.1] also have a responsibility for personally building relationships with key customers [3.2c] (creating a bidirectional relationship).
D	Leaders [1.1] use analyses of data [4.3] to monitor organizational performance and understand relationships among performance, employee satisfaction, customers, markets, and financial success. These analyses are also used for decision making at all levels to set priorities for action and allocate resources for maximum advantage.

Continued on next page

	Nature of Relationship (continued)
E	Leaders [1.1] at all levels work to improve the organization's work and job design [5.1a] and ensure that the compensation and recognition system [5.1b] encourages employees at all levels to achieve the organization's performance objectives including customer satisfaction and performance excellence. Leaders [1.1] are also responsible for supporting appropriate skill development of all employees through training and development systems and the use of learning on the job [5.2] as well as creating effective systems to enhance employee satisfaction, well-being, and motivation [5.3]. Leaders are also responsible for evaluating and refining all of these processes.
F	Leaders [1.1] at all levels are responsible for creating an environment that supports high performance, including monitoring processes for design and delivery [6.1], support services [6.2], and better supplier and partner performance [6.3]. Leaders must ensure that design, production/delivery, support, and supplier performance processes are aligned and consistently evaluated and refined.
G	Leaders [1.1a(2)] at all levels use performance results data [Category 7] for many activities including strategic planning [2.1] and for setting goals and priorities, allocating resources [2.2], reinforcing or rewarding employee performance [5.1b], and for improving the leadership system [1.1a(2)].

1.1 Leadership System—Sample Effective Practices

A. Leadership System

- All senior leaders are personally involved in performance improvement.
- Senior leaders spend a significant portion of their time on quality and performance improvement activities.
- Senior leaders carry out many visible activities (for example, goal setting, planning, and recognition and reward of performance and process improvement).
- Senior leaders regularly communicate quality values to managers and ensure that managers demonstrate those values in their work.
- Senior leaders participate on performance improvement teams and use quality tools and practices.
- Senior leaders spend time with suppliers and customers.
- Senior leaders mentor managers and ensure that promotion criteria reflect organizational values.
- Senior leaders study and learn about the improvement practices of other organizations.
- Senior leaders clearly and consistently articulate values (customer focus, customer satisfaction, role model leadership, continuous improvement, work force involvement, and performance optimization) throughout the organization.
- Senior leaders base their business decisions on reliable data and facts pertaining to customers, operational processes, and employee performance and satisfaction.
- Senior leaders ensure that organizational values are used to provide direction to all employees in the organization to help achieve the mission, vision, and quality goals.
- Senior leaders hold regular meetings to review performance data and communicate problems, successes, and effective approaches to improve work.
- Senior leaders use effective and innovative approaches to reach out to all employees to spread the organization's values and align its work to support organizational goals.
- Senior leaders effectively surface problems and encourage employee risk taking.
- Senior leaders conduct monthly reviews of organizational and key supplier performance. This requires that subordinates conduct biweekly reviews and that workers and work teams provide daily performance updates. Corrective actions are developed to improve performance that deviates from planned performance.

- Roles and responsibilities of managers are clearly defined, understood by them, and used to judge their performance.
- Managers walk the talk (serve as role models) in leading quality and systematic performance improvement.
- Job definitions with quality indices are clearly delineated for each level of the organization, objectively measured, and presented in a logical and organized structure.
- Many different communication strategies are used to reinforce quality values.
- Leader behavior (not merely words) clearly communicates what is expected of the organization and its employees.
- Systems and procedures are deployed that encourage cooperation and a cross-functional approach to management, team activities, and problem solving.
- Leaders monitor employee acceptance and adoption of vision and values using annual surveys, employee focus groups, and e-mail questions.
- Reviews against measurable performance standards are held frequently.
- Actions are taken to assist units that are not meeting goals or performing to plan.
- A systematic process is in place for evaluating and improving the integration or alignment of quality values throughout the organization.
- Senior leaders systematically and routinely check the effectiveness of their leadership activities (for example, seeking annual feedback from employees and peers (upward evaluation)), and take steps to improve.
- Leaders at all levels determine how well they carried out their activities (what went right or wrong and how they could be done better).
- There is evidence of adopting changes to improve leader effectiveness.
- Priorities for organizational improvement are driven by customer, performance, and financial data.

1.2 Company Responsibility and Citizenship (30 Points)
Approach/Deployment Scoring

Describe how the company addresses its responsibilities to the public and how the company practices good citizenship.

In your response, address the following Areas:

a. **Societal Responsibilities**
   How the company addresses the current and potential impacts on society of its products, services, and operations. Include:
   (1) key practices, measures, and targets for regulatory, legal, and ethical requirements and for risks associated with company products, services, and operations; and
   (2) how the company anticipates public concerns with current and future products, services, and operations, and addresses these concerns in a proactive manner.

b. **Support of Key Communities**
   How the company, its senior leaders, and its employees support and strengthen their key communities.

Notes:
N1. Public responsibilities in areas critical to the business also should be addressed in Strategy Development Process (Item 2.1) and in Process Management (Category 6). Key results, such as results of regulatory/legal compliance, environmental improvements through use of "green" technology or other means, should be reported as Company-Specific Results (Item 7.5).

N2. Areas of community support appropriate for inclusion in 1.2b may include efforts by the company to strengthen local community services, education, the environment, and practices of trade, business, or professional associations.

N3. Health and safety of employees are not addressed in Item 1.2; they are addressed in Item 5.3.

This item addresses how the organization integrates its values and expectations regarding its public responsibilities and citizenship into its performance management practices.

Area 1.2a calls for information on how the company addresses two basic aspects of societal responsibility in planning products, services, and operations.
- Making legal and ethical requirements and risk factors an integral part of performance management and improvement
- Sensitivity to issues of public concern, whether or not these issues are currently embodied in law or regulation

Fulfilling societal responsibilities means not only meeting all local, state, and federal laws and regulatory requirements, but also treating these and related requirements as areas for improvement "beyond mere compliance." This means that the organization should maintain constant awareness of potential public concerns related to its products, services, facilities, and operations.

Area 1.2b calls for information on how the organization promotes good citizenship in its key communities as a contributing member and as a positive influence upon other organizations. Opportunities for involvement and leadership include efforts by the organization, its senior leaders, and its employees to strengthen community services, education, health care, the environment, and practices of trade, business, and professional associations. The level of involvement and leadership is dependent on organization size and resources, with larger organizations expected to do more. Levels of involvement and leadership are dependent upon company size and resources.
- Good citizenship activities may include community service by employees that is encouraged, supported, and recognized by the organization. For example, organizations and their employees could help to influence the adoption of higher standards in education by communicating employability requirements to schools and to other education organizations. Organizations could also sponsor programs to encourage employees to volunteer in local schools, provide charitable donations to education institutions, or provide scholarships to students.
- Organizations could partner with other organizations and health care providers to improve health in the local community by providing education and volunteer services to address public health or education issues.
- Organizations also could partner to influence trade and business associations to engage in generally beneficial cooperative activities, such as the sharing of best practices to improve overall U.S. global competitiveness.

Finally, as part of the need to learn and improve, programs and practices should be systematically evaluated and refined to ensure that resources are effectively used and that public responsibility and commitment is optimum.

1.2 Company Responsibility and Citizenship

How the organization addresses societal responsibilities and practices good citizenship

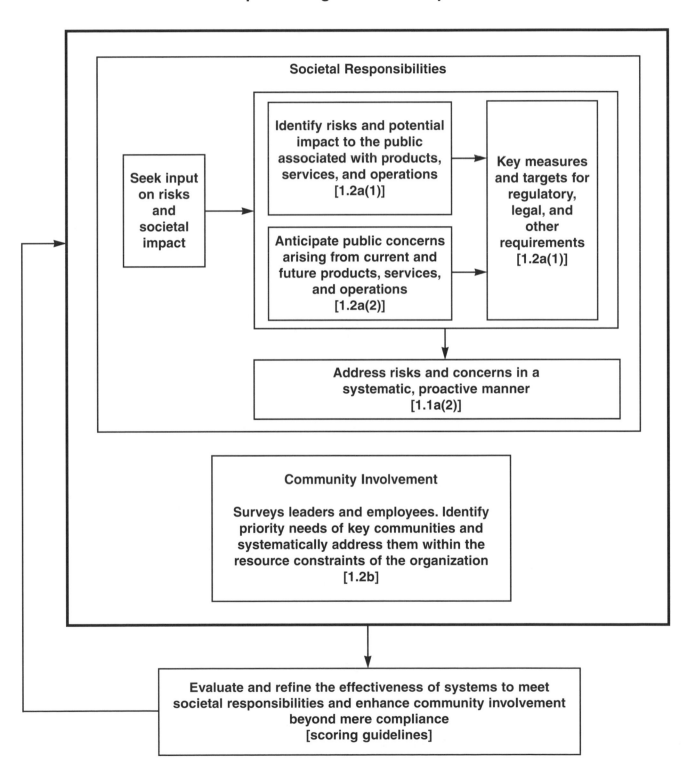

1.2 Company Responsibility and Citizenship Item Linkages

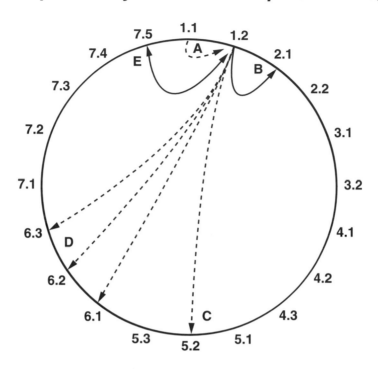

	Nature of Relationship
A	Leaders [1.1] have a responsibility for setting policies and ensuring that practices and products of the organization and its employees do not adversely impact society or violate ethical standards, regulations, or law [1.2a]. Leaders are also responsible for ensuring that the organization and its employees strengthen key communities in areas such as local community services, education, the environment, business and professional associations, and health and welfare [1.2b].
B	Public health and safety concerns, environmental protection, and waste management issues [1.2] are important factors to consider in strategy development [2.1].
C	Training [5.2] is provided to ensure all employees understand organization ethical and business practices as well as the importance of strengthening key communities [1.2].
D	Managers at all levels have responsibility for ensuring that work practices of the organization [6.1 and 6.2] and its suppliers [6.3] are consistent with the organization's standards of ethics and public responsibility [1.2].
E	Key results, such as results of regulatory compliance, environmental improvements, and support to key communities, are reported in Company-Specific Results [7.5]. In addition, these results are monitored to determine if process changes are needed. (Compliance results in areas of employee safety are reported in 7.3, based on processes described in Item 5.3, Employee Well-Being and Satisfaction, and are not a part of the requirements in 1.2.)

1.2   Company Responsibility and Citizenship—Sample Effective Practices

A. Societal Responsibilities

- The organization's principal business activities include systems to analyze, anticipate, and minimize public hazards or risk.
- Indicators for risk areas are identified and monitored.
- Continuous improvement strategies are used consistently, and progress is reviewed regularly.
- The organization considers the impact its operations, products, and services might have on society and considers those impacts in planning.
- The effectiveness of systems to meet or exceed regulatory or legal requirements is systematically evaluated and improved.

B. Support of Key Communities

- Employees at various levels in the organization are encouraged to be involved in professional organizations, committees, task forces, or other community activities.
- Organizational resources are allocated to support involvement in community activities outside the organization.
- Employees participate in local, state, or national quality award programs and receive recognition from the organization.
- Employees participate in a variety of professional quality and business improvement associations.
- The effectiveness of processes to support and strengthen key communities is systematically evaluated and improved.

2 Strategic Planning—80 Points

The **Strategic Planning** category examines how the company sets strategic directions, and how it develops the critical strategies and action plans to support the directions. Also examined are how plans are deployed and how performance is tracked.

The Strategic Planning category stresses that customer-driven quality and operational performance excellence are key strategic business issues that need to be an integral part of overall company planning.

Specifically:
- Customer-driven quality is a strategic view of quality. The focus is on the drivers of customer satisfaction, customer retention, new markets, and market share—key factors in competitiveness, profitability, and business success.
- Operational performance improvement contributes to short-term and longer-term productivity growth and cost/price competitiveness. Building operational capability—including speed, responsiveness, and flexibility—represents an investment in strengthening competitive fitness.

The criteria emphasize that improvement and learning must be integral parts of company work processes. The special role of strategic planning is to align work processes with the company's strategic directions, thereby ensuring that improvement and learning reinforce company priorities.

The Strategic Planning category examines how organizations
- Understand the key customer, market, and operational requirements as input to setting strategic directions. This is to help ensure that ongoing process improvements are aligned with the company's strategic directions.
- Optimize the use of resources, ensure the availability of trained human resources, and ensure bridging between short-term and longer-term requirements that may entail capital expenditures, supplier development, etc.

- Ensure that deployment will be effective—that there are mechanisms to transmit requirements and achieve alignment on three basic levels: (1) company/executive level; (2) the key process level; and (3) the work-unit/individual-job level.

The requirements for the Strategic Planning category are intended to encourage strategic thinking and acting—to develop a basis for a distinct competitive position in the marketplace. These requirements do not imply formalized plans, planning systems, departments, or specific planning cycles. Rather, the category recognizes that an effective improvement system combines improvements of many types and extents and requires clear strategic guidance, particularly when improvement alternatives compete for limited resources. In most cases, priority setting depends heavily upon a cost rationale. However, there also might be critical requirements such as societal responsibilities that are not driven by cost considerations alone.

This category addresses how the organization develops its view of the future, sets strategic directions, and translates these directions into a clear, actionable, and measurable basis for communicating, deploying, and aligning work and critical performance requirements. Without measures it is difficult to communicate clearly and monitor progress, ensuring all critical work is aligned and workers are pulling in the same direction.

Unless the strategic planning process yields measurable goals, it is difficult to ensure alignment of work at all levels in the organization.

2.1 Strategy Development Process (40 points)
Approach/Deployment Scoring

Describe how the company sets strategic directions to strengthen its business performance and competitive position.

In your response, address the following Area:

a. Strategy Development Process
Provide a brief description or diagram of the strategy development process. Include how the company takes the following factors into account:
(1) customers; market requirements, including price; customer and market expectations; and new opportunities;
(2) the competitive environment: industry, market, and technological changes;
(3) risks: financial and societal;
(4) human resource capabilities and needs;
(5) company capabilities—technology and technology management, research and development, innovation, and business processes—to seek or create new opportunities and/or to prepare for key new requirements; and
(6) supplier and/or partner capabilities.

Notes:

N1. The strategy development process refers to the company's approach, formal or informal, to a future-oriented basis for making or guiding business decisions, resource allocations, and companywide management. This process might use models, market or sales forecasts, scenarios, analyses, business intelligence, and/or key customer requirements and plans.

N2. Strategy should be interpreted broadly. It might include any or all of the following: new products, services, and markets; revenue growth; cost reduction; and new partnerships and alliances. Company strategy might be directed toward making the company a preferred supplier, a low-cost producer, a market innovator, a high-end or customized service provider.

Strategy might depend upon many different kinds of capabilities, including rapid response, customization, lean or virtual manufacturing, relationships, rapid innovation, technology management, leveraging assets, business process excellence, and information management. Responses to Item 2.1 should address the factors from the point of view of the company, how it plans to operate, and the capabilities most critical to its performance.

N3. Item 2.1 addresses overall company directions and strategy, including changes in services, products, and/or product lines. However, the Item does not address product and service design; these are addressed in Item 6.1.

This item addresses how the organization develops its view of the future and sets strategic directions.

The focus of the item is on achieving competitive leadership. Such organizational leadership usually depends on revenue growth as well as on operational effectiveness. This requires the creation of a view of the future that takes into account not only the markets or segments within which to compete, but also how to compete. *How to compete* presents many options and requires good understanding of the organization's and competitors' (or similar providers') strengths and weaknesses.

Clear and measurable performance objectives are critical to success. These objectives serve to guide the design and management of key processes. Measurable objectives should also serve to align communications and compensation and recognition systems with performance objectives. Although no specific time horizon is required, the thrust of the item is to produce a plan to achieve sustained competitive leadership.

Item 2.1 calls for information on all the key influences, challenges, and requirements that might affect the organization's future opportunities and directions—taking as long a view as possible. The main purpose of the item is to provide a thorough and realistic context for the development of a customer- and market-focused strategy to guide ongoing decision making, resource allocation, and organizationwide management. An increasingly important part of strategic planning is projecting the competitive environment. The purposes of such projections are to detect and reduce competitive threats, to shorten reaction time, and to identify and act on opportunities. Depending on the size and type of business, organizations might use a variety of modeling, scenario, or other techniques and judgments to project the competitive environment.

Pricing is also increasingly important to competitive success and customer satisfaction. Often this means that organizations' strategies need to address cost levels dictated by the anticipated price levels of customers, rather than merely setting prices to cover costs.

2.1 Strategy Development Process

**How the organization sets strategic direction to define
and strengthen competitive position**

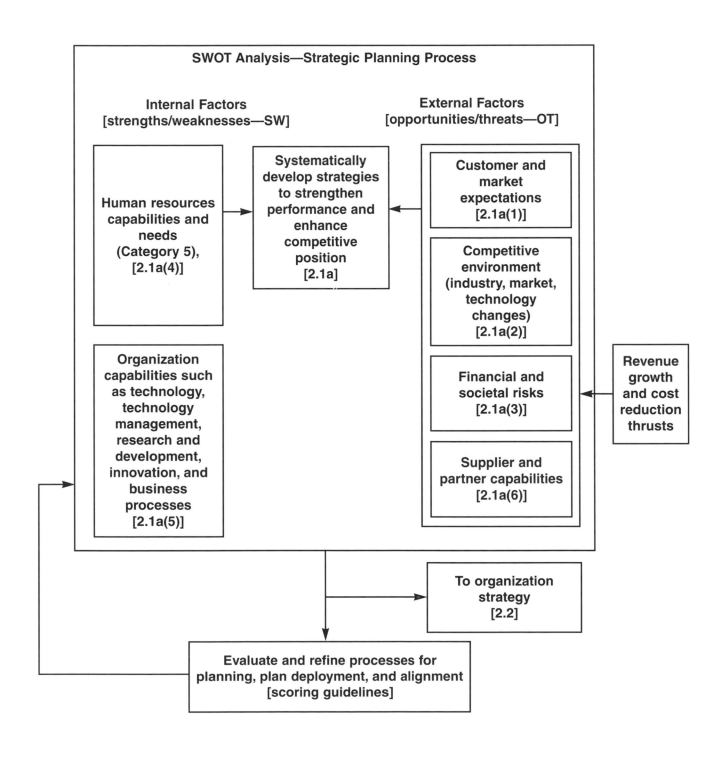

2.1 *Strategy Development Process Item Linkages*

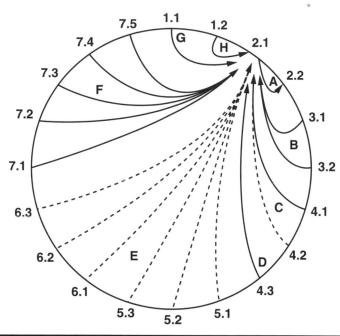

	Nature of Relationship
A	The planning process [2.1] produces a plan [2.2] and sets of actionable items.
B	The business planning process [2.1] includes information on current and potential customer requirements and the projected competitive environment [3.1] as well as intelligence obtained from customer-contact people (complaints and comments) [3.2a].
C	Key organizational [4.1] and competitive comparison data [4.2] are used for planning [2.1].
D	Analytical data [4.3] including data on work process improvement strategies, realigning work processes, improving operational performance, and reducing waste are used in the planning process [2.1].
E	Information on human resource capabilities [Category 5] and work process capabilities [Category 6] is considered in the strategic planning process as part of the determination of internal strengths and weaknesses. To avoid cluttering diagrams 5.1–6.3, these arrows will not be repeated there.
F	Organization customer satisfaction, market, and competitive results [7.1 and 7.2] and human resource, supplier, and organization performance results [7.3, 7.4, and 7.5] are used in the planning process [2.1] to set priorities and goals (which are reported in 2.2).
G	The planning process [2.1] includes senior leader participation and guidance as well as participation by leaders at all levels [1.1].
H	Public health, environmental, waste management, and related concerns [1.2a] are considered, as appropriate, in the strategy development process [2.1].

NOTE: The many inputs to strategy development will not all be repeated on other linkage diagrams to avoid clutter.

2.1   Strategy Development Process—Sample Effective Practices

A. Strategy Development Process

- Business goals, strategies, and issues are addressed and reported in measurable terms. Goals consider future requirements needed to achieve organizational leadership after considering the quality levels other organizations are likely to achieve.
- The planning and goal-setting process encourages input (but not necessarily decision making) from a variety of people at all levels throughout the organization.
- Data on customer requirements, key markets, benchmarks, supplier, human resource, and organizational capabilities are used to develop business plans.
- Plans are evaluated each cycle for accuracy and completeness—more often if needed to keep pace with changing business requirements.
- Areas for improvement in the planning process are identified systematically and carried out each planning cycle.
- Refinements in the process of planning, plan deployment, and receiving input from work units have been made. Improvements in plan cycle time, plan resources, and planning accuracy are documented.

2.2 Company Strategy (40 points)
Approach/Deployment Scoring

Summarize the company's strategy and action plans, how they are deployed and how performance is tracked. Include key performance requirements and measures, and an outline of related human resource plans. Estimate how the company's performance projects into the future relative to competitors and/or key benchmarks.

In your response, address the following Areas:

a. **Strategy and Action Plans**

Provide a summary of the action plans and related human resource plans derived from the company's overall strategy. Briefly explain how critical action plan requirements, including human resource plans, key processes, performance measures and/or indicators, and resources are aligned and deployed. Describe how performance relative to plans is tracked. Note any important differences between short- and longer-term plans and the reasons for the differences.

b. **Performance Projection**

Provide a two- to five-year projection of key measures and/or indicators of performance based on the likely changes resulting from the company's action plans. Include appropriate comparisons with competitors and/or key benchmarks. Briefly explain the comparisons, including any estimates or assumptions made in projecting competitor performance and/or benchmark data.

Notes:

N1. The development and implementation of company strategy and action plans are closely linked to other Items in the criteria and to the overall performance excellence framework as indicated on page 43 *[of the 1998 Baldrige Criteria booklet]*. Specific linkages include:

- Item 1.1 and how senior leaders set and communicate company directions;
- Category 3 for gathering customer and market knowledge as input to strategy and action plans, and for implementing action plans for building and enhancing relationships;
- Category 4 for information and analysis to support development of company strategy and track progress relative to strategies and action plans;
- Items 5.1 and 5.2 for work system and employee education, training, and development needs resulting from company action plans and related human resource plans;
- Category 6 for process requirements resulting from company action plans.

N2. Projected measures and/or indicators of performance (2.2b) also might include changes resulting from new business ventures, new value creation, major market shifts, and/or significant anticipated innovations in products, services, and/or technology.

This item addresses the organization's action plans and how they are deployed. The item also calls for a projection of the organization's performance. The main intent of the item is effective deployment of the organization's directions, incorporating measures that permit clear communication and the tracking of progress and performance.

Area 2.2a calls for information on the organization's action plans and how these plans are deployed. This includes spelling out key performance requirements and measures, as well as alignment of work unit, supplier, and/or partner plans. Of central importance in this Area is how alignment and consistency are achieved—for example, via key processes and key measurements. The alignment and consistency are intended also to provide a basis for setting priorities for ongoing improvement activities—part of the daily work of all work units.

Without effective alignment, routine work and acts of improvement can be random and serve to suboptimize organizational performance. In Figure 2.2-1, the arrows represent the well-intended work carried out by employees of organizations who lack a clear set of expectations and direction. Each person, each manager, and each work unit works diligently to achieve goals they believe are important. Each is pulling hard—but not necessarily in ways that ensure performance excellence. This encourages the creation of "feifdoms" within organizations.

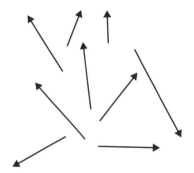

Figure 2.2-1—Nonaligned Work

With a clear, well-communicated strategic plan, it is easier to know when daily work is out of alignment. The large arrow in Figure 2.2-2 represents the strategic plan pointing the direction the organization must take to be successful and achieve its mission and vision. The strategic plan and accompanying measures make it possible to know when work is not aligned and help employees, including leaders, to know when adjustments are required.

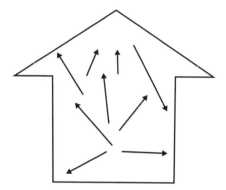

Figure 2.2-2—Strategic Direction

A well-deployed and understood strategic plan helps everyone in the organization distinguish between random acts of improvement and aligned improvement. Random acts of improvement give a false sense of accomplishment and rarely benefit the organization. For example, a decision to improve a business process that is not aligned with the strategic plan (as the small bold arrow in Figure 2.2-3 represents) usually results in a wasteful expenditure of time, money, and human resources—improvement without benefiting customers or enhancing operating effectiveness.

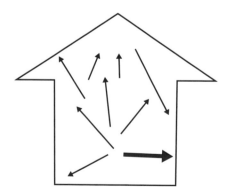

Figure 2.2-3—Random Improvement

On the other hand, by working systematically to strengthen processes that are aligned with the strategic plan, the organization moves closer to achieving success, as Figure 2.2-4 indicates. Ultimately, all processes and procedures of an organization should be aligned to maximize the achievement of strategic plans, as Figure 2.2-5 demonstrates.

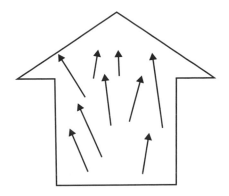

Figure 2.2-4—Moving Toward Alignment

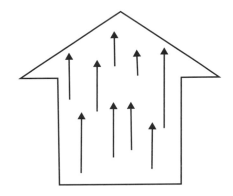

Figure 2.2-5—Systematic Alignment

Critical action plan requirements include human resource plans to support the overall strategy. Examples of human resource plan elements that might be part of a comprehensive plan are the following:

- Redesign of work, organization structure and function, and/or jobs to increase employee responsibility and decision making
- Initiatives to promote labor-management cooperation, such as partnerships with union
- Creation or modification of compensation and recognition systems based on building shareholder value and/or customer satisfaction
- Creation or redesign of employee surveys to assess the factors in the work climate that contribute to or inhibit high performance
- Prioritization of employee problems based on potential impact on productivity
- Development of hiring criteria and/or standards to produce a work force with necessary skills
- Creation of opportunities for employees to learn and use skills that go beyond current job assignments through redesign of processes or organizations
- Education and training initiatives, including those that involve developmental assignments
- Formation of partnerships with educational institutions to develop employees or to help ensure the future supply of well-prepared employees
- Establishment of partnerships with other organizations and/or networks to share training and/or spread job opportunities

- Introduction of distance learning or other technology-based learning approaches
- Integration of customer and employee surveys to focus on critical human resource development needs for meeting customer requirements

Area 2.2b calls for a two- to five-year projection of key measures and/or indicators of the organization's performance. It also calls for a comparison of projected performance versus competitors and/or key benchmarks. This projection comparison is intended to encourage organizations to improve their ability to understand and track dynamic, competitive performance factors. Through this tracking process, organizations should be better prepared to take into account their rates of improvement and change relative to competitors as a diagnostic management tool and ensure that plans will position the organization for future success.

In addition to improvement relative to past performance and competitors, projected performance also might include changes resulting from new business ventures, market shifts, product/service innovations, or other strategic thrusts. Goals should be rigorous and force the organization to stretch. It is critical to be able to project the future performance levels of competitors or similar providers to ensure that the organization, after achieving its strategic goals, is able to command a leadership position.

2.2 Company Strategy

Summary of strategy, action plans, and performance projections, how they are deployed, and how performance is tracked.

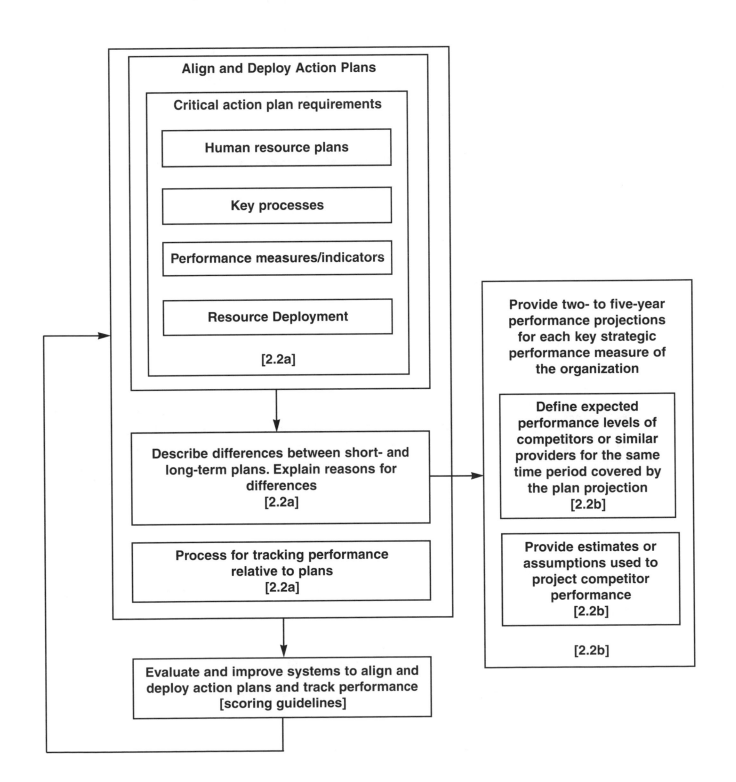

2.2 Company Strategy Item Linkages

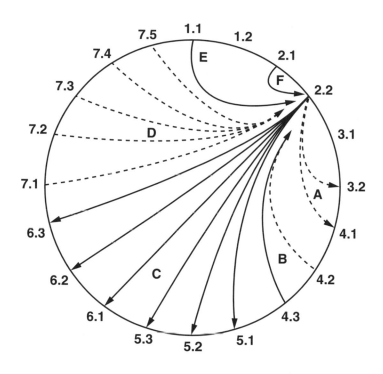

	Nature of Relationship
A	The goals and strategy [2.2] will influence the data and measures that need to be collected to monitor alignment [4.1], customer relations management, and customer satisfaction determination [3.2].
B	Benchmarking comparison data [4.2] and analytical processes [4.3] are used to set organizational measures and objectives [2.2].
C	Measures, objectives, and plans, deployed to the work force [2.2], are used to drive and align actions to achieve improved performance [Category 6] and develop human resources [Category 5].
D	Results data [Category 7] are used to help set goals [2.2]. (To avoid clutter, these relationships will not be repeated on the Category 7 linkage diagrams.)
E	The leadership team [1.1] sets the organization's goals and objectives [2.2].
F	The planning process [2.1] produces the strategic plan [2.2].

2.2 Company Strategy—Sample Effective Practices

A. Strategy and Action Plans

- Plans are in place to optimize operational performance and improve customer focus using tools such as reengineering, streamlining work processes, and reducing cycle time.
- Strategies to retain or establish leadership positions exist for major products and services for key customers or markets.
- Strategies to achieve key organizational results (operational performance requirements) are defined.
- Planned quality and productivity levels are defined in measurable terms for key features of products and services.
- Planned actions are challenging, realistic, achievable, and understood by employees throughout the organization. Each employee understands his or her role in achieving strategic and operational goals and objectives.
- Resources are available and committed to achieve the plans (no unfunded mandates).
- Plans are realistic and used to guide operational performance improvements.
- Incremental (short-term) strategies to achieve long-term plans are defined in measurable terms.
- Business plans, short- and long-term goals, and performance measures are understood and used to drive actions throughout the organization.
- Each individual in the organization, at all levels, understands how his or her work contributes to achieving organizational goals and plans.
- Plans are followed to ensure that resources are deployed and redeployed as needed to support goals.
- Capital projects are funded according to business improvement plans.
- Human resource plans support strategic plans and goals. Plans show how the work force will be developed to enable the organization to achieve its strategic goals.
- Key issues of training and development, hiring, retention, employee participation, involvement, empowerment, and recognition and reward are addressed as a part of the human resource plan.
- Innovative strategies may involve one or more of the following:
  - Redesign of work to increase employee responsibility
  - Improved labor-management relations (that is, prior to contract negotiations, train both sides in effective negotiation skills so that people focus on the merits of issues, not on positions. The goal is to improve relations and shorten negotiation time by 50 percent.)

- Forming partnerships with education institutions to develop employees and ensure a supply of well-prepared future employees
- Developing gain-sharing or equity-building compensation systems for all employees to increase motivation and productivity
- Broadening employee responsibilities; creating self-directed or high performance work teams
- Key performance measures (for example, employee satisfaction or work climate surveys) have been identified to gather data to manage progress. (Note: Improvement results associated with these measures should be reported in 7.3.)
- The effectiveness of human resource planning and alignment with strategic plans is evaluated systematically.
- Data are used to evaluate and improve performance and participation for all types of employees (for example, absenteeism, turnover, grievances, accidents, recognition and reward, and training participation).
- Routine, two-way communication about performance of employees occurs.

B. Performance Projection

- Projections of two- to five-year changes in performance levels are developed and used to track progress.
- Data from competitors and/or key benchmarks form a valid basis for comparison. The organization has strategies and goals in place to exceed the planned levels of performance for these competitors and benchmarks.
- Plans include expected future levels of competitor or comparison performance and are used to set and validate the organization's own plans.

3 Customer and Market Focus— 80 Points

The **Customer and Market Focus** category examines how the company determines requirements, expectations, and preferences of customers and markets. Also examined is how the company builds relationships with customers and determines their satisfaction.

The Customer and Market Focus category is the focal point within the criteria for examining how the organization systematically understands the requirements and expectations of customers and of the marketplace. The category stresses relationship enhancement as an important part of an overall listening and learning strategy. Vital information for understanding the voices of customers and of the marketplace also comes from customer satisfaction results. In many cases, such results and trends provide the most meaningful information, not only on customers' views but also on their marketplace behaviors and loyalty—resulting in repeat business and positive referrals. Therefore, it is critical that the processes used to obtain customer satisfaction and loyalty data are complete and accurate. To ensure this, data from multiple sources should be collected.

3.1 Customer and Market Knowledge (40 points)
Approach/Deployment Scoring

Describe how the company determines longer-term requirements, expectations, and preferences of target and/or potential customers and markets. Describe also how the company uses this information to understand and anticipate needs and to develop business opportunities.

In your response, address the following Area:

a. Customer and Market Knowledge
Provide a brief description of how the company learns, from its former, current, and potential customers and markets, to support the company's business needs and to seek market opportunities. Include:
(1) how customer groups and/or market segments are determined or selected, including the consideration of customers of competitors, other potential customers, and future markets. Describe how the approaches to listening and learning vary for different groups;
(2) how the company determines and/or projects key product and service features, their relative importance/value to customers, and new product, service, or market opportunities. Describe how key information from former and current customers and markets, including customer retention and complaint information, is used in this determination; and
(3) how the company's approach to listening to and learning from customers, potential customers, and markets is evaluated, improved, and kept current with changing business needs and strategies.

Notes:

N1. The company's products and services might be sold to end users via other businesses such as retail stores or dealers. Customer groups [3.1a(1)] should take into account the requirements and expectations of both the end users and intermediate businesses.

N2. Product and service features [3.1a(2)] refer to all important characteristics and to the performance of products and services throughout their full life cycle and the full "consumption chain." The focus should be primarily on features that bear upon customer preference and repurchase loyalty—for example, those features that differentiate products and services from competing offerings. Those features might include price, value, delivery, customer or technical support, and the sales relationship.

N3. Information about customers and markets is requested as key input to strategic planning (Item 2.1). However, strategic plans could also result in a need for new or additional customer and market information, new ways to gather information, and/or new customers and segments from which to gather information.

This item examines how the organization determines emerging customer requirements and expectations. In a rapidly changing competitive environment, many factors may affect customer preference and loyalty, making it necessary to listen and learn on a continuous basis. To be effective, such listening and learning need to have a close connection with the organization's overall business strategy. For example, if the organization customizes its products and services, the listening and learning strategy needs to be backed by a capable information system—one that rapidly accumulates information about customers and makes this information available where needed throughout the organization or the overall value chain.

A wide variety of listening and learning strategies should be used, depending on the type and size of business and other factors.

Examples of approaches that might be part of listening and learning strategies are as follows:
- Relationship building, including close integration with customers;
- Rapid innovation and field trials of products and services to better link research and development (R&D) and design to market and customer requirements;
- Close tracking of technological, competitive, societal, environmental, economic, and demographic factors that may bear upon customer requirements, expectations, preferences, or alternatives;
- Seeking to understand in detail customers' value chains and how they are likely to change;
- Focus groups with demanding or leading-edge customers;
- Training frontline employees in customer listening;
- Using critical incidents data such as complaints to understand key service attributes from the point of view of customers and frontline employees;
- Interviewing lost customers to determine the factors they use in their purchase decisions and factors that drive loyalty;
- Conducting won/lost analysis relative to competitors;
- Conducting post-transaction follow-up to determine if requirements were met; and
- Conducting analyses of major factors affecting key customers.

This item seeks information on how organizations recognize market segments, customers of competitors, and other potential customers. Accordingly, the item addresses how the organization tailors its listening and learning to different customer groups and market segments.

For example, a relationship strategy might be possible with some customers, but not with others. Other information sought relates to customers' reactions to specific product and service requirements and their relative importance or value to customer groups. This is vital to determining and refining an understanding of their requirements and expectations and should be supported by use of information and data, such as complaints and gains and losses of customers. As with all other processes, high performing organizations systematically evaluate and improve the processes for understanding customer requirements.

This item also addresses how the company improves its listening and learning strategies, with a focus on keeping current with changing business needs.

3.1 Customer and Market Knowledge

How the organization determines longer-term requirements, expectations, and preferences of target or potential customers and markets to anticipate their needs and to develop business opportunities

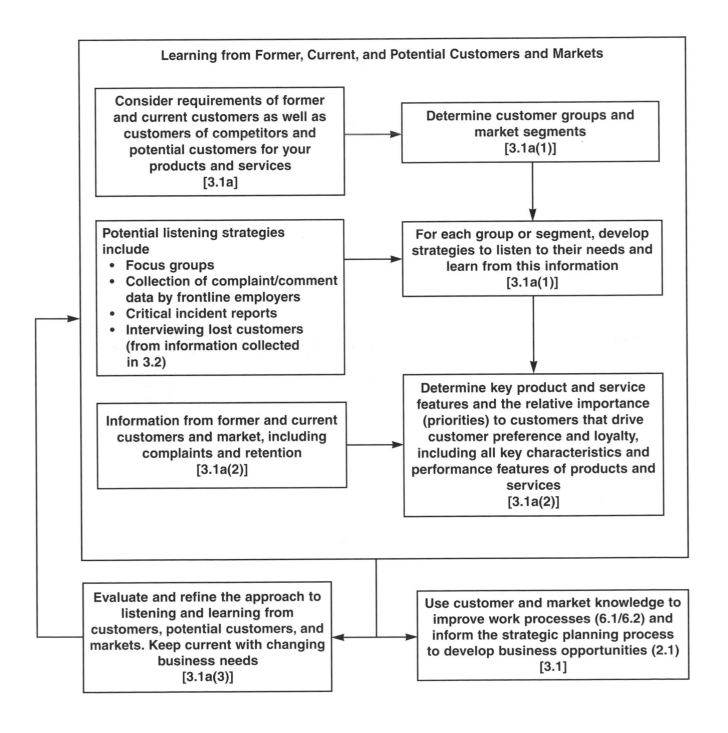

3.1 *Customer and Market Knowledge Item Linkages*

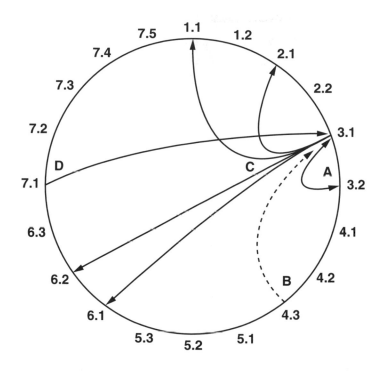

	Nature of Relationship
A	Customer complaints [3.2a] are used to help assess current customer expectations and refine requirements [3.1]. Information about customer requirements [3.1] is used to build instruments to assess customer satisfaction [3.2b].
B	Information from customer satisfaction data are analyzed [4.3] and used to help determine ways to assess current and potential customer requirements [3.1].
C	Information about current and future customer and market requirements [3.1] is used for strategic planning [2.1] to design products and services and revise work processes [6.1 and 6.2], and to help leaders set directions for the organization [1.1].
D	Customer satisfaction data and complaints [7.1] are used to assess customer expectations and refine requirements [3.1].

3.1   Customer and Market Knowledge—Sample Effective Practices

A. Customer and Market Knowledge

- Various systematic methods are used to gather data and identify current requirements and expectations of customers (for example, surveys, focus groups).
- Key product and service features are defined. Product and service features refer to all important characteristics and to the performance of products and services that customers experience or perceive throughout their use. The focus is primarily on factors that bear on customer preference and loyalty—for example, those features that enhance or differentiate products and services from competing offerings.
- Customer segments are identified or grouped by customer requirements.
- Customer data such as complaints and gains or losses of customers are used to support the identification of key customer requirements.
- Various systematic methods are used to identify the future requirements and expectations of customers.
- Customers of competitors are considered and processes are in place to gather expectation data from potential customers.
- Effective listening and learning strategies include
  - Close monitoring of technological, competitive, societal, environmental, economic, and demographic factors that may bear on customer requirements, expectations, preferences, or alternatives
  - Focus groups with demanding or leading-edge customers
  - Training of frontline employees in customer listening
  - Use of critical incidents in product or service performance or quality to understand key service attributes from the point of view of customers and frontline employees
  - Interviewing lost customers
  - Won/lost analysis relative to competitors
  - Analysis of major factors affecting key customers
- Methods to listen and learn from customer are evaluated and improved through several cycles. Examples of factors that are evaluated include
  - The adequacy and timeliness of customer-related information
  - Improvement of survey design
  - Approaches for getting reliable and timely information—surveys, focus groups, customer-contact personnel
  - Improved aggregation and analysis of information
  - Effective listening/learning strategies
- Best practices for gathering customer requirements and forecasting are gathered and used to make improvements.

3.2 Customer Satisfaction and Relationship Enhancement (40 points)
Approach/Deployment Scoring

Describe how the company determines and enhances the satisfaction of its customers to build relationships, to improve current offerings, and to support customer- and market-related planning.

In your response, address the following Areas:

a. Accessibility and Complaint Management
How the company provides access and information to enable customers to seek assistance, to conduct business, and to voice complaints. Include:
(1) how the company determines customer contact requirements, deploys the requirements to all employees who are involved in meeting the requirements, and evaluates and improves customer contact performance; and
(2) a description of the company's complaint management process. Explain how the company ensures that complaints are resolved effectively and promptly, and that complaints received by all company units are aggregated and analyzed for use throughout the company.

b. Customer Satisfaction Determination
How the company determines customer satisfaction and dissatisfaction. Include:
(1) a brief description of processes, measurements, and data used to determine customer satisfaction and dissatisfaction. Describe how the measurements capture actionable information that reflects customers' future business with the company and/or positive referral. Indicate significant differences, if any, in methods and/or measurement scales for different customer groups or market segments;
(2) how the company follows up with customers on products, services, and recent transactions to receive prompt and actionable feedback; and
(3) how the company obtains objective and reliable information on customer satisfaction relative to its competitors.

c. Relationship Building
Describe:
(1) how the company builds loyalty, positive referral, and relationships with its customers. Indicate significant differences, if any, for different customer groups or market segments.
(2) how the company's processes for providing access, determining customer satisfaction, and building relationships are evaluated, improved, and kept current with changing business needs and strategies.

Continued on next page

Notes:

N1. Customer satisfaction and dissatisfaction determination (3.2b) might include any or all of the following: surveys, formal and informal feedback from customers, use of customer account data, and complaints

N2. Customer satisfaction measurements might include both a numerical rating scale and descriptors for each unit in the scale. Effective (actionable) customer satisfaction measurement provides reliable information about customer ratings of specific product, service, and relationship features, the linkage between these ratings, and the customer's likely future actions—repurchase and/or positive referral. Product and service features might include overall value and price.

N3. Customer relationships (3.2c) might include the development of partnerships or alliances.

N4. Customer satisfaction and dissatisfaction results should be reported in Item 7.1. Information on operational measures that contribute to customer satisfaction or dissatisfaction should be reported in Item 7.5. For example, information on trends and levels in measures and/or indicators of complaint handling effectiveness such as complaint response time, effective resolution, and percent of complaints resolved on first contact should be reported in Item 7.5.

This item addresses how the organization effectively manages its responses to and follow-up with customers. Relationship enhancement provides a potentially important means for organizations to understand and manage customer expectations and to develop new business. Also, frontline employees may provide vital information to build partnerships and other longer-term relationships with customers.

This item also addresses how the organization determines customer satisfaction and satisfaction relative to competitors. Satisfaction relative to competitors, and the factors that lead to preference, are of critical importance to managing in a competitive environment.

Overall, Item 3.2 emphasizes the importance of capturing actionable information such as complaints and feedback from customer contacts. To be actionable, the information gathered should meet two conditions: (1) responses are tied directly to key business processes, so that opportunities for improvement are clear; and (2) responses are translated into cost/revenue implications to provide a rationale that supports the setting of improvement priorities.

Area 3.2a requires the organization to manage its relationships with customers effectively. Relationship enhancement provides an important means for organizations to understand and manage expectations, and even strengthen customer loyalty. Also, appropriately trained and authorized (empowered) frontline employees can strengthen partnerships and help build longer-term relationships with customers by resolving their problems quickly.

Area 3.2a calls for information on how the organization provides easy access for customers to obtain information or assistance and/or to comment and complain. The Area calls for information on how customer contact requirements (scrvice standards) are determined and deployed. Such deployment needs to take account of all key points in the response chain—all units or individuals in the organization that make effective responses possible. Area 3.2a also addresses thc complaint management process. The principal issue is prompt and effective resolution of complaints, resulting in recovery of customer confidence. In addition, the area addresses how the organization learns from complaints and ensures that production/delivery process employees receive information needed to eliminate the causes of complaints and meet customer requirements better. Effective elimination of the causes of complaints involves aggregation of complaint information from all sources for evaluation and use throughout the organization. Complaints should cause systematic action to improve.

The effective complaint management process includes analysis and priority setting for improvement projects based on potential cost impact of complaints, including the cost of losing customers. The process should also have an evaluation and improvement cycle. Effective complaint management processes can enable an organization to recover from problems and convert a dissatisfied customer to a satisfied, loyal customer.

Area 3.2b addresses how the organization determines the customer satisfaction of its customers as well as satisfaction relative to competitors. Satisfaction relative to competitors, and the factors that lead to preference, are of critical importance to managing in a competitive environment. It is important to note this item includes direct measures of customer satisfaction, such as those gathered through questions or observations of customers, including complaints and accolades.

Area 3.2b addresses how the organization determines customer satisfaction. Three types of requirements are considered.
- How the organization follows up with customers regarding products, services, and recent transactions to determine satisfaction and to resolve problems quickly

- How the organization gathers information on customer satisfaction, including any important differences in approaches for different customer groups or market segments. This highlights the importance of the measurement scale in determining those factors that best reflect customers' market behaviors—repurchase, new business, and positive referral
- How satisfaction relative to competitors is determined. Such information might be derived from organization-based comparative studies or studies made by independent organizations. The purpose of this comparison is to develop information that can be used for improving performance relative to competitors and to better understand the factors that drive markets

Area 3.2c addresses relationship building—how the organization builds loyalty and positive referral. Increasingly, business success, business development, and product/service innovation depend upon maintaining close relationships with customers. Approaches to relationship building vary greatly, depending on products/services and types of customers. Hence, Area 3.2c addresses how relationship building is tailored to customer groups and market segments. Avenues to, and bases for, relationship building change quickly. Accordingly, this Area addresses how the organization evaluates and improves its customer relationship building and ensures that approaches are kept current with changing business needs.

3.2 Customer Satisfaction and Relationship Enhancement

How customer satisfaction is determined, relationships strengthened, and current products and services enhanced to support customer- and market-related planning

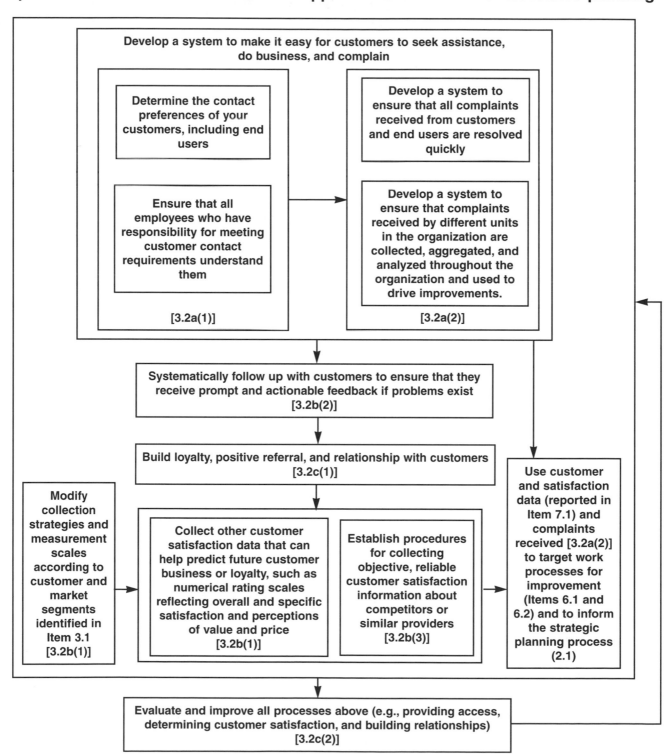

3.2 Customer Satisfaction and Relationship Enhancement Item Linkages

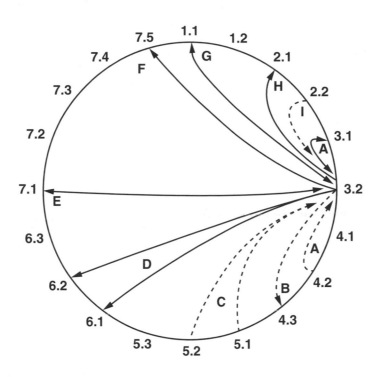

Nature of Relationship	
A	Information concerning customer requirements and expectations [3.1] and benchmark data [4.2] are used to set and deploy customer contact requirements (service standards) [3.2a]. Customer complaint data [3.2a] are used to help assess customer requirements and expectations [3.1].
B	Customer relations data [3.2] are analyzed and used to set priorities for action [4.3].
C	Training [5.2] and improved flexibility and self-direction [5.1] can enhance the development and effectiveness of customer-contact employees [3.2a].
D	Information collected through customer relations employees [3.2a] is used to enhance design of products and services and to improve operational and support processes [6.1 and 6.2].
E	Information from customer relations processes [3.2a] can help in the design of customer satisfaction measures [3.2b] and even produce data on customer satisfaction [7.1]. In addition, customer satisfaction results data [7.1] are used to set customer contact requirements (service standards) [3.2a].

Continued on next page

	Nature of Relationship (continued)
F	Efforts of improved accessibility and responsiveness in complaint management [3.2a] should result in improved complaint response time, effective complaint resolution, and a higher percentage of complaints resolved on first contact. These results should be reported in 7.5.
G	Priorities and customer contact requirements (service standards) for customer service personnel [3.2a] are driven by top leadership [1.1]. Leaders at all levels [1.1] personally interact with and build better relationships with customers. They receive useful information from those customers to improve management decision making.
H	Information about customer complaints and satisfaction collected by customer-contact employees [3.2a] is used in the planning process [2.1].
I	Goals and strategy [2.2] influence customer relations management [3.2c] and customer satisfaction determination processes [3.2b].

3.2 Customer Satisfaction and Relationship Enhancement—Sample Effective Practices

A. Accessibility and Complaint Management

- Several methods are used to ensure ease of customer contact, 24 hours a day if necessary (for example, toll-free numbers, pagers for contact personnel, surveys, interviews, focus groups, electronic bulletin boards).
- Customer-contact employees are empowered to make decisions to address customer concerns.
- Adequate staff are available to maintain effective customer contact.
- Performance expectations are set for employees whose job brings them in regular contact with customers.
- The performance of employees against these expectations is measured and tracked.
- A system exists to ensure that customer complaints are resolved promptly and effectively.
- Complaints and customer concerns are resolved at first contact. This often means training customer-contact employees and giving them authority for resolving a broad range of problems.
- Complaint data are tracked and used to initiate prompt corrective action to prevent the problem from recurring.
- Procedures are in place and evaluated to ensure that customer contact is initiated to follow up on recent transactions to build relationships.
- Training and development plans and replacement procedures exist for customer-contact employees.
- Objective customer contact requirements (service standards) have been derived from customer expectations (for example, timeliness, courtesy, efficiency, thoroughness, and completeness).

B. Customer Satisfaction Determination

- An actionable customer satisfaction measurement system exists that provides the organization with reliable information about customer ratings of specific product and service features and the relationship between these ratings and the customer's likely future market behavior (loyalty).
- Several customer satisfaction indicators are used (for example, repeat business measures, praise letters, and direct measures using survey questions and interviews).

- Comprehensive satisfaction and dissatisfaction data are collected and segmented or grouped to enable the organization to predict customer behavior (likelihood of remaining a customer).
- Several means of collecting customer satisfaction data are used (for example, surveys, interviews, and third-party contractors).
- Customer satisfaction measurement includes both a numerical rating scale and descriptors assigned to each unit in the scale. An effective (actionable) customer satisfaction measurement system provides the organization with reliable information about customer ratings of specific product and service features and the relationship between these ratings and the customer's likely market behavior.
- Customer dissatisfaction indicators include complaints, claims, refunds, recalls, returns, repeat services, litigation, replacements, performance rating downgrades, repairs, warranty work, warranty costs, misshipments, and incomplete orders.
- Satisfaction data are collected from former customers.
- Competitors' customer satisfaction is determined using various means such as external or internal studies.
- Methods are in place to ensure objectivity of these data.
- Organization-based or independent organization comparative studies take into account one or more indicators of customer dissatisfaction as well as satisfaction. The extent and types of such studies depend on industry and organization size.

C. Relationship Building

- Requirements for building relationships are identified and may include factors such as product knowledge, employee responsiveness, and various customer contact methods.
- Problem resolution priority setting is based on the potential cost impact of customer decisions to repurchase or recommend the product or service to others.
- Feedback is sought on the effectiveness of service.
- A systematic approach exists to evaluate and improve service and customer relationships.
- Feedback from customers and employees is systematically used in the improvement process.
- The process of collecting complete, timely, and accurate customer satisfaction and dissatisfaction data is regularly evaluated and improved. Several improvement cycles are evident.

4 *Information and Analysis—80 Points*

> The **Information and Analysis** category examines the selection, management, and effectiveness of use of information and data to support key company processes and action plans, and the company's performance management system.

The Information and Analysis category is the main point within the criteria for examining all key information to manage the organization and to drive improvement of organization performance and competitiveness. Category 4 is the "brain center" or "central processing unit" (CPU) for the alignment of an organization's operations with its strategic directions. However, since information, information technology, and analysis might themselves be primary sources of competitive advantage and productivity growth, the category also includes such strategic considerations.

Leaders at all levels use information to plan, set strategic direction and performance goals, monitor performance, set priorities, allocate resources, and take corrective action. Employees use data and information to manage their work processes and adjust them when they are out of control. Access to data and tools for decision making is a prerequisite to effective employee involvement, increased initiative, and self-directed responsibility. Without this information and the skill to use it, decisions are left to intuition—and decisions based on intuition are usually retained by more senior leaders and managers.

Finally, information, information technology, and analysis may also be primary sources of competitive advantage and productivity growth.

4.1 Selection and Use of Information and Data (25 points)
Approach/Deployment Scoring

Describe the company's selection, management, and use of information and data needed to support key company processes and action plans, and to improve company performance.

In your response, address the following Area:

a. Selection and Use of Information and Data
Describe:
(1) the main types of information and data, financial and nonfinancial, and how each type relates to key company processes and action plans;
(2) how the information and data are deployed to all users to support the effective management and evaluation of key company processes;
(3) how key user requirements, including rapid access and ongoing reliability, are met; and
(4) how information and data, their deployment, and effectiveness of use are evaluated, improved, and kept current with changing business needs and strategies.

Notes:
N1. Users [4.1a(2,3)] refers to company work units and to those outside the company who have access to information and data—customers, suppliers, and business partners, as appropriate.

N2. Deployment of information and data might be via electronic or other means. Reliability [4.1a(3)] includes reliability of software and delivery systems.

This item examines the organization's selection, use, and management of information and data to support overall business goals, with strong emphasis on the data needed for effective process management, action plans, and performance improvement. Overall, the item represents a key foundation for a performance-oriented organization that effectively utilizes nonfinancial and financial information and data.

The item examines the main types of data, financial and nonfinancial, and how each type relates to key organization processes and action plans. In addition, the item examines a central requirement in an effective performance management system—the integration of information and data into measurements that are used for decision making. Also examined is the deployment of information and data to users, with emphasis on alignment of data and information with key organization processes and goals. The effective management of the information/data system itself, ensuring rapid access and reliability, is examined in connection with user requirements. Finally, the item examines how overall data and information requirements, including effectiveness of use, deployment, and ability to keep current with changing business needs and strategies are evaluated.

Although the main focus of this item is on information and data for the effective management of performance, information, data, and information technology often have major strategic significance as well. For example, information technology could be used to accumulate and disseminate unique knowledge about customers and markets, which would enable the organization to customize products and services quickly. Also, information technology and the information and data made available through such technology could be of special advantage in business networks, alliances, and supply chains. Responses to this item should take into account such strategic use of information and data. Accordingly, "users" would include business partners as well as organization units.

4.1 Selection and Use of Information and Data

How the organization selects, manages, and uses information and data to support decision making for key processes and to improve performance

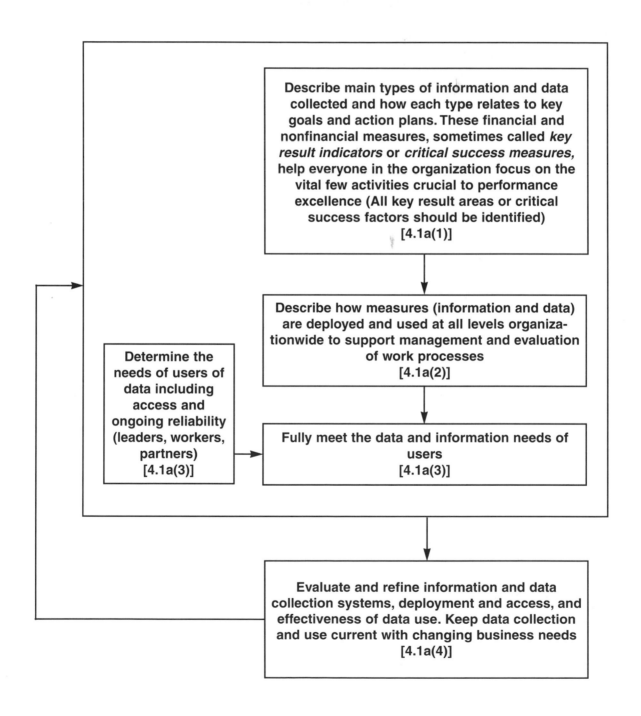

Describe main types of information and data collected and how each type relates to key goals and action plans. These financial and nonfinancial measures, sometimes called *key result indicators* or *critical success measures,* help everyone in the organization focus on the vital few activities crucial to performance excellence (All key result areas or critical success factors should be identified)
[4.1a(1)]

Describe how measures (information and data) are deployed and used at all levels organizationwide to support management and evaluation of work processes
[4.1a(2)]

Determine the needs of users of data including access and ongoing reliability (leaders, workers, partners)
[4.1a(3)]

Fully meet the data and information needs of users
[4.1a(3)]

Evaluate and refine information and data collection systems, deployment and access, and effectiveness of data use. Keep data collection and use current with changing business needs
[4.1a(4)]

4.1   Selection and Use of Information and Data Item Linkages

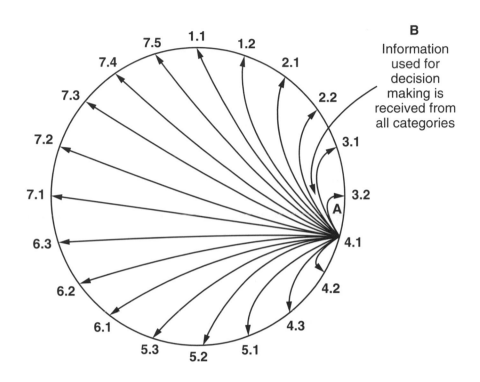

Nature of Relationship	
A	Information collected [4.1] is used for planning [2.1], goal setting [2.2], analysis [4.3], benchmarking priority setting [4.2], day-to-day leadership [1.1], setting social responsibility standards (regulatory, legal, ethical) for community involvement [1.2], monitoring of quality and operational performance results [7.2, 7.3, 7.4, 7.5], improving work processes [6.1, 6.2, 6.3] and human resource systems [5.1, 5.2, 5.3], determining customer requirements [3.1], managing customer complaints [3.2a], building customer relations [3.2c], and determining customer satisfaction [3.2b] and reporting customer satisfaction [7.1].
B	Information used for decision making and continuous improvement [4.1] is collected from all categories.

NOTE: Because the information collected and used for decision-making links with all other items, the linkage arrows will not all be repeated on the other item maps. The more relevant connections will be identified.

4.1 Selection and Use of Information and Data—Sample Effective Practices

A. Selection and Use of Information and Data

- Data collected at the individual worker level are consistent across the organization to permit consolidation and organizationwide performance monitoring.
- Every person has access to the data they need to make decisions about their work, from top leaders to individual workers or teams of workers.
- Quality and operational data are collected and routinely used for management decisions.
- Internal and external data are used to describe customer satisfaction and product and service performance.
- The cost of quality and other financial concerns are measured for internal operations and processes.
- Data are maintained on employee-related issues of satisfaction, morale, safety, education and training, use of teams, and recognition and reward.
- Supplier performance data are maintained.
- The data collection and analysis system is systematically evaluated and refined.
- Improvements have been made to reduce cycle time for data collection and to increase data access and use.
- Formal processes are in place to ensure data reliability and objectivity.
- Employees, customers, and suppliers are involved in validating data.
- A systematic process exists for data review and improvement, standardization, and easy employee access to data. Training on the use of data systems is provided as needed.
- Data used for management decisions' focus on critical success factors are integrated with work processes for the planning, design, and delivery of products and services.
- Users of data help determine what data systems are developed and how data are accessed.

4.2 Selection and Use of Comparative Information and Data (15 points)
Approach/Deployment Scoring

Describe the company's selection, management, and use of comparative information and data to improve the company's overall performance and competitive position.

In your response, address the following Area:

a. Selection and Use of Comparative Information and Data
Describe:
(1) how needs and priorities for comparative information and data are determined, taking into account key company processes, action plans, and opportunities for improvement;
(2) the company's criteria and methods for seeking sources of appropriate comparative information and data—from within and outside the company's industry and markets;
(3) how comparative information and data are deployed to all potential users and used to set stretch targets and/or to stimulate innovation; and
(4) how comparative information and data, their deployment, and effectiveness of use are evaluated and improved. Describe how priorities and criteria for selecting benchmarks and comparisons are kept current with changing business needs and strategies.

Note:
Comparative information and data include benchmarking and competitive comparisons. Benchmarking refers to processes and results that represent best practices and performance for similar activities, inside or outside the company's industry. Competitive comparisons refer to performance relative to competitors in the company's markets.

This item addresses external drivers of performance improvement—data and information related to competitive position and best practices. Such data usually have both operational and strategic value.

The item examines how competitive comparisons and benchmarking information are selected and used to help drive improvement of overall organization performance. The item also examines the key aspects of effective selection and use of competitive comparisons and benchmarking information and data; determination of needs and priorities; criteria for seeking appropriate information—from within and outside the organization's industry and markets; and use of information and data to set stretch targets and to promote major improvements in areas most critical to the organization's competitive strategy.

The item also calls for information on how the organization evaluates and improves its processes for selecting and using competitive and benchmark information to improve planning, to drive improvement of performance and competitive position, and to keep current with changing business needs and strategies.

The major premises underlying the requirements of this item are as follows:
- Organizations facing tough competition need to know where they stand relative to competitors and to best practices.
- Comparative and benchmarking information often provide impetus for significant (breakthrough) improvement and might alert organizations to competitive threats and new practices.
- Organizations need to understand their own processes and the processes of others before they compare performance levels. Benchmarking information may also support business analysis and decisions relating to core competencies, alliances, and outsourcing.

It is important to develop and use systematic methods to set priorities for determining targets for collecting competitive comparison and benchmarking information. This will help organizations avoid wasting resources on frivolous or fruitless searches for information. It is also important to be able to implement the lessons learned from collecting this information. Otherwise, the act of collecting the information will waste resources and not add the value needed to compete effectively. Finally, it is important to learn from and improve the processes of collecting and using comparison and benchmarking information.

4.2 Selection and Use of Comparative Information and Data

How the organization selects, manages, and uses comparative information and data to improve overall performance and competitive position

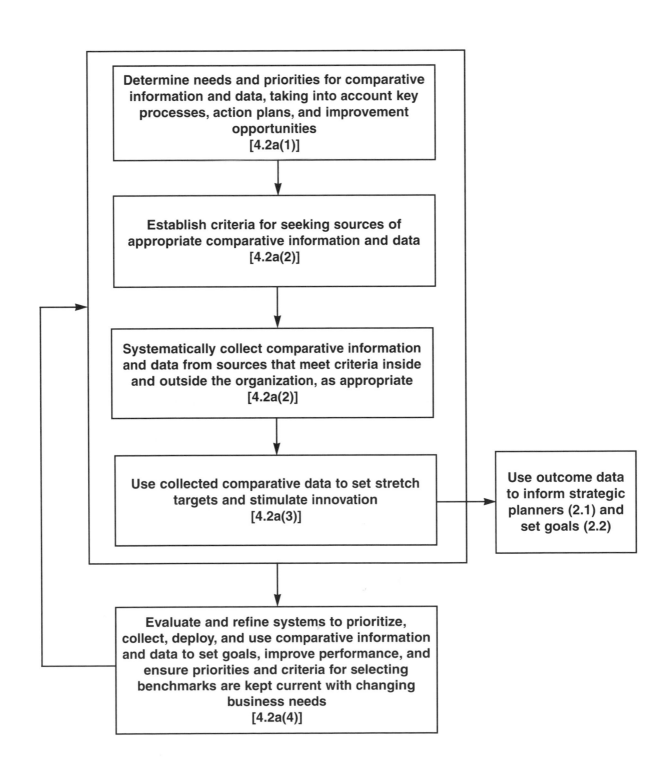

4.2 Selection and Use of Comparative Information and Data Item Linkages

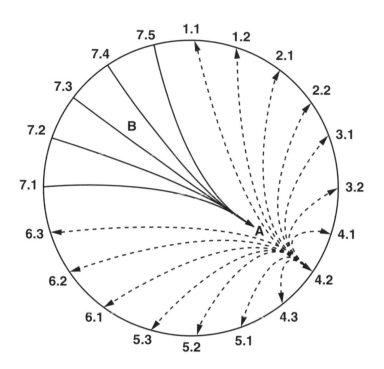

	Nature of Relationship
A	Comparison data [4.2] can be used to improve data collection, benchmarking, data analysis [4.1, 4.2, 4.3], leadership effectiveness [1.1], and public responsibility and citizenship [1.2]; to encourage breakthrough improvements in customer-related areas [3.1, and 3.2], in design, development, and delivery of products and services [6.1], support services [6.2], and supplier performance [6.3]; for planning [2.1] and to set stretch objectives and goals [2.2]; and to improve employee morale [5.3], employee performance, reward and recognition [5.1], and training [5.2]. Process information is also used to help set improvement priorities [4.3].
B	The need for information to help set priorities for selecting comparison organizations [4.2] is driven by work processes that need improvement as determined by performance [Category 7] results.

NOTE: Because comparison information links with most items, the linkage arrows will not be repeated on all other item maps; however, the most relevant connections will be identified.

4.2 Selection and Use of Comparative Information and Data—Sample Effective Practices

A. Selection and Use of Comparative Information and Data

- A systematic process is in place for identifying and prioritizing comparative information and benchmark targets.
- Research has been conducted to identify best-in-class organizations, which may be competitors or noncompetitors.
- Key processes or functions are the subject of benchmarking. Activities such as those that support the organization's goals and objectives, action plans, and opportunities for improvement and innovation are the subject of benchmarking.
- Benchmarking covers key products, services, customer satisfiers, suppliers, employees, and support operations.
- The organization reaches beyond its own business to conduct comparative studies.
- Benchmark or comparison data are used to improve the understanding of work processes and to discover the best levels of performance that have been achieved. Based on this knowledge, the organization sets goals or targets to stretch performance as well as drive innovations.
- A systematic approach is used to evaluate and improve processes for selecting, gathering, and using comparative information.
- Benchmarking processes are fully documented.
- Systematic actions have been taken to evaluate and improve the quality and use of comparative information and benchmark data.

4.3 Analysis and Review of Company Performance (40 points)
Approach/Deployment Scoring

Describe how the company analyzes and reviews overall performance to assess progress relative to plans and goals and to identify key areas for improvement.

In your response, address the following Areas:

a. Analysis of Data

How performance data from all parts of the company are integrated and analyzed to assess overall company performance in key areas. Describe how the principal financial and nonfinancial measures are integrated and analyzed to determine:

(1) customer-related performance;

(2) operational performance, including human resource and product/service performance;

(3) competitive performance; and

(4) financial and market-related performance.

b. Review of Company Performance

Describe:

(1) how company performance and capabilities are reviewed to assess progress relative to action plans, goals, and changing business needs. Describe the performance measures regularly reviewed by the company's senior leaders.

(2) how review findings are translated into priorities for improvement, decisions on resource allocation, and opportunities for innovation. Describe also how these findings are deployed throughout the company and, as appropriate, to the company's suppliers and/or business partners.

Notes:

N1. Analysis includes trends, projections, comparisons, and cause-effect correlations intended to support the setting of priorities for resource use. Accordingly, analysis draws upon all types of data: customer-related, operational, competitive, financial, and market.

N2. Performance results should be reported in Items 7.1, 7.2, 7.3, 7.4, and 7.5.

This item addresses organization-level analysis and performance—the principal basis for guiding an organization's process management toward key business results.

Despite the importance of individual facts and data, standing alone they do not usually provide a sound basis for effectively making decisions, taking actions, or setting priorities. To be effective, these activities depend on developing a solid understanding of the relationships among processes and between processes and business results. Process actions may have many resource implications; results may have many cost and revenue implications as well. Given that resources for improvement are limited and cause-effect connections are often unclear, there is a critical need to provide a sound analytical basis for decisions.

A close connection between analysis and performance review helps to ensure that analysis is kept relevant to decision making. This item is the central analysis point in an integrated information and data system. This system is built around financial and nonfinancial information and data.

Area 4.3a examines how information and data from all parts of the organization are aggregated and analyzed to assess overall organization performance. The Area covers four key aspects of performance—customer-related, operational, competitive, and financial/market.

Analyses that organizations perform to gain understanding of performance vary widely. Selection depends on many factors, including business type, size, and competitive position. Examples include
- How the organization's product and service improvements correlate with key customer indicators such as customer satisfaction, customer retention, and market share
- Cost/revenue implications of customer-related problems and problem resolution effectiveness
- Interpretation of market share changes in terms of customer gains and losses and changes in customer satisfaction
- Improvement trends in key operational performance indicators such as productivity, cycle time, waste reduction, new product introduction, and defect levels
- Relationships between employee/organization learning and value added per employee
- Financial benefits derived from improved employee safety, absenteeism, and turnover
- Benefits and costs associated with education and training

- How the organization's ability to identify and meet employee requirements correlates with employee retention, motivation, and productivity
- Cost/revenue implications of employee-related problems and problem resolution effectiveness
- Trends in individual measures of productivity such as labor productivity
- Working capital productivity relative to competitors
- Individual or aggregate measures of productivity relative to competitors
- Performance trends relative to competitors on key measures and indicators
- Cost trends relative to competitors
- Relationships between product/service quality and operational performance indicators and overall organization financial performance trends as reflected in indicators such as operating costs, revenues, asset utilization, and value added per employee
- Allocation of resources among alternative improvement projects based on cost/revenue implications and improvement potential
- Net earnings derived from quality/operational/human resource performance improvements
- Comparisons among business units showing how quality and operational performance improvement affect financial performance
- Contributions of improvement activities to cash flow, working capital use, and shareholder value
- Profit impacts of customer retention
- Market share versus profits
- Trends in aggregate measures such as total factor productivity and
- Trends in economic and/or market indicators of value.

Area 4.3b examines how the organization reviews performance and capabilities and uses the review findings to improve performance and capabilities relative to action plans, goals, and changing business needs. An important part of this review is the translation of review findings into an action plan sufficiently specific so that deployment throughout the organization and to suppliers/partners is possible.

4.3 Analysis and Review of Company Performance

How the organization analyzes and reviews overall performance to assess progress relative to plans and goals and to identify key areas for improvement

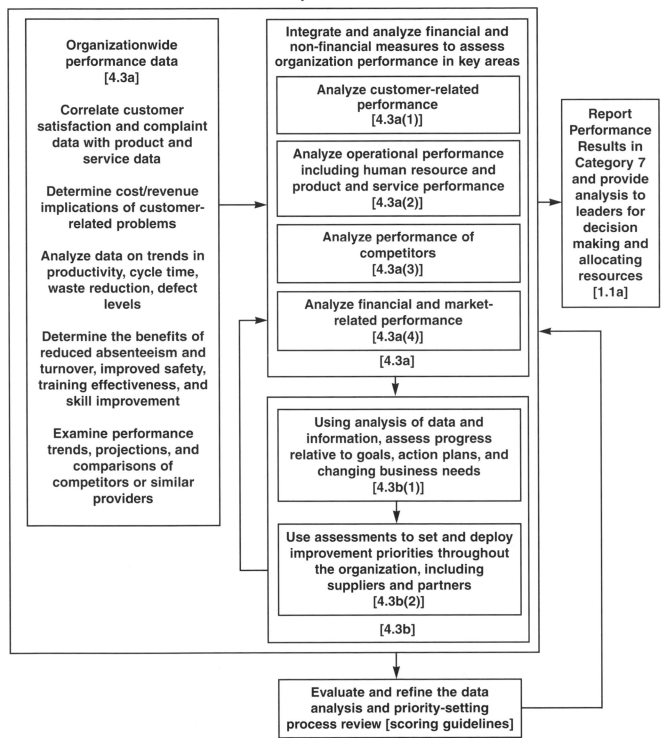

Organizationwide performance data [4.3a]

Correlate customer satisfaction and complaint data with product and service data

Determine cost/revenue implications of customer-related problems

Analyze data on trends in productivity, cycle time, waste reduction, defect levels

Determine the benefits of reduced absenteeism and turnover, improved safety, training effectiveness, and skill improvement

Examine performance trends, projections, and comparisons of competitors or similar providers

Integrate and analyze financial and non-financial measures to assess organization performance in key areas

Analyze customer-related performance [4.3a(1)]

Analyze operational performance including human resource and product and service performance [4.3a(2)]

Analyze performance of competitors [4.3a(3)]

Analyze financial and market-related performance [4.3a(4)]

[4.3a]

Report Performance Results in Category 7 and provide analysis to leaders for decision making and allocating resources [1.1a]

Using analysis of data and information, assess progress relative to goals, action plans, and changing business needs [4.3b(1)]

Use assessments to set and deploy improvement priorities throughout the organization, including suppliers and partners [4.3b(2)]

[4.3b]

Evaluate and refine the data analysis and priority-setting process review [scoring guidelines]

4.3 Analysis and Review of Company Performance Item Linkages

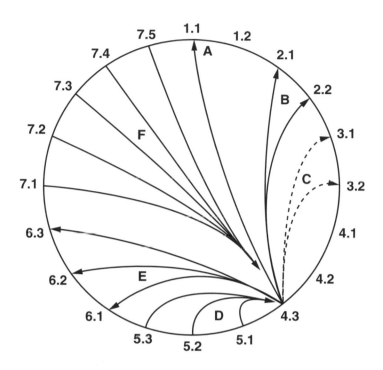

	Nature of Relationship
A	Leaders at all levels [1.1] use data and information [4.3b] to review overall performance, assess progress relative to plans, and identify key areas for improvement.
B	Aggregated information is analyzed [4.3a] and used in the strategic planning process [2.1] and to help set goals [2.2b].
C	Information from customer satisfaction data are analyzed [4.3a] and used to help determine ways to assess customer requirements [3.1], to determine standards or required levels of customer service and relationship development [3.2a and c], and to design instruments to assess customer satisfaction [3.2b].
D	Information regarding human resources capabilities, including work system efficiency, initiative, and self-direction [5.1], training and development [5.2], and well-being and satisfaction [5.3] is used to set priorities [4.3b] and improve safety, retention, absenteeism, and organizational effectiveness.
E	Data are aggregated and analyzed and used to set priorities [4.3] and improve work processes [6.1, 6.2, 6.3] that will reduce cycle time, waste, and defect levels.
F	Performance data from all parts of the organization are integrated and analyzed [4.3a] to assess performance in key areas such as customer-related performance [7.1], operational performance [7.5], financial and market performance [7.2], human resource performance [7.3], and supplier performance [7.4], relative to competitive performance in all areas.

4.3 Analysis and Review of Company Performance— Sample Effective Practices

A. Analysis of Data

- Systematic processes are in place for analyzing customer-related data and results (including complaint data) and setting priorities for action.
- Facts, rather than intuition, are used to support decision making at all levels based on the analyses conducted to make sense out of the data collected.
- The analysis process itself is analyzed to make the results more timely and useful for decision making for quality improvement at all levels.
- Analysis processes and tools, and the value of analyses to decision making, are systematically evaluated and improved.

B. Review of Company Performance

- Customer and operational performance data, including financial performance data, are used to support performance reviews relative to action plans, planning, and resource allocation.
- Data are used to help leaders improve operations-related decision making, such as determining improvement priorities; evaluating the cost impact of improvement initiatives and trends in key operational indicators (such as cycle time, waste and rework, and product/service quality); and using benchmark data to set improvement priorities and targets.
- Data regarding improvements in performance and financial performance are used in planning, goal setting, and establishing priorities.
- The impacts of improvement activities on customer satisfaction, operational effectiveness, and financial indicators (for example, operating costs, production value per employee, cost per employee) are used to set improvement priorities.

5 Human Resource Focus—100 Points

> The **Human Resource Focus** category examines how the company enables employees to develop and utilize their full potential, aligned with the company's objectives. Also examined are the company's efforts to build and maintain a work environment and work climate conducive to performance excellence, full participation, and personal and organizational growth.

The Human Resource Focus category is the focal point within the criteria for all key human resource practices—those directed toward creating a high performance workplace and toward developing employees that enable them and the organization to adapt to change. The category addresses human resource development and management requirements in an integrated way, aligned with the organization's strategic directions.

In order to ensure the basic alignment of human resource management with organization strategy, the criteria also address human resource planning as an integral part of organization planning in the Strategic Planning category.

It is important to note that human resource focus encompasses all activities related to the development and optimum use of human resources, not just the activities of the Human Resource department.

5.1 Work Systems (40 Points)
Approach/Deployment Scoring

Describe how all employees contribute to achieving the company's performance and learning objectives, through the company's work design, and compensation and recognition approaches.

In your response, address the following Areas:

a. Work Design
How work and jobs are designed and how employees, including all managers and supervisors, contribute to ensure:
(1) design, management, and improvement of company work processes that support company action plans and related human resource plans. Include how work processes are designed and managed to encourage individual initiative and self-directed responsibility;
(2) communication, cooperation, and knowledge and skill sharing across work functions, units, and locations; and
(3) flexibility, rapid response, and learning in addressing current, and changing customer, operational, and business requirements.

b. Compensation and Recognition
How the company's compensation and recognition approaches for individuals and groups, including all managers and supervisors, reinforce overall company objectives for customer satisfaction, performance improvement, and employee and company learning. Describe significant differences, if any, among different categories or types of employees.

Notes:

N1. For purposes of the criteria, employees include the company's permanent, temporary, and part-time personnel, as well as any contract employees supervised by the company. Any contract employees supervised by the contractor should be addressed in Item 6.3.

N2. Work design refers to how employees are organized and/or organize themselves in formal and informal, temporary, or longer-term units. This includes work teams, process teams, customer action teams, problem-solving teams, centers of excellence, functional units, cross-functional teams, and departments—self-managed or managed by supervisors. Job design refers to responsibilities, authorities, and tasks of individuals. In some work systems, jobs might be shared by a team based upon cross-training.

N3. Compensation and recognition refer to all aspects of pay and reward, including promotions and bonuses, that might be based upon performance, skills acquired, and other factors. This includes monetary and nonmonetary, formal and informal, and individual and group compensation and recognition.

This item addresses how the organization's work and job design and compensation and recognition approaches enable and encourage all employees to contribute effectively. The item is not only concerned with current and near-term performance objectives, but also with individual and organizational learning—enabling adaptation to change.

Area 5.1a examines the extent to which work and job design and work organizations enable employees to exercise discretion and decision making, leading to flexibility, innovation, knowledge and skill sharing, and rapid response to the changing requirements of the marketplace. Examples of approaches to create flexibility in work and job design might include simplification of job classifications, cross-training, job rotation, and changes in work layout and work locations. It might also entail use of technology and changed flow of information to support local decision making.

Effective job design and flexible work organizations are necessary, but may not be sufficient to ensure high performance. High performance work systems require information systems [Category 4], education, and appropriate training [5.2] to ensure that information flow supports the job and work designs. Also important is effective communication across functions and work units to ensure a focus on customer requirements and to ensure an environment of encouragement, trust, and mutual commitment. In some cases, teams might involve individuals in different locations linked via computers or conferencing technology.

Area 5.1b addresses the important alignment of incentives with the achievement of key organization objectives. The basic thrust of this Area is the consistency between the organization's compensation and recognition system and its work structures and processes.

The Area calls for information on employee compensation and recognition—how these reinforce high performance job design, a focus on customer satisfaction, and learning. To be effective, compensation and recognition might need to be based, wholly or in part, on demonstrated skills and/or evaluation by peers in teams and networks.

Compensation and recognition approaches could include profit sharing and compensation based on skill building, use of new skills, demonstrations of self-learning, and knowledge sharing. Compensation and recognition approaches could also be based on the linkage to customer retention or other specific performance objectives.

5.1 Work Systems

How the organization's work and job design, and compensation and recognition approaches enable and encourage all employees to contribute effectively to achieving high performance and learning objectives

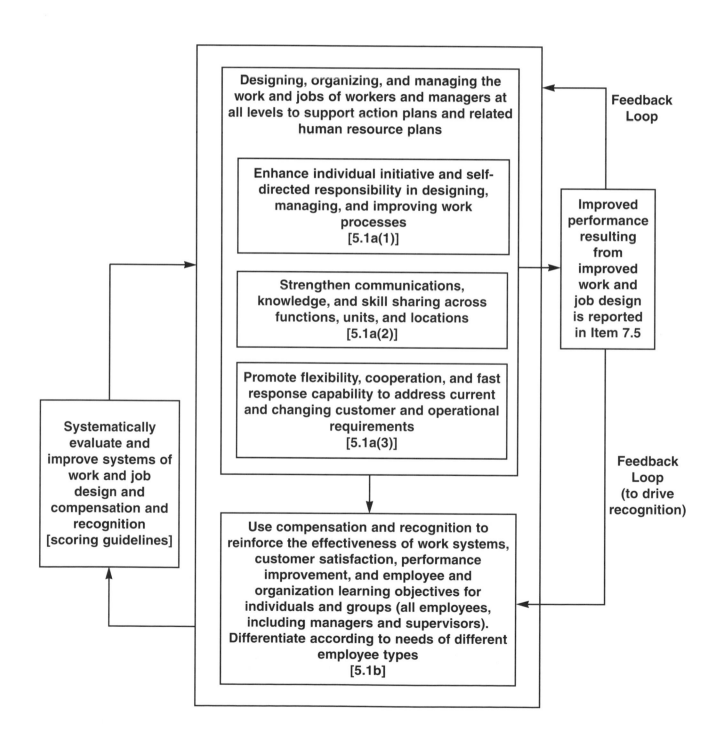

5.1 Work Systems Item Linkages

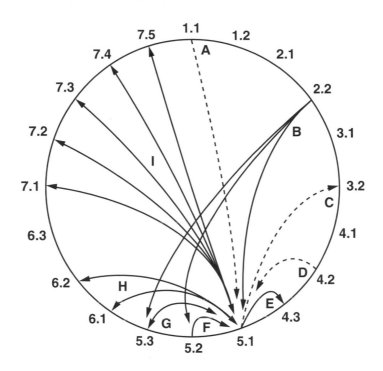

	Nature of Relationship
A	Leaders at all levels [1.1] set the policies and role model actions essential to improving work and job design to enhance employee performance, initiative, self-direction, and involvement in quality improvement [5.1a].
B	Human resource development plans and goals [2.2] address ways to improve employee performance and involvement [5.1], training [5.2], and satisfaction and well-being [5.3].
C	Improved flexibility and self-direction [5.1a] can enhance the effectiveness of customer-contact employees [3.2a].
D	Key comparison data [4.2] are often used to improve work systems, and reward and recognition [5.1].
E	Information regarding work systems effectiveness, design effectiveness, and employee involvement and recognition [5.1] is used to gain a better understanding of operational performance and organizational capabilities and to set priorities for improvement actions [4.3].
	Continued on next page

	Nature of Relationship (continued)
F	Effective training [5.2] is critical to enable employees or managers at all levels to improve skills and improve their ability to manage, organize, and design better work processes [5.1a].
G	High morale [5.3] enhances employee participation, self-direction, and initiative [5.1] and vice versa.
H	High-performance, streamlined work systems, and effective compensation and recognition [5.1] are essential to improving operational and support processes [6.1 and 6.2]. In addition, the analysis of work processes (identifying inefficiencies) is used to inform or drive the improvements in flexibility and job design [5.1a].
I	Recognition or rewards [5.1b] are based in part on performance results [Category 7], particularly in areas of operating effectiveness [7.5], financial performance [7.2], and customer satisfaction [7.1]. Improvements in work and job design [5.1] result in improved employee motivation and satisfaction [7.3] and improved operating effectiveness [7.5]. Processes to improve initiative and flexibility [5.1a] can enhance all performance results [Category 7].

5.1 Work Systems—Sample Effective Practices

A. Work Design

- Fully using the talents of all employees is a basic organizational value.
- Managers use cross-functional work teams to break down barriers, improve effectiveness, and meet goals.
- Teams have access to data and are authorized to take responsibility for decisions affecting their work.
- Employee opinion is sought regarding work design and work processes.
- Prompt and regular feedback is provided to teams regarding their performance. Feedback covers both results and team process.
- Lower-performing organizations use teams for special improvement projects, while the "regular work" is performed using traditional approaches. In higher-performing organizations, using teams and self-directed employees is the way regular work is done.
- Self-directed or self-managed work teams are used throughout the organization. They have authority over matters such as budget, hiring, and team membership and roles.
- A systematic process is used to evaluate and improve the effectiveness and extent of employee involvement.
- Many indicators of employee involvement effectiveness exist, such as the improvements in time or cost reduction produced by teams.

B. Compensation and Recognition

- Recognition and rewards are provided for generating improvement ideas. Also, a system exists to encourage and provide rapid reinforcement for submitting improvement ideas.
- Recognition and rewards are provided for results, such as for reductions in cycle time and exceeding target schedules with error-free products or services at less-than-projected cost.
- Employees, as well as managers, participate in creating the recognition and rewards system and help monitor its implementation and systematic improvement.
- The organization evaluates its approaches to employee performance and compensation, recognition, and rewards to determine the extent to which employees are satisfied with them, the extent of employee participation, and the impact of the system on improved performance (reported in Item 7.3).
- Evaluations are used to make improvements. Top-scoring organizations have several improvement cycles. (Many improvement cycles can occur in one year.

- Performance measures exist, and goals are expressed in measurable terms. These measurable goals form the basis for performance recognition.
- Recognition, reward, and compensation are influenced by customer satisfaction ratings as well as other performance measures.

5.2 Employee Education, Training, and Development (30 points)
Approach/Deployment Scoring

Describe how the company's education and training support the accomplishment of key company action plans and address company needs, including building knowledge, skills, and capabilities, and contributing to improved employee performance and development.

In your response, address the following Area:

a. Employee Education, Training, and Development
Describe:
   (1) how education and training support the company's key action plans and address company needs, including longer-term objectives for employee development and learning, and for leadership development of employees;
   (2) how education and training are designed to support the company's work systems. Include how the company seeks input from employees and their supervisors/managers in education and training design;
   (3) how education and training, including orientation of new employees, are delivered;
   (4) how knowledge and skills are reinforced on the job; and
   (5) how education and training are evaluated and improved, taking into account company and employee performance, employee development and learning objectives, leadership development, and other factors, as appropriate.

Notes:
N1. Education and training delivery [5.2a(3)] might occur inside or outside the company and involve on-the-job, classroom, computer-based, distance education, or other types of delivery.

N2. Other factors [5.2a(5)] might include: effectiveness of incentives in promoting skill building; benefits and costs of education and training; most effective means and timing for training delivery; and effectiveness of cross-training.

This item addresses how the organization develops the work force via education, training, and on-the-job reinforcement of knowledge and skills. Development is intended to meet the needs of employees and a high performance workplace, accommodating to change.

Education and training address the knowledge and skills employees need to meet their overall work and personal objectives and the organization's need for leadership development of employees. Depending on the nature of the organization's work and the employees' responsibilities and stage of development, education and training needs might vary greatly. Examples include leadership skills, communications, teamwork, problem solving, interpreting and using data, meeting customer requirements, process analysis, process simplification, waste reduction, cycle time reduction, error-proofing, priority setting based on cost and benefit data, quality tools, and other training that affects employee effectiveness, efficiency, and safety. It might also include basic skills such as reading, writing, language, and arithmetic if required to ensure employee competence in the workplace.

The item examines key performance and learning objectives, and how education and training are designed, delivered, reinforced, and evaluated, with special emphasis on on-the-job application of knowledge and skills.

The item emphasizes the importance of involving employees and their managers in the design of training, including clear identification of specific needs. This involves job analysis—understanding the types and levels of the skills required and the timeliness of training. Determining specific education and training needs might include the use of organization assessment or employee self-assessment to determine and/or compare skill levels for progression within the organization or elsewhere.

Education and training delivery might occur inside or outside the organization and involve on-the-job, classroom, computer-based, distance education, or other types of delivery. This includes the use of developmental assignments within or outside the organization to enhance employees' career opportunities and employability.

It is also important for managers at all levels to reinforce training and education on the job. Without such reinforcement, newly learned skills are easily forgotten—wasting resources and suboptimizing performance.

The item also emphasizes evaluating and improving education and training. Evaluation could take into account managers' evaluation, employee self-evaluation, and peer evaluation of value received through education and training relative to needs identified in design. Evaluation might also address factors such as the effectiveness of education and training delivery, impact on work unit and organization performance, costs of delivery alternatives, and cost/benefit ratios.

Training for customer-contact employees is often essential in developing performance excellence and competitive advantage. Such training usually entails the following:

- Acquiring key knowledge and skills, including knowledge of products and services
- Listening to customers
- Soliciting comments from customers
- Anticipating and handling problems or failures (recovery)
- Developing skills in customer retention
- Learning how to effectively manage expectations

5.2 Employee Education, Training, and Development

How the organization's education and training address organization plans, including building knowledge and capabilities and contributing to achieving action plans and improving employee skills, capabilities, performance, and development

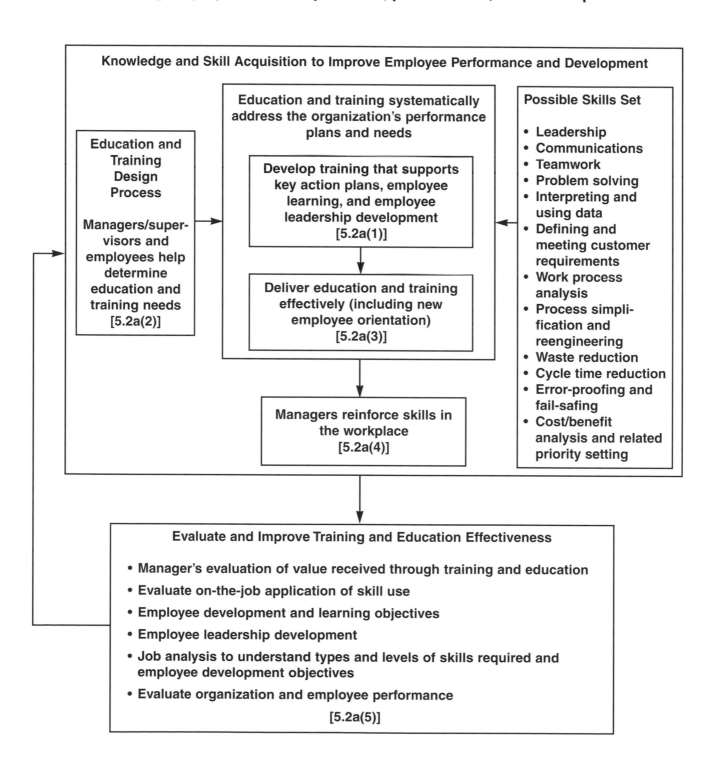

Knowledge and Skill Acquisition to Improve Employee Performance and Development

Education and Training Design Process

Managers/supervisors and employees help determine education and training needs [5.2a(2)]

Education and training systematically address the organization's performance plans and needs

Develop training that supports key action plans, employee learning, and employee leadership development [5.2a(1)]

Deliver education and training effectively (including new employee orientation) [5.2a(3)]

Managers reinforce skills in the workplace [5.2a(4)]

Possible Skills Set

- Leadership
- Communications
- Teamwork
- Problem solving
- Interpreting and using data
- Defining and meeting customer requirements
- Work process analysis
- Process simplification and reengineering
- Waste reduction
- Cycle time reduction
- Error-proofing and fail-safing
- Cost/benefit analysis and related priority setting

Evaluate and Improve Training and Education Effectiveness

- Manager's evaluation of value received through training and education
- Evaluate on-the-job application of skill use
- Employee development and learning objectives
- Employee leadership development
- Job analysis to understand types and levels of skills required and employee development objectives
- Evaluate organization and employee performance

[5.2a(5)]

5.2 Employee Education, Training, and Development Item Linkages

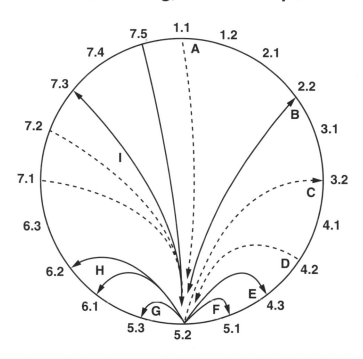

	Nature of Relationship
A	Leaders at all levels [1.1] reinforce training on the job to ensure its effectiveness [5.2].
B	Human resource development plans [2.2a] are used to help align training [5.2] to support the organizational goals [2.2b].
C	Training [5.2] can enhance capabilities of customer-contact employees [3.2a] and strengthen customer relationships [3.2c].
D	Key measures and benchmarking data [4.2] are used to improve training [5.2].
E	Information regarding training effectiveness [5.2] is analyzed to set priorities for improvement actions [4.3].
F	Effective training [5.2] enables employees and managers at all levels to improve skills and their ability to manage, organize, and design better work processes [5.1a].
G	Effective training [5.2] is often critical to maintaining and improving a safe, healthful work environment [5.3a].
H	Training [5.2] is essential to improving work in process effectiveness and innovation [6.1 and 6.2].
I	Results of improved training and development [5.2a] are reported in 7.3. In addition, customer satisfaction [7.1], financial and market [7.2], and operational performance and product and service quality results [7.5] are monitored, in part, to assess training effectiveness [5.2].

5.2 Employee Education, Training, and Development—Sample Effective Practices

A. Employee Education Training and Development

- Systematic needs analyses are conducted by managers and employees to ensure that skills required to perform work are routinely assessed, monitored, and maintained.
- Clear linkages exist between strategic plans and the education and training that are provided. Skills are developed based on work demands and employee needs.
- Employee input is considered when developing training plans.
- Employee career and personal development options, including development for leadership, are enhanced through formal education and training and through on-the-job training such as rotational assignments or job exchange programs.
- The organization uses various methods to deliver training to ensure that it is suitable for employee knowledge and skill levels.
- Training is linked to work requirements, which managers reinforce on the job. Just-in-time training is preferred (rather than just-in-case training) to help ensure that the skills will be used immediately after training.
- Employee feedback on the appropriateness of the training is collected and used to improve course delivery and content.
- The organization systematically evaluates training effectiveness on the job. Performance data are collected on individuals and groups at all levels to assess the impact of training.
- Employee satisfaction with courses is tracked.
- Training is systematically refined and improved based on these evaluations.

5.3 Employee Well-Being and Satisfaction (30 points)
Approach/Deployment Scoring

Describe how the company maintains a work environment and work climate that support the well-being, satisfaction, and motivation of employees.

In your response, address the following Areas:

a. Work Environment
How the company maintains a safe and healthful work environment. Describe how health, safety, and ergonomics are addressed in improvement activities. Briefly describe key measures and targets for each of these environmental factors and how employees take part in establishing these measures and targets. Note significant differences, if any, based upon different work environments for employee groups or work units.

b. Work Climate
How the company builds and enhances its work climate for the well-being, satisfaction, and motivation of all employees. Describe:
(1) company services, benefits, and actions to support employees; and
(2) a brief summary of how senior leaders, managers, and supervisors encourage and motivate employees to develop and utilize their full potential.

c. Employee Satisfaction
How the company assesses the work environment and work climate. Include:
(1) a brief description of formal and/or informal methods and measures used to determine the key factors that affect employee well-being, satisfaction, and motivation. Note important differences in methods, factors, or measures for different categories or types of employees, as appropriate; and
(2) how the company relates employee well-being, satisfaction, and motivation results to key business results and/or objectives to identify improvement priorities.

Notes:
N1. Approaches for supporting and enhancing employee well-being, satisfaction, and motivation [5.3b(1)] might include: counseling; career development and employability services; recreational or cultural activities; non-work-related education; day care; job sharing; special leave for family responsibilities and/or for community service; safety off the job; flexible work hours; outplacement; and retiree benefits, including extended health care.

Continued on next page

N2. Specific factors that might affect well-being, satisfaction, and motivation [5.3c(1)] include: effective employee problem or grievance resolution; safety factors; employee views of management; employee training, development, and career opportunities; employee preparation for changes in technology or the work organization; work environment and other work conditions; workload; cooperation and teamwork; recognition; benefits; communications; job security; compensation; equal opportunity; and capability to provide required services to customers.

N3. Measures and/or indicators of well-being, satisfaction, and motivation (5.3c) might include safety, absenteeism, turnover, turnover rate for customer-contact employees, grievances, strikes, other job actions, and worker's compensation claims, as well as results of surveys. Results relative to such measures and/or indicators should be reported in Item 7.3.

This item examines the work environment and motivational climate, and how they are tailored to foster the well-being, satisfaction, and motivation of all employees.

Area 5.3a calls for information regarding a safe and healthful work environment. High performing organizations include such factors in their planning and improvement activities. Important factors in this Area include establishing appropriate measures and targets and recognizing that various employee groups might experience very different environments and, as a result, may need different safety procedures, measures, and plans.

Area 5.3b calls for information on the organization's approach to enhance employee well-being, satisfaction, and motivation based on a holistic view of employees as key stakeholders who are critical to the organization's success. The Area emphasizes that the organization needs to consider a variety of services, facilities, activities, and opportunities to build well-being, satisfaction, and motivation. Senior leaders, managers, and supervisors have a specific responsibility to encourage employees, and to ensure good communication with and between employees.

Most organizations, regardless of size, have many opportunities to contribute to employee well-being, satisfaction, and motivation. Examples of services, facilities, activities, and other opportunities include the following:
- Personal and career counseling
- Career development and employability services
- Recreational or cultural activities
- Formal and informal recognition
- Non-work-related education

- Day care
- Special leave for family responsibilities or for community services
- Safety off the job
- Flexible work hours
- Outplacement
- Retiree benefits, including extended health care

These services also might include career enhancement activities such as skills assessment, helping employees develop learning objectives and plans, and employability assessment.

Area 5.3c calls for information on how the organization determines employee satisfaction, well-being, and motivation. The Area recognizes that many factors might affect employees. Although satisfaction with pay and promotion potential is important, these factors might not be adequate to assess the overall climate for motivation and high performance. For this reason, the organization might need to consider a variety of factors in the work environment to determine the key factors in motivation. Examples of specific factors that might affect satisfaction, well-being, and motivation include:
- Effective employee problem or grievance resolution
- Safety
- Employee views of leadership and management
- Employee development and career opportunities
- Employee preparation for changes in technology or work organization
- Work environment
- Workload
- Cooperation and teamwork
- Recognition
- Benefits
- Communications
- Job security
- Compensation
- Equal opportunity
- Capability to provide required services to customers

In addition to formal or informal survey results, other measures and/or indicators of satisfaction, well-being, and motivation might include safety, absenteeism, turnover, turnover rate for customer-contact employees, grievances, strikes, and worker's compensation claims. Factors inhibiting motivation need to be prioritized and addressed. Further understanding of these factors could be developed through exit interviews with departing employees.

The Area also addresses how the information and data on the well-being, satisfaction, and motivation of employees are systematically used in identifying improvement priorities. Decisions about such activities might be based, in part, on human resource results presented in Item 7.3. Leaders should use these data to develop priorities for addressing employee problems based on impact on organization performance.

5.3 Employee Well-Being and Satisfaction

How the organization maintains a work environment and a work climate that support the well-being, satisfaction, and motivation of employees

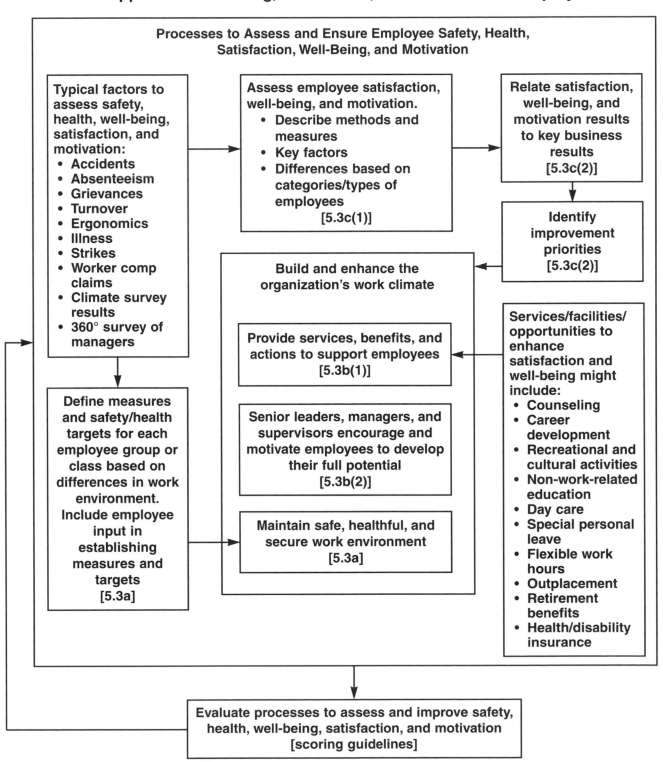

Processes to Assess and Ensure Employee Safety, Health, Satisfaction, Well-Being, and Motivation

Typical factors to assess safety, health, well-being, satisfaction, and motivation:
- **Accidents**
- **Absenteeism**
- **Grievances**
- **Turnover**
- **Ergonomics**
- **Illness**
- **Strikes**
- **Worker comp claims**
- **Climate survey results**
- **360° survey of managers**

Assess employee satisfaction, well-being, and motivation.
- **Describe methods and measures**
- **Key factors**
- **Differences based on categories/types of employees [5.3c(1)]**

Relate satisfaction, well-being, and motivation results to key business results [5.3c(2)]

Identify improvement priorities [5.3c(2)]

Define measures and safety/health targets for each employee group or class based on differences in work environment. Include employee input in establishing measures and targets [5.3a]

Build and enhance the organization's work climate

Provide services, benefits, and actions to support employees [5.3b(1)]

Senior leaders, managers, and supervisors encourage and motivate employees to develop their full potential [5.3b(2)]

Maintain safe, healthful, and secure work environment [5.3a]

Services/facilities/opportunities to enhance satisfaction and well-being might include:
- **Counseling**
- **Career development**
- **Recreational and cultural activities**
- **Non-work-related education**
- **Day care**
- **Special personal leave**
- **Flexible work hours**
- **Outplacement**
- **Retirement benefits**
- **Health/disability insurance**

Evaluate processes to assess and improve safety, health, well-being, satisfaction, and motivation [scoring guidelines]

5.3   Employee Well-Being and Satisfaction Item Linkages

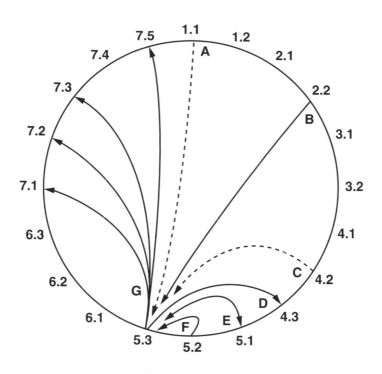

Nature of Relationship	
A	Leaders at all levels [1.1] have responsibility for enhancing employee morale and well-being [5.3].
B	Human resource development plans [2.2a] address morale and well-being concerns [5.3].
C	Key benchmarking data [4.2] are used to design processes to enhance employee morale and well-being [5.3].
D	Information regarding employee well-being and morale [5.3c] is used to gain a better understanding of problems and performance capabilities and to set priorities for improvement actions [4.3].
E	High morale [5.3] enhances employee participation, self-direction, and initiative [5.1], and vice versa.
F	Training systems [5.2] enhance employee development, leading to improved employee morale and well-being [5.3].
G	Systems that enhance employee satisfaction and well-being [5.3] can boost performance [7.2 and 7.5] and customer satisfaction [7.1]. Specific results of employee well-being and satisfaction systems are reported in 7.3.

5.3   *Employee Well-Being and Satisfaction—Sample Effective Practices*

A. Work Environment

- Quality activities consider issues relating to employee health, safety, and workplace environment. Plans exist to optimize these conditions and eliminate adverse conditions.
- Root causes for health and safety problems are systematically identified and eliminated. Corrective actions are communicated widely to help prevent the problem in other parts of the organization.

B. Work Climate

- Special activities and services are available for employees. These can be quite varied, depending on the needs of employees, such as the following:
  - Flexible benefits plan including health care, on-site day care, dental, portable retirement, education (both work and non-work-related), maternity, paternity, and family illness leave.
  - Group purchasing power program where the number of participating merchants is increasing steadily.
  - Special facilities for employee meetings to discuss their concerns.
- Senior leaders motivate employees by building a work climate that addresses the well-being of all employees.

C. Employee Satisfaction

- Key employee satisfaction opinion indicators are gathered periodically based on the stability of the organization (organizations in the midst of rapid change conduct assessments more frequently).
- Satisfaction data are derived from employee focus groups, e-mail data, employee satisfaction survey results, turnover, absenteeism, stress-related disorders, and other data that reflect employee satisfaction. (A key employee satisfaction indicator is one that reflects conditions affecting employee morale and motivation.)
- On-demand electronic surveys are available for quick response and tabulations any time managers seek employee satisfaction feedback.
- Managers use the results of these surveys to focus improvements in work systems and enhance employee satisfaction.
- Employee satisfaction indicators are correlated with drivers of business success to help identify where resources should be placed to provide maximum business benefit.

6   *Process Management—100 Points*

The **Process Management** category examines the key aspects of
process management, including customer-focused design, product and
service delivery, support, and supplier and partnering processes involving
all work units. The category examines how key processes are designed,
implemented, managed, and improved to achieve better performance.

The Process Management category is the focal point within the criteria for all
key work processes. Built into the category are the central requirements for
efficient and effective process management—effective design, a prevention
orientation, evaluation and continuous improvement, linkage to suppliers and
partners, cycle time, and overall high performance.

An increasingly important concept in all aspects of process management and
organizational design is flexibility. In simplest terms, flexibility refers to the
ability to adapt quickly and effectively to changing requirements—
minimizing bureaucratic rigidity and "system craziness."

Depending on the nature of the business's strategy and markets, flexibility
might mean rapid changeover from one product to another, rapid response to
changing demands, or the ability to produce a wide range of customized
services. Flexibility might demand special strategies such as modular
designs, sharing of components, sharing of manufacturing lines, and
specialized training. Flexibility also increasingly involves outsourcing
decisions, agreements with key suppliers, and innovative partnering
arrangements. Flexibility in process management is facilitated by the work
systems designed and examined in Item 5.1.

6.1 Management of Product and Service Processes (60 points)
Approach/Deployment Scoring

Describe how products and services are designed, implemented, and improved. Describe also how production/delivery processes are designed, implemented, managed, and improved.

In your response, address the following Areas:

a. Design Processes

How new, modified, and customized products and services, and production/delivery processes are designed and implemented. Include:

(1) how changing customer and market requirements and technology are incorporated into product and service designs;

(2) how production/delivery processes are designed to meet customer, quality, and operational performance requirements;

(3) how design and production/delivery processes are coordinated and tested to ensure trouble-free and timely introduction and delivery of products and services; and

(4) how design processes are evaluated and improved to achieve better performance, including improvements to products and services, transfer of learning to other company units and projects, and reduced cycle time.

b. Production/Delivery Processes

How the company's key product and service production/delivery processes are managed and improved. Include:

(1) a description of the key processes and their principal requirements;

(2) how the processes are managed to maintain process performance and to ensure products and services will meet customer and operational requirements. Include a description of key in-process measurements and/or customer information gathering, as appropriate; and

(3) how production/delivery processes are evaluated and improved to achieve better performance, including improvements to products and services, transfer of learning to other company units and projects, and reduced cycle time.

Continued on next page

Notes:

N1. The relative importance of, and relationships between, design processes and production/delivery processes depend upon many factors, including the nature of the products and services, technology requirements, issues of modularity and parts commonality, customer and supplier relationships and involvement, product and service customization, and overall company strategy. Design, production, and delivery might depend upon and/or utilize new technology in ways that differ greatly among companies. Responses to Item 6.1 should address the most critical requirements to business success.

N2. Responses to 6.1a(1) should include how customers are involved in design, as appropriate.

N3. Responses to 6.1a(3) should include key supplier and partner participation, as appropriate.

N4. Process evaluation and improvement [6.1a(4) and 6.1b(3)] might include process analysis, research and development results, technology management, benchmarking, use of alternative technology, and information from internal and external customers.

N5. Results of improvements in product and service design and delivery processes, product and service quality results, and results of improvements in products and services should be reported in Item 7.5.

This item examines how the organization designs, introduces, produces, delivers, and improves its products and services. It also examines how production/delivery processes are designed, managed, and improved. Important to the management of these processes is the trouble-free introduction of new products and services. This requires effective coordination of all entities key to design and delivery, starting early in the product and service design phase. The item also examines organizational learning, through a focus on how learning in one process or organization unit is replicated and added to the knowledge base of other projects or organization units.

Area 6.1a calls for information on the design of products, services, and their production/delivery processes. Four aspects of this design are examined.
  • How changing customer and market requirements and technology are incorporated into product and service designs
  • How production/delivery processes are designed to meet customer, quality, and operational performance requirements

- How design and production/delivery processes are coordinated to ensure trouble-free and timely introduction and delivery of products and services
- How design processes are evaluated and improved to achieve better performance.

Design approaches could differ appreciably depending on the nature of the products/services—whether they are entirely new, variants of existing ones, or major or minor process changes. Responses should reflect the key requirements for the organization's products and services.

Factors that might need to be considered in design include health, safety, long-term performance, environmental impact, "green" manufacturing, measurement capability, process capability, manufacturability, maintainability, supplier capability, and documentation. Effective design must also consider cycle time and productivity of production and delivery processes. This might entail detailed mapping of production or service processes and redesigning or reengineering them to achieve efficiency as well as to meet changing customer requirements.

Many organizations also need to consider requirements for suppliers and/or business partners at the design stage. Overall, effective design must take into account all stakeholders in the value chain. If many design projects are carried out in parallel, or if the organization's products utilize parts, equipment, and facilities used for other products, coordination of resources might be a major concern and might offer the means to reduce unit costs and time to market significantly. This should be addressed in responding to Area 6.1a.

Coordination of design and production/delivery processes involves all organization units and/or individuals who will take part in production and delivery and whose performance materially affects overall process outcome. This might include groups such as research and development (R&D), marketing, design, and product/process engineering.

Area 6.1b examines the management and improvement of the organization's key production and delivery processes. Key processes, their specific requirements, and how performance relative to these requirements is determined and maintained must be described. It is also important to identify in-process measurements and customer interactions early in the production process, rather than relying on end-process inspection. This requires the identification of critical points in processes for measurement, observation, or interaction. The intent is that these activities occur at the earliest points possible in processes, to minimize problems that may result from deviations from expected (design) performance. Expected performance frequently requires setting performance levels or standards to guide decision making. When deviations occur, a remedy—usually called corrective action—is required to restore the performance of the process to its design performance. Depending on the nature of the process, the correction could involve technical and/or human factors. Proper correction involves changes at the source (root cause) of the deviation. Such corrective action should minimize the likelihood of this type of variation recurring anywhere in the organization.

When customer interactions are involved, differences between customers must be taken into account in evaluating how well the process is performing. This might entail specific or general contingencies depending on the customer information gathered. This is especially true of professional and personal services.

Areas 6.1a and 6.1b call for information on how processes are systematically improved to achieve better performance. Better performance means not only better quality from the customers' perspective, but also better financial and operational performance—such as improved productivity and cycle time— from the organization's perspective. Area 6.1b anticipates that organizations use a variety of process improvement approaches such as:
- The sharing of successful strategies across the organization
- Process analysis and research (for example, process mapping, optimization experiments, and error-proofing)
- Research and development results
- Benchmarking
- Use of alternative technology
- Information from customers of the processes—within and outside the organization.

Process improvement approaches might utilize financial data to evaluate alternatives and set priorities. Together, all of these approaches offer a wide range of possibilities, including the complete redesign (reengineering) of processes.

6.1 Management of Product and Service Processes

How products and services as well as production/delivery processes are designed, implemented, managed, and improved

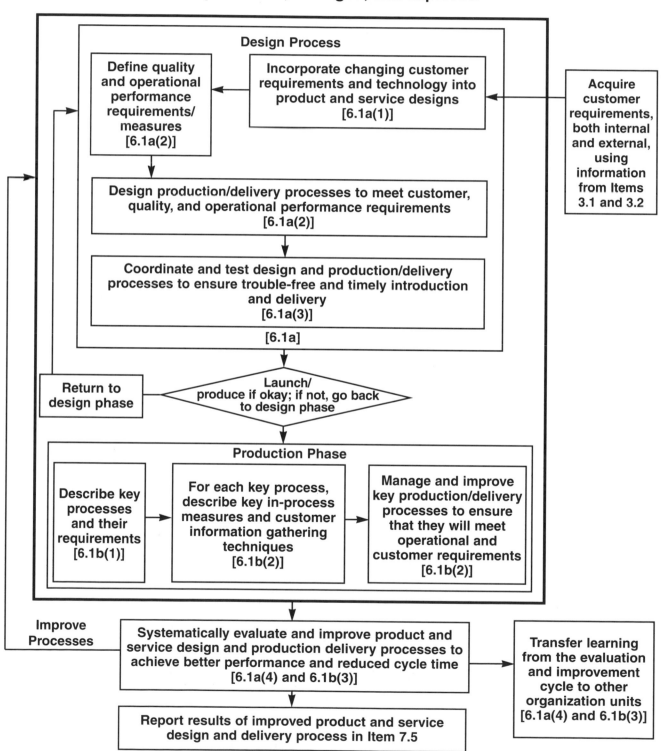

6.1 Management of Product and Service Processes Item Linkages

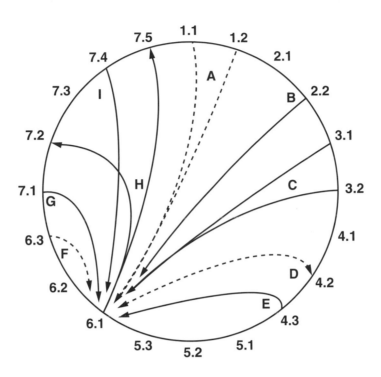

	Nature of Relationship
A	Leaders at all levels [1.1] have a responsibility for ensuring that work processes are designed [6.1a] consistent with organizational objectives, including those relating to public responsibility and corporate citizenship [1.2].
B	Goals, deployed to the work force [2.2], are used to drive and align actions to achieve improved performance [6.1].
C	Information about customer requirements [3.1] and information from customer hot lines (complaints) through customer-contact employees [3.2a] is used to design or modify products and services to better meet requirements.
D	Critical work processes [6.1] are used to help identify and prioritize benchmarking or comparison targets [4.2]. Benchmarking and comparison data [4.2] are used to improve work processes [6.1].
	Continued on next page

	Nature of Relationship (continued)
E	Priorities for work process improvements [6.1] are set based on performance data analysis [4.3].
F	Effective management of supplier and partner performance [6.3] can result in improved operations processes [6.1] by reducing error, rework, and delay.
G	Information about customer satisfaction [7.1] is used to target improvement efforts in product and service design and development processes [6.1].
H	Processes to ensure that products and services are designed to meet customer requirements and have a trouble-free introduction [6.1a] affect product and service production and delivery [6.1b], product and service operating performance [7.5], and financial results [7.2].
I	Information about supplier performance [7.4] is essential to the design and implementation of new, modified, or customized products and services [6.1a].

6.1 Management of Product and Service Processes—Sample Effective Practices

A. Design Processes

- A systematic iterative process (such as quality function deployment) is used to maintain a focus on the voice of the customer and convert customer requirements into product or service design, production, and delivery.
- Product design requirements are systematically translated into process specifications, with measurement plans to monitor process consistency.
- The work of various functions is coordinated to bring the product or service through the design-to-delivery phases. Functional barriers between units have been eliminated organizationwide.
- Concurrent engineering is used to operate several processes (for example, product and service planning, R&D, manufacturing, marketing, supplier certification) in parallel as much as possible, rather than operating in sequence. All activities are closely coordinated through effective communication and teamwork.
- Internal process capacity and supplier capability, using measures such as C_{pk}, are reviewed and considered before production and delivery process designs or plans are finalized.
- Market, design, production, service, and delivery reviews occur at defined intervals or as needed.
- Steps are taken (such as design testing or prototyping) to ensure that the production and delivery process will work as designed, and will meet customer requirements.
- Design processes are evaluated and improvements have been made so that future designs are developed faster (shorter cycle time), at lower cost, and with higher quality, relative to key product or service characteristics that predict customer satisfaction.
- The results of improved design process performance are reported in 7.5.

B. Production/Delivery Processes

- Performance requirements (from Item 6.1a design processes and customer requirements) are set using facts and data and are monitored using statistical process control techniques.
- Production and service delivery processes are measured and tracked. Measures (quantitative and qualitative) should reflect or assess the extent

to which customer requirements are met, as well as production consistency.

- For processes that produce defects (out-of-control processes), root causes are systematically identified and corrective action is taken to prevent their recurrence.
- Corrections are monitored and verified. Process used and results obtained should be systematic and integrated throughout the organization.
- Processes are systematically reviewed to improve productivity, reduce cycle time and waste, and increase quality.
- Tools are used—such as flowcharting, work redesign, and reengineering—throughout the organization to improve work processes.
- Benchmarking, competitive comparison data, or information from customers of the process (in or out of the organization) are used to gain insight to improve processes.

6.2 Management of Support Processes (20 points)
Approach/Deployment Scoring

Describe how the company's key support processes are designed, implemented, managed, and improved.

In your response, address the following Area:

a. Management of Support Processes

How key support processes are designed, implemented, managed, and improved so that current and future requirements are met. Include:

(1) how key requirements are determined or set, incorporating input from internal and external customers, as appropriate;

(2) how key support processes are designed and implemented to meet customer, quality, and operational performance requirements;

(3) a description of the key support processes and their principal requirements;

(4) how the processes are managed to maintain process performance and to ensure results will meet customer and operational requirements. Include a description of key in-process measurements and/or customer information gathering, as appropriate; and

(5) how the processes are evaluated and improved to achieve better performance, including transfer of learning to other company units and projects, and reduced cycle time.

Notes:

N1. The purpose of Item 6.2 is to permit companies to highlight separately the processes that support the product and service design, production, and delivery processes addressed in Item 6.1. The support processes included in Item 6.2 depend on the company's business and how it operates. Together, Items 6.1, 6.2, and 6.3 should cover all key operations, processes, and activities of all work units.

N2. Process evaluation and improvement [6.2a(5)] might include process analysis and research, benchmarking, use of alternative technology, and information from internal and external customers. Information from external customers could include information described in Items 3.2 and 4.3.

N3. Results of improvements in key support processes and key support process performance results should be reported in Item 7.5.

This item examines how the organization designs, maintains, and improves its support processes. Support processes are those that support the organization's product or service delivery, but are not usually designed in detail with the products and services themselves, because their requirements do not usually depend a great deal on product and service characteristics. Support process design requirements usually significantly depend on internal requirements and must be coordinated and integrated to ensure efficient and effective performance.

Support processes generally include the following:
- Finance and accounting
- Software services
- Sales
- Marketing
- Public relations
- Information services
- Personnel and payroll
- Legal services
- Plant and facilities management
- Logistics
- Security
- Research and development
- Secretarial and other administrative services

The item examines how the organization maintains the performance of the key support processes. The organization should describe key support processes, their principal requirements, and a description of key in-process measurements and customer interactions. These principal requirements are similar to those for operational performance requirements in Item 6.1b.

Item 6.2 also calls for information on how the organization evaluates and improves the performance of its key support processes. Four key approaches the organization might consider or use are as follows:
- Process analysis and research
- Benchmarking
- Use of alternative technology
- Information from customers of the processes—within and outside the organization

Together, these approaches may help organizations improve or reengineer key processes.

6.2 Management of Support Processes

How key support processes are designed, implemented, managed, and improved

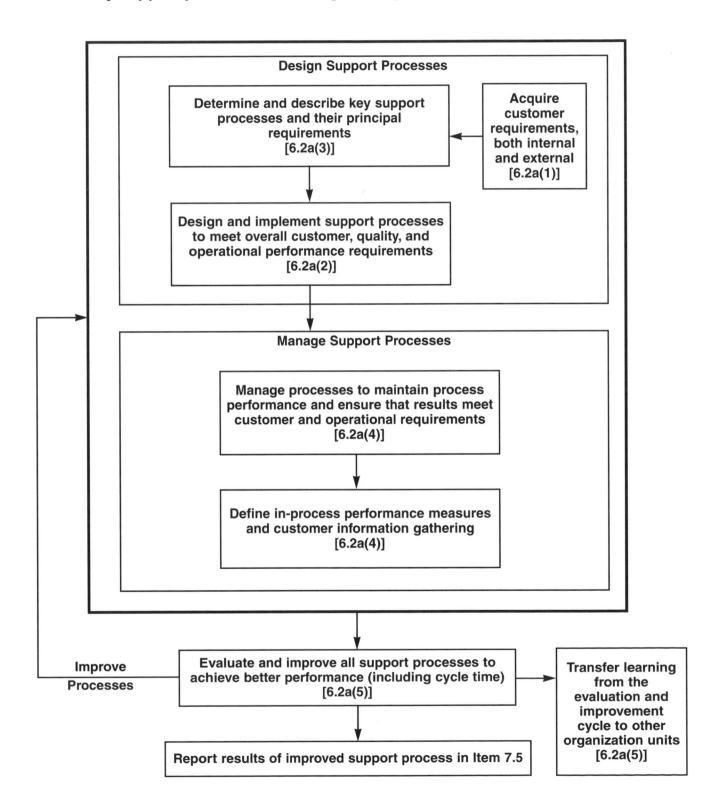

6.2 Management of Support Processes Item Linkages

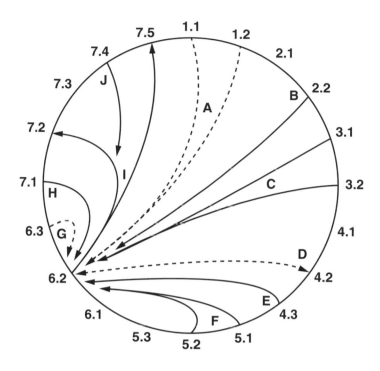

	Nature of Relationship
A	Leaders at all levels [1.1] ensure that support processes [6.2] are aligned with organization priorities, including regulatory and public responsibilities [1.2].
B	Goals deployed to the work force [2.2], are used to drive and align actions to achieve improved support performance [6.2].
C	Information about customer requirements [3.1] and from customer contact personnel [3.2a] is used to identify improvement opportunities in support work processes [6.2].
D	Critical work processes in the support area [6.2] are used to help identify and prioritize benchmarking targets [4.2]. Benchmarking data [4.2] are used to improve support work processes [6.2].
E	Priorities for support work processes improvement [6.2] are set based on performance data and analysis [4.3].
	Continued on next page

	Nature of Relationship (continued)
F	High-performance flexible work systems [5.1a] and effective recognition [5.1b] and training [5.2] are essential to improving support work processes [6.2].
G	Effective management of supplier and partner performance [6.3] may be required to improve support work processes [6.2] by reducing rework, error, and delay.
H	Information about customer satisfaction [7.1] is used to target improvement efforts in support work processes [6.2].
I	Improved support work processes [6.2] produce better product and service quality, operational efficiency [7.5], and financial results [7.2].
J	Supplier and partner capabilities, as indicated by performance results [7.4] are considered in the design process for support services [6.2].

6.2 Management of Support Processes—Sample Effective Practices

A. Management of Support Processes

- A formal process exists to understand internal customer requirements, translate those requirements into efficient service processes, and measure their effectiveness.
- Specific improvements in support services are made with the same rigor and concern for the internal and external customer as improvements in operating processes.
- All support services are subject to continuous review and improvements in performance and customer satisfaction.
- Systems to ensure process performance are maintained, and customer requirements are met.
- Root causes of problems are systematically identified and corrected for processes that produce defects.
- Corrections are monitored and verified. Process used and results obtained should be systematic and integrated throughout the organization.
- Support processes are systematically reviewed to improve productivity, reduce cycle time and waste, and increase quality.
- Work process simplification or improvement tools are used with measurable sustained results.
- Stretch goals are used to drive higher levels of performance.
- Benchmarking, competitive comparison data, or information from customers of the process (in or out of the organization) are used to gain insight to improve processes.

6.3 Management of Supplier and Partnering Processes (20 points)
Approach/Deployment Scoring

Describe how the company's supplier and partnering processes and relationships are designed, implemented, managed, and improved. Describe also how supplier and partner performance is managed and improved.

In your response, address the following Area:

a. Management of Supplier and Partnering Processes
   Describe:
   (1) how supplier and partnering processes are designed and implemented to meet overall performance requirements and to help suppliers and partners meet these requirements. Include a brief summary of the principal performance requirements for key suppliers and partners, and describe how partners and preferred suppliers are selected, as appropriate.
   (2) how the company ensures that its performance requirements are met. Describe how suppliers' and partners' performance is evaluated, including key measures, expected performance levels, any incentive systems used, and how performance information is fed back to suppliers and partners; and
   (3) how the company evaluates and improves its management of supplier and partnering processes. Summarize current actions and plans to improve suppliers' and partners' abilities to contribute to achieving your company's performance goals. Include actions to minimize costs associated with inspection, testing, or performance audits; and actions to enhance supplier and partner knowledge of your company's current and longer-term needs and their ability to respond to those needs.

Notes:
N1. Supplier and partnering processes could include company processes for supply chain improvement and optimization, beyond direct suppliers and partners.

N2. In 6.3a(1), key suppliers and partners are those selected on the basis of volume of business or criticality of their supplied products and/or services; preferred suppliers and partners are those selected on the basis of performance criteria.

N3. Results of improvements in supplier and partnering processes and supplier/partner performance results should be reported in Item 7.4.

Item 6.3 examines how the organization designs, implements, manages, and improves its supplier and partnering processes, relationships, and performance. The term *supplier* refers to other organizations as well as to other units of the parent organization that provide goods and services.

The use of these goods and services may occur at any stage in the production, design, delivery, and use of the organization's products and services. Thus, suppliers include organizations such as distributors, dealers, warranty repair services, transportation, contractors, and franchises, as well as those that provide materials and components. Suppliers also include service suppliers, such as health care, training, and education providers.

The item places particular emphasis on the unique relationships that organizations are building with key and preferred suppliers, including establishing longer-term partnering relationships. For many organizations, key suppliers and partners are an increasingly important part of achieving not only high performance and lower-cost objectives, but also strategic objectives. For example, suppliers and partners might provide unique design, integration, and marketing capabilities. Item 6.3 requests information on the criteria for selecting partners and preferred suppliers.

Organizations must identify the principal performance requirements for key suppliers and partners. These requirements are the principal factors involved in the organization's purchases, for example, quality, delivery, and price. Processes for determining whether or not requirements are met might include audits, process reviews, receiving inspection, certification, testing, and rating systems.

Item 6.3 also requests information on actions and plans to improve suppliers' and partners' abilities to contribute to achieving performance goals. These actions and plans might include one or more of the following:
- Improving procurement and supplier management processes (including seeking feedback from suppliers and internal customers)
- Joint planning and rapid information and data exchanges
- Using benchmarking and comparative information
- Forming customer-supplier teams
- Training suppliers and partners
- Developing long-term agreements
- Incentives and recognition
- Changing supplier selection methods, leading to a reduction in the number of suppliers and enhancing the strength and performance of remaining partnership agreements

6.3 Management of Supplier and Partnering Processes

How the supplier and partnering process, relationship, and performance are designed, implemented, managed, and improved

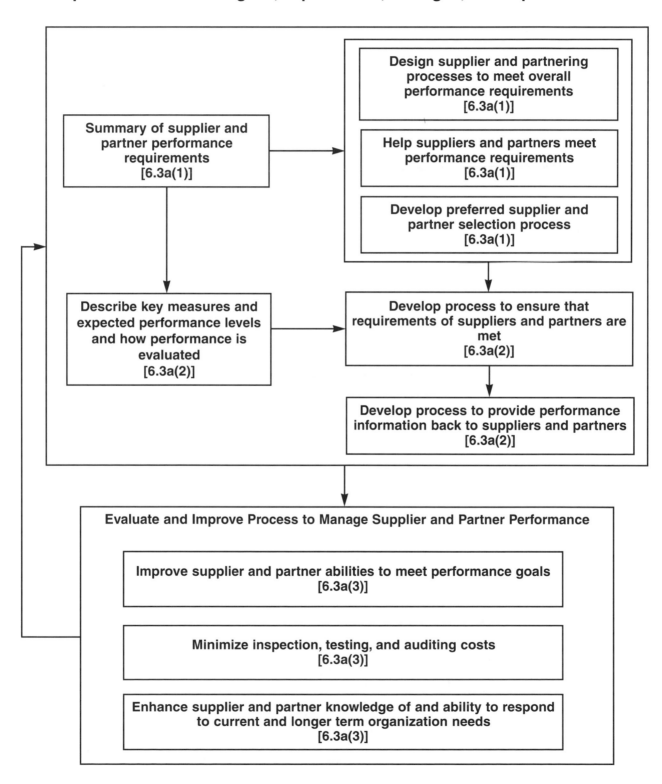

6.3 Management of Supplier and Partnering Processes Item Linkages

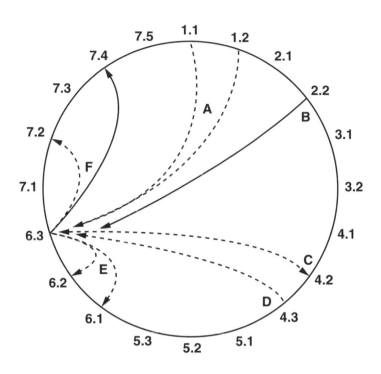

Nature of Relationship
A   Leaders at all levels [1.1] who interact with suppliers and partners have a responsibility to ensure systematic improvement of performance on key indicators [6.3] and ensure that suppliers and partners do not act in a manner inconsistent with the organization's commitment to the public, including regulatory compliance [1.2].
B   Stretch goals [2.2], deployed through the key supplier chain, are used to drive improved supplier performance [6.3] in critical areas.
C   Problems and issues with supplier performance [6.3] are used to help identify and prioritize benchmarking targets [4.2]. Benchmarking and comparison data [4.2] are used to improve supplier performance initiatives [6.3].
D   Data are analyzed and used to set priorities [4.3] to help improve supplier and partner work processes and performance [6.3].
E   Improved supplier performance [6.3] may be required to, and typically helps to, improve work processes [6.1 and 6.2].
F   Improved supplier processes [6.3] result in better supplier performance [7.4] and possibly better financial performance [7.2].

6.3 Management of Supplier and Partnering Processes— Sample Effective Practices

A. Management of Supplier and Partnering Processes

- Performance requirements are clearly defined in measurable terms and communicated to suppliers.
- Decisions on which suppliers are selected are driven by measurable performance characteristics of the supplier, rather than primarily on price.
- Measures of expected supplier performance are in place.
- Data on supplier and partner performance are provided to suppliers frequently so that they can adjust and improve performance.
- The organization has a system in place to review and improve its own procurement processes and processes for communicating with and selecting suppliers and partners.
- Procedures are in place to improve supplier and partner performance (for example, fewer defective parts, less rework and scrap, faster response time) that include training or certification programs. The organization systematically helps its key suppliers improve their own performance and capabilities.
- Actions are taken to reduce unnecessary costs—such as incoming inspection or testing—by improving the internal performance systems of suppliers and partners.

7 *Business Results—450 Points*

The **Business Results** category examines the company's performance and improvement in key business areas—customer satisfaction, financial and marketplace performance, human resource results, supplier and partner performance, and operational performance. Also examined are performance levels relative to competitors.

The Business Results category provides a focus that encompasses the customer's evaluation of the organization's products and services, the organization's overall financial and market performance, and the results of all key human resource, supplier, and operational processes and process improvement activities. Through this focus, the criteria's dual purposes— superior value of offerings as viewed by customers and the marketplace, and superior organization performance reflected in operational and financial indicators—are maintained. Category 7 thus provides real-time measures of progress for evaluation and improvement of processes, products, and services, aligned with overall business strategy. Analysis of business results data are carried out using the processes examined in Item 4.3.

Item 7.5 provides an opportunity to summarize key performance results, not covered in Items 7.1–7.4, that contribute significantly to customer satisfaction, operational, and financial/marketplace performance.

7.1 Customer Satisfaction Results (125 points)
Results Scoring

Summarize the company's customer satisfaction and dissatisfaction results.

In your response, address the following Area:

a. Customer Satisfaction Results
Summarize current levels and trends in key measures and/or indicators of customer satisfaction and dissatisfaction, including satisfaction relative to competitors. Address different customer groups and market segments, as appropriate.

Notes:

N1. Customer satisfaction and dissatisfaction results reported in this Item derive from determination methods described in Item 3.2.

N2. Measures and/or indicators of customer satisfaction and satisfaction relative to competitors might include information on customer-perceived value.

N3. Measures and/or indicators of customer satisfaction relative to competitors might include objective information and data from customers and independent organizations. Comparative performance of products and services and operational performance measures that serve as indicators of customer satisfaction should be addressed in Item 7.5.

This item addresses the principal customer-related results—customer satisfaction, customer dissatisfaction, and customer satisfaction relative to competitors.

The item calls for all relevant data and information to examine the organization's performance *as viewed by the customer*. Results relating to the organization's performance *as viewed by the organization* through internal measures such as response time to resolve customer complaints, should be reported in item 7.5.

Relevant data and information from the viewpoint of the customer include the following:
- Customer satisfaction and dissatisfaction measures
- Retention, gains and losses of customers, and customer account growth or decline
- Customer complaints and warranty claims
- Customer-perceived value based on customer's opinion of quality and price
- Competitive awards, ratings, and recognition from customers and independent organizations

In order to determine whether results, trends, and levels are good or not, comparative data must be provided.

It is also important to provide data segmented by markets and product or service lines if those groupings are made in plans or operations. For example, if an organization offers three different products to different customer groups, it is important to differentiate customer satisfaction levels for each product and group—although all data can be presented on one graph. It would be inappropriate to aggregate the data into one trend line because it tends to obscure trends and levels for the component segments. This would likely result in a lower score during the examination process.

7.1 Customer Satisfaction Results

The organization's customer satisfaction and customer dissatisfaction results using key measures and/or indicators of these results

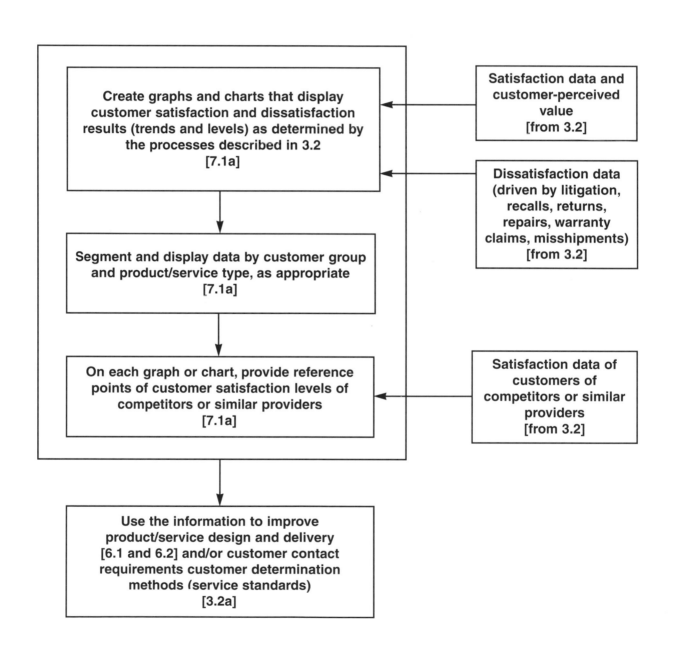

7.1 Customer Satisfaction Results Item Linkages

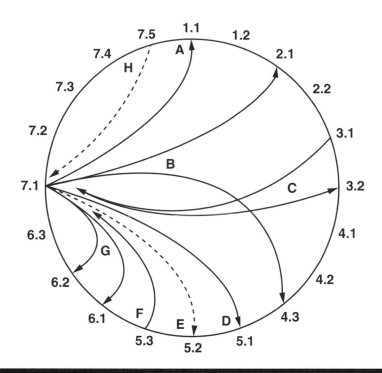

	Nature of Relationship
A	Data on levels of satisfaction of customers [7.1] are monitored by leaders at all levels [1.1].
B	Data on levels of satisfaction of customers [7.1] are collected and used to set organizational improvement priorities and to allocate resources [4.3b], and for strategic planning [2.1].
C	Processes used to gather intelligence about current customer requirements [3.1], strengthen customer relations [3.2a], and determine customer satisfaction [3.2b] are used to produce customer satisfaction results data [7.1]. In addition, customer satisfaction results [7.1] are used to set customer contact requirements (service standards) [3.2a].
D	Recognition and rewards [5.1b] must be based, in part, on customer satisfaction results [7.1].
E	Customer satisfaction data [7.1], are monitored, in part, to assess training effectiveness [5.2].
F	Systems to enhance employee satisfaction and well-being [5.3] can produce higher levels of customer satisfaction [7.1], especially from customer-contact employees.
G	Data on satisfaction or dissatisfaction of customers [7.1] are used to help design products and services and to improve operational [6.1] and support [6.2] processes.
H	Organization-specific results [7.5] provide an adverse indicator of customer satisfaction results [7.1].

7.1 Customer Satisfaction Results—Sample Effective Results

A. Customer Satisfaction Results

- Trends and indicators of customer satisfaction and dissatisfaction (including complaint data), segmented by customer groups, are provided in graph and chart form for all key measures. Multiyear data are provided.
- All indicators show steady improvement. (Indicators include data collected in Item 3.2b such as customer assessments of products and services, customer awards, and customer retention.)
- All indicators compare favorably to competitors or similar providers.
- Customer satisfaction graphs and information are accurate and easy to understand.
- Data are not missing.
- Results data are supported by customer feedback, customers' overall assessments of products and services, and customer awards.
- Data are presented concerning customer dissatisfaction for the most relevant product or service quality indicators collected through the processes described in Item 3.2b (some of which may be referenced in the business overview).

7.2 Financial and Market Results (125 points)
Results Scoring

Summarize the company's key financial and marketplace performance results.

In your response, address the following Area:

a. Financial and Market Results
Provide results of:
(1) financial performance, including aggregate measures of financial return and/or economic value, as appropriate; and
(2) marketplace performance, including market share/position, business growth, and new markets entered, as appropriate.
For all quantitative measures and/or indicators of performance, provide current levels and trends. Include appropriate comparative data.

Note:
Aggregate measures such as return on investment (ROI), asset utilization, operating margins, profitability, liquidity, debt to equity ratio, value added per employee, and financial activity measures are appropriate for responding to 7.2a(1).

This item addresses those factors that best reflect the organization's financial and marketplace performance. Measures reported in this item will frequently be those key financial and market measures tracked by senior leadership on an ongoing basis to monitor overall organization performance, and often used to determine incentive compensation for senior leaders in the private sector.

Measures of financial performance could include return on equity, return on investment, operating profit, pretax profit margin, earnings per share, profit forecast reliability, and other liquidity and financial activity measures. For support organizations, such as management information systems (MIS), financial indicators could include asset utilization and cost reductions.

Marketplace performance could include market share measures of business growth, new product and geographic markets entered, and percent new product sales, as appropriate.

To score high, use comparative information so that results reported can be meaningfully evaluated. Comparative data might include industry best, best competitor, industry average, and appropriate benchmarks. Such data might be derived from independent surveys, studies, or other sources.

7.2 Financial and Market Results

Results of improvement efforts using key measures and/or indicators of financial and market performance

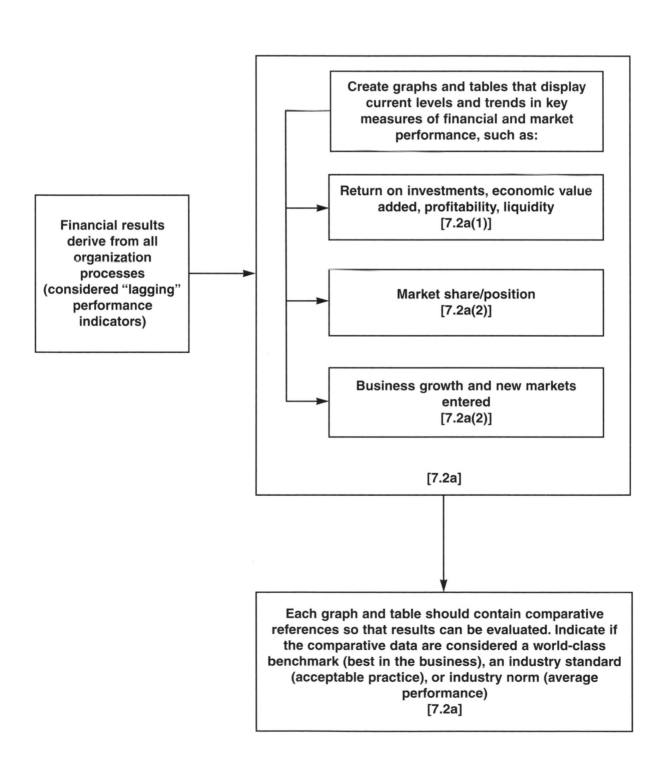

Financial results derive from all organization processes (considered "lagging" performance indicators)

Create graphs and tables that display current levels and trends in key measures of financial and market performance, such as:

Return on investments, economic value added, profitability, liquidity
[7.2a(1)]

Market share/position
[7.2a(2)]

Business growth and new markets entered
[7.2a(2)]

[7.2a]

Each graph and table should contain comparative references so that results can be evaluated. Indicate if the comparative data are considered a world-class benchmark (best in the business), an industry standard (acceptable practice), or industry norm (average performance)
[7.2a]

7.2   *Financial and Market Results Item Linkages*

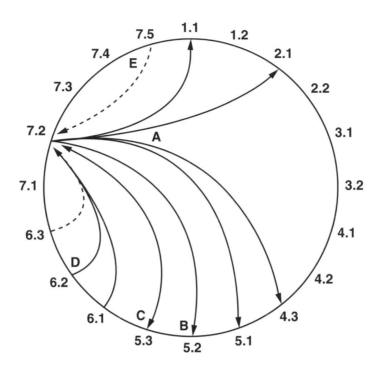

Nature of Relationship	
A	Financial and market results data [7.2] are used for strategic planning [2.1], leadership monitoring and decision making [1.1], and priority setting [4.3], and may be used as a basis for compensation, recognition, and reward [5.1b].
B	Financial data [7.2] are monitored, in part, to assess training effectiveness [5.2].
C	Employee morale and well-being [5.3] affect financial performance results [7.2], and vice-versa.
D	Financial and market results [7.2] are enhanced by improvements in design and development and by better operational processes [6.1], support processes [6.2], and supplier and partner effectiveness [6.3].
E	Organization-specific results [7.5] form the basis for financial and market results [7.2].

7.2 Financial and Market Results—Sample Effective Results

A. Financial and Market Results

- Key measures and indicators of organization market and financial performance address the following areas.
    - Effective use of materials, energy, capital, and assets
    - Cost reductions, asset utilization, and cost/benefit results from improvement efforts
    - Market share, business growth, new markets entered, and market shifting
    - Return on equity
    - Operating margins
    - Pre-tax profit
    - Earnings per share
    - Generating enough revenue to cover expenses (not-for-profit and public sector)
    - Operating within budget (government sector)
- All measures and indicators show steady improvement.
- All important financial and market data are presented.
- Comparative data include industry best, best competitor, and appropriate benchmarks.

7.3 Human Resource Results (50 Points)
Results Scoring

Summarize the company's human resource results, including employee well-being, satisfaction, development, and work system performance.

In your response, address the following Area:

a. Human Resource Results
Summarize current levels and trends in key measures and/or indicators of employee well-being, satisfaction, development, work system performance, and effectiveness. Address all categories and types of employees, as appropriate. Include appropriate comparative data.

Notes:
N1. The results reported in this Item should address results from activities described in Category 5. The results should be responsive to key process needs described in Category 6, and the company action plans and related human resource plans described in Item 2.2

N2. For appropriate measures of employee well-being, satisfaction, and motivation see notes to Item 5.3. Appropriate measures and/or indicators of employee development and effectiveness might include innovation and suggestion rates, courses completed, learning, on-the-job performance improvements, and cross-training.

N3. Appropriate measures and/or indicators of work system improvements and effectiveness might include job and job classification simplification, job rotation, work layout, work locations, and changing supervisory ratios.

This item addresses the organization's human resource results—those relating to employee well-being, satisfaction, development, motivation, work system performance, and effectiveness—that result from the processes described in Category 5.

Results reported could include generic and business- or organization-specific factors. Generic factors include the following:
- Safety
- Absenteeism
- Turnover
- Employee satisfaction

Business- or organization-specific factors include those commonly used in the industry or created by the organization for purposes of tracking progress. Other results might include input data, such as extent of training, but the main emphasis should be placed on measures of effectiveness (outcomes). If different processes are applied to different employee groups, results data should be segmented and reported accordingly.

Results reported for work system performance should include those relevant to the organization and might include measures of improvement in job classification, job rotation, work layout, and changes in local decision making.

Provide comparative information so that results can be evaluated meaningfully against competitors or other relevant external measures of performance. For some measures, such as absenteeism and turnover, local or regional comparisons may be appropriate.

7.3 Human Resource Results

Results of human resource improvement efforts using key measures and/or indicators of such performance

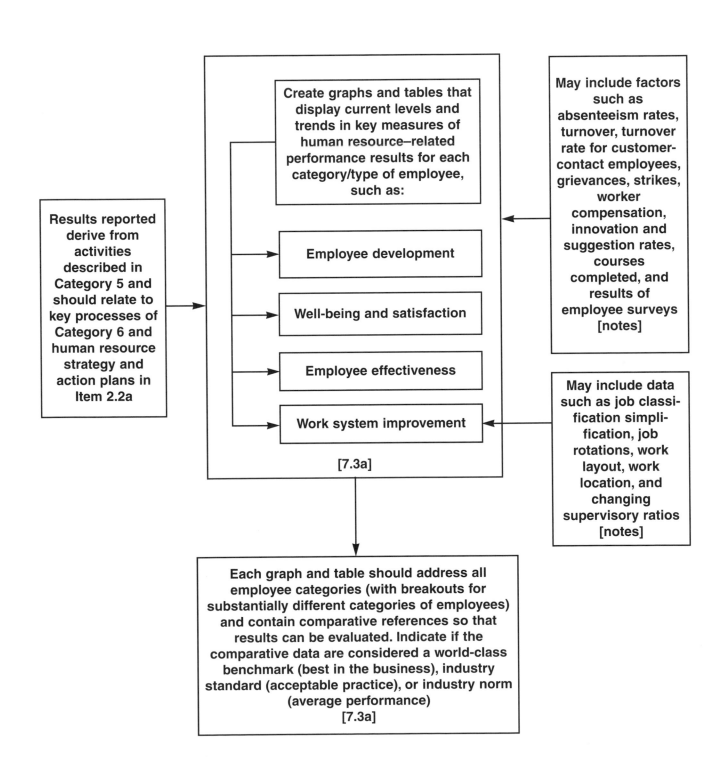

Results reported derive from activities described in Category 5 and should relate to key processes of Category 6 and human resource strategy and action plans in Item 2.2a

Create graphs and tables that display current levels and trends in key measures of human resource–related performance results for each category/type of employee, such as:

Employee development

Well-being and satisfaction

Employee effectiveness

Work system improvement

[7.3a]

May include factors such as absenteeism rates, turnover, turnover rate for customer-contact employees, grievances, strikes, worker compensation, innovation and suggestion rates, courses completed, and results of employee surveys [notes]

May include data such as job classi-fication simpli-fication, job rotations, work layout, work location, and changing supervisory ratios [notes]

Each graph and table should address all employee categories (with breakouts for substantially different categories of employees) and contain comparative references so that results can be evaluated. Indicate if the comparative data are considered a world-class benchmark (best in the business), industry standard (acceptable practice), or industry norm (average performance) [7.3a]

7.3 Human Resource Results Item Linkages

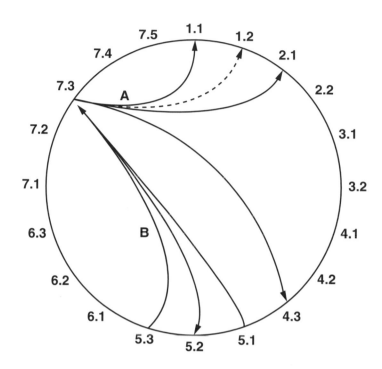

	Nature of Relationship
A	Human resource results data [7.3] are collected and used for planning [2.1], for leader decision making [1.1], to provide feedback to organizational managers [1.1], and for priority setting [4.3]. In addition, results in the area of employee safety [7.3] are used to ensure compliance with regulatory requirements [1.2].
B	Human resource results derive from and are enhanced by improving work systems and enhancing flexibility [5.1a] and by strengthening employee recognition systems [5.1b], training [5.2], and well-being and satisfaction [5.3]. In addition, human resource results data [7.3] are monitored, in part, to assess training effectiveness [5.2].

7.3   Human Resource Results—Sample Effective Results

A. Human Resource Results

- The results reported in Item 7.3 derive from activities described in Category 5.
- Multiyear data are provided to show sustained performance.
- All results show steady improvement.
- Data are not missing—if human resource results data are declared important, they are reported.
- Comparison data for benchmark or competitor organizations are reported.
- Trend data are reported for employee satisfaction with working conditions, safety, retirement package, and other employee benefits. Satisfaction with management is also reported.
- Trends for declining absenteeism, grievances, employee turnover, strikes, and worker compensation claims are reported.
- Data are reported for all employee categories.

7.4 Supplier and Partner Results (25 Points)
Results Scoring

Summarize the company's supplier and partner performance results.

In your response, address the following Area:

a. Supplier and Partner Results

Summarize current levels and trends in key measures and/or indicators of supplier and partner performance. Include company performance and/or cost improvements attributed to supplier and partner performance, as appropriate. Include appropriate comparative data.

Note:

The results reported in this Item should relate directly to processes and performance requirements described in Item 6.3.

This item examines current levels and trends in key measures and/or indicators of supplier and partner performance. Suppliers and partners are organizations or individuals that provide upstream and/or downstream materials and services. The focus should be on the most critical requirements from the point of view of the organization—the buyer or end user of the products and services.

Data reported should reflect results of the processes described in Item 6.3 by whatever means they occur—via improvements in the performance of current suppliers and partners and/or through the selection of new, better-performing suppliers and partners.

Measures and indicators of performance should relate to the principal factors involved in the organization's purchases, for example, quality, delivery, price, and performance. Examiners will look for alignment between the key requirements of suppliers and performance results against those requirements.

Data reported should also reflect how suppliers and partners have contributed to achieving the organization's performance goals. Results reported typically include the following:
- Cost savings
- Reductions in scrap, waste, or rework
- Cycle time or productivity enhancements

The item calls for comparative information so that results reported can be meaningfully evaluated against competitors or other relevant external measures of performance. Comparative data might include industry best, best competitor, industry average, and appropriate benchmarks. Such data might be derived from independent surveys, studies, laboratory testing, or other sources.

7.4 Supplier and Partner Results

Results of supplier and partner performance improvement efforts using key measures and/or indicators of such performance

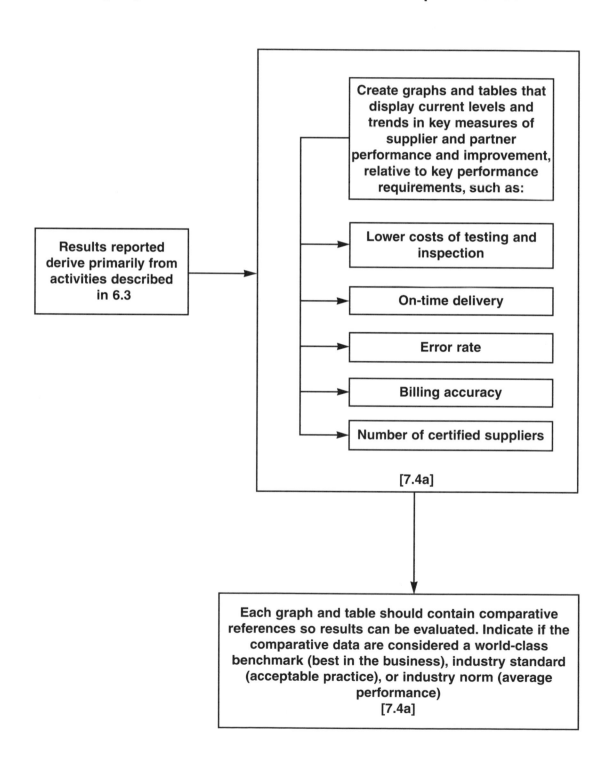

Results reported derive primarily from activities described in 6.3

Create graphs and tables that display current levels and trends in key measures of supplier and partner performance and improvement, relative to key performance requirements, such as:

Lower costs of testing and inspection

On-time delivery

Error rate

Billing accuracy

Number of certified suppliers

[7.4a]

Each graph and table should contain comparative references so results can be evaluated. Indicate if the comparative data are considered a world-class benchmark (best in the business), industry standard (acceptable practice), or industry norm (average performance)
[7.4a]

7.4 Supplier and Partner Results Item Linkages

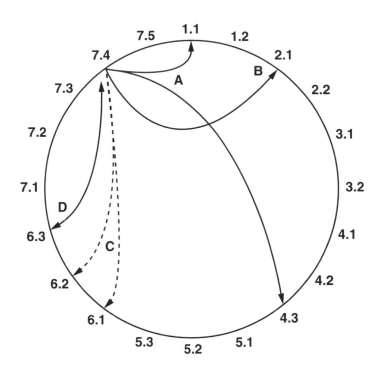

	Nature of Relationship
A	Supplier and partner performance results data [7.4] are collected and used to provide feedback to organizational managers [1.1], and to help set priorities [4.3] relative to supplier and partner performance.
B	Supplier and partner performance results [7.4] are used to determine supplier capabilities during the strategic planning process [2.1a].
C	Supplier and partner capabilities as reflected in the results data [7.4] are considered in the design process for both operations [6.1] and support activities [6.2] to help determine the overall process capability of the organization to deliver products and services that meet customer requirements.
D	Processes to improve supplier and partner capability [6.3a] affect supplier and partner results [7.4].

7.4   Supplier and Partner Results—Sample Effective Results

A. Supplier and Partner Results

- Results are broken out by key suppliers or supplier types as appropriate. Data are presented using the measures and indicators of supplier performance described in the Business Overview, 6.3, 4.1, and relevant goals in 2.2b.
- If the organization's supplier management efforts include factors such as building supplier partnerships or reducing the number of suppliers, data related to these efforts are included in responses.
- Supplier performance measures include defect rate, on-time delivery, and number of certified suppliers.
- Multiyear data are provided to demonstrate steady improvement.
- Data are not missing—all data declared to be important are reported.
- Comparison data for suppliers of benchmark or competitor organizations are reported.
- Data are broken out by meaningful supplier categories to demonstrate consistent improvement in each category.

7.5 Company-Specific Results (125 Points)
Results Scoring

Summarize company operational performance results that contribute to the achievement of key company performance goals—customer satisfaction, product and service quality, operational effectiveness, and financial/marketplace performance.

In your response, address the following Area:

a. Company-Specific Results

Summarize key company-specific results derived from: product and service quality and performance; key process performance; productivity, cycle time, and other effectiveness and efficiency measures; regulatory/legal compliance; and other results supporting accomplishment of the company's strategy and action plans, such as new product/service introductions. For all quantitative measures and/or indicators of performance, provide current levels and trends. Include appropriate comparative data.

Notes:

N1. Results reported in Item 7.5 should address key company requirements and progress toward accomplishment of key company performance goals as presented in the Business Overview, Items 1.1, 2.2, 6.1, and 6.2. Include results not reported in Items 7.1, 7.2, 7.3, and 7.4.

N2. Results reported in Item 7.5 should provide key information for analysis and review of company performance (Item 4.3) and should provide the operational basis for customer satisfaction results (Item 7.1) and company financial and market results (Item 7.2).

N3. Regulatory/legal compliance results reported in Item 7.5 should address requirements described in Item 1.2.

This item calls for data describing key performance results not covered in Items 7.1–7.4 that contribute significantly to the organization's goals—customer satisfaction, product and service quality, operational effectiveness, and financial/marketplace performance. The item encourages the use of any unique measures the organization has developed to track performance in areas important to the organization.

- Results should reflect key product, service, and process performance measures, including those that serve as predictors of customer satisfaction, such as customer complaints and warranty claims, not direct measures of customer satisfaction, which should be reported in item 7.1.

- Measures of productivity and operational effectiveness in all key design areas, support areas, and product/service delivery areas are appropriate for inclusion.
- Results of compliance with regulatory/legal requirements should also be reported.
- Measures and/or indicators of product and service performance should relate to requirements that matter to the customer and to the marketplace. These features are derived from the voice-of-the-customer processes in Items 3.1 and listening posts, such as complaints discussed in Item 3.2. If the features have been properly selected, these measures should show a strong positive correlation with customer and marketplace improvement indicators—reported in Items 7.1 and 7.2.

The correlation between product/service performance and customer indicators is a critical management tool—a device for defining and focusing on key quality and customer requirements and for identifying product/service differentiators in the marketplace. In addition, the correlation might reveal emerging or changing market segments, the changing importance of requirements, or even the potential obsolescence of products and/or services.

Product/service performance appropriate for inclusion might be based upon one or more of the following: internal (organization) measurements; field performance; data collected by the organization or on behalf of the organization; or customer surveys on product and service performance. Although data appropriate for inclusion are primarily based upon internal measurements and field performance, data collected by the organization or other organizations through follow-up might be included for attributes that cannot be accurately assessed through direct measurement (such as ease of use) or when variability in customer expectations makes the customer's perception the most meaningful indicator (such as courtesy).

Measures and/or indicators of operational effectiveness could include the following:
- Environmental improvements reflected in lower emissions levels, waste stream reductions, by-product use, and recycling
- Cycle time, lead times, set-up times, and other responsiveness indicators
- Process assessment results such as customer assessment or third-party assessment (such as ISO 9000)
- Organization-specific indicators such as innovation rates, innovation effectiveness, cost reductions through innovation, time to market, product/process yield, complete and accurate shipments, and measures of strategic goal achievement.

Organizations should report any unique measures that track performance in areas important to the organization, even if comparison data do not exist.

To score in the upper levels, organizations should also provide comparative information so that most results reported can be evaluated against competitors or other relevant external measures of performance. These comparative data might include industry best, best competitor, industry average, and appropriate benchmarks. Such data might be derived from independent surveys, studies, laboratory testing, or other sources.

7.5 Company-Specific Results

Results of improvement efforts that contribute to organizational goals of customer satisfaction, product and service quality, operational effectiveness, and financial/marketplace performance

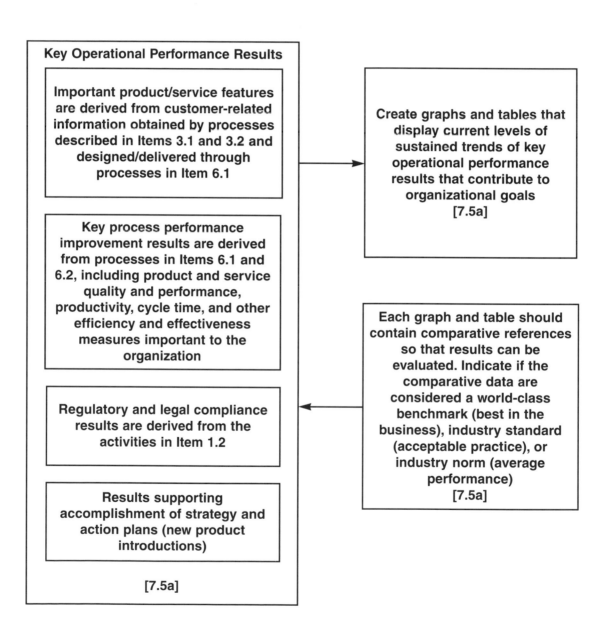

7.5   Company-Specific Results Item Linkages

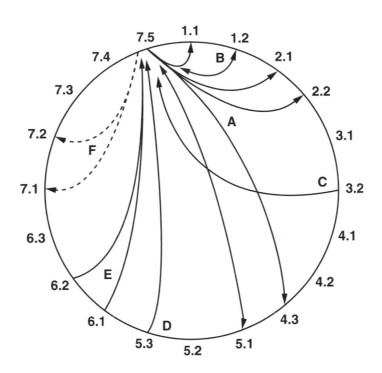

Nature of Relationship

A	Product and service quality characteristics and operational performance results data [7.5] are collected and used for planning [2.1], goal setting [2.2], management, monitoring, and decision making [1.1], analysis and priority setting [4.3], and reward and recognition determination [5.1b]. In addition, processes to improve employee initiative and flexibility [5.1a] can enhance performance results [7.5].
B	Regulatory and legal compliance resulting from the activities in Item 1.2 should be reported in 7.5. In addition, these results are monitored to determine if process changes are needed.
C	Customer relations systems [3.2a] result in improved complaint response time, effective complaint resolution, and percentage of complaints resolved on first contact. These results should be reported in 7.5.
D	Employee morale and well-being [5.3] affect product and service quality results [7.5].
E	Designing products and services to meet customer requirements, improved operational performance [6.1], and support performance [6.2] affect product and service quality [7.5].
F	Organization-specific results [7.5] provide the basis for financial and market results [7.2] and customer satisfaction results [7.1].

7.5 Company-Specific Results—Sample Effective Results

A. Company-Specific Results

- Indices and trend data are provided in graph and chart form for all operational performance measures identified in 6.1, 6.2, 4.1, 1.2, relevant organizational goals (2.2), and the key business factors identified in the business overview and not reported elsewhere in Category 7. Multiyear data are reported.
- All indicators show steady improvement.
- Results data reflect performance relative to specific nonprice product and service key quality requirements that relate closely to customer satisfaction and customer retention.
- Product and service quality measures and indicators address requirements such as accuracy, timeliness, and reliability and are key to predicting customer behavior. Examples include defect levels, repeat services, meeting product or service delivery or response times, availability levels, and complaint levels.
- Operational performance measures address
  - Productivity, efficiency and effectiveness such as productivity indices, human resource utilization, waste reduction, energy efficiency, cycle time reduction, and product/service design improvement measures
  - Public responsibilities such as environmental improvements
  - Cycle time reductions
- Comparative data include industry best, best competitor, industry average, and appropriate benchmarks. Data are also derived from independent surveys, studies, laboratory testing, or other sources.
- Data are not missing. (For example, do not show a steady trend from 1991 to 1997, but leave out 1993.)
- Data are not aggregated since aggregation tends to hide poor performance by blending it with good performance. Break out and report trends separately.

Tips on Preparing a Baldrige Award Application

Preparing the Business Overview

The Business Overview is an outline of the applicant's business that addresses what is most important to the business, key influences on how the business operates, and where the business is headed. The Business Overview is intended to help examiners understand what is relevant and important to the applicant's business.

The Business Overview is of critical importance to the applicant because
- It is the starting point for writing and reviewing the application, helping to ensure focus on key business issues and consistency in responses, especially in reporting business results.
- It is used by the examiners and judges in the application review, including the site visit.

Guidelines for Preparing the Business Overview

The Business Overview consists of five sections as follows:

Basic Description of the Organization
This section should provide basic information on the following:
- The nature of the applicant's business: products and services
- Organization size, location(s), and whether it is publicly or privately owned
- The applicant's major markets (local, regional, national, or international) and principal customer types (consumers, other businesses, government, and so on) (Note any special relationships, such as partnerships, with customers or customer groups.)
- A profile of the applicant's employee base, including number, types, educational level, bargaining units, and special safety requirements
- Major equipment, facilities, and technologies used
- The regulatory environment affecting the applicant, such as occupational health and safety, environmental, financial, food and drug, Americans with disabilities, to name a few.

If the applicant is a subunit of a larger organization, a brief description of the organizational relationship to the parent and percentage of employees the subunit represents should be given. Briefly describe how the applicant's products and services relate to those of the parent and/or other units of the parent organization. If the parent organization provides key support services, these should also be described.

Customer Requirements

This section should provide information on key customer and market requirements (for example, on-time delivery, low defect levels, price demands, reliability, ease of access, and after-sales services) for products and services. Briefly describe all important requirements, and note significant differences, if any, in requirements among customer groups and market segments.

Supplier and Partnering Relationships

This section should provide information on the following:
- Types and numbers of suppliers of goods and services
- The most important types of suppliers, dealers, and other businesses
- Any limitations, special relationships, or special requirements that may exist with some or all suppliers and partners

Competitive Factors

This section should provide information on the following:
- The applicant's position (relative size, growth) in the industry
- Numbers and types of competitors or similar providers
- Principal factors that determine competitive success, such as productivity growth, cost reduction, and product innovation
- Changes taking place that affect competition.
- Changes taking place that *might* affect competition

Strategic Context and Other Factors Important to the Applicant

This section should provide information, as appropriate, on the following:
- Major new thrusts for the organization, such as entry into new markets or segments
- New business alliances
- Introduction of new technologies
- The role of and approaches to process, product, and service innovation;
- Changes in strategy
- Unique factors such as the impact of new acquisitions, restructuring, new leadership, and litigation, to name a few

Page Limit

The Business Overview is limited to five pages. These pages are not counted in the overall application page limit.

The Business Overview should be prepared first and then used to guide the applicant in writing and reviewing the application.

Guidelines for Responding to Approach/Deployment Items

The criteria focus on key performance results. However, results by themselves offer little help in diagnosing why performance is not at required levels. For example, if some results are poor or are improving at rates slower than the competition's, it is important to understand why this is so and what might be done to accelerate improvement.

Approach/deployment items permit diagnosis of the applicant's most important systems, activities, and processes—the ones that offer the greatest potential for fast-paced performance improvement. Diagnosis and feedback depend heavily on the content and completeness of approach/deployment item responses. For this reason, it is important to respond to these items by providing key process information. Guidelines for organizing and reviewing such information follow. Basic approach/deployment terms are provided on page 181.

Understand the Meaning of "How"

Items that request information on approach include Areas to Address that begin with the word "how." Responses to such areas should provide a complete picture to enable meaningful evaluation and feedback. Responses should outline key process details such as methods, measures, deployment, and evaluation factors. Information lacking sufficient detail to permit an evaluation and feedback, or merely providing an example, is referred to in the scoring guidelines as anecdotal information.

Show What and How

Describe your system for meeting the requirements of each item. Ensure that methods, processes, and practices are fully described. Use flowcharts to help examiners visualize your key processes.

It is important to give basic information about what the key processes are and how they work. Although it is helpful to include who performs the work, merely stating *who* does not permit effective communication or feedback. For example, stating that "customer satisfaction data are analyzed for improvement by the customer service department" does not set the stage for useful feedback, because potential strengths and weaknesses in the analysis cannot be identified from this very limited information. This makes it impossible to determine if a systematic process is in place.

Show That Activities Are Systematic	Ensure that the response describes a systematic approach, not merely an anecdotal example.
	Systematic approaches are repeatable, predictable, and involve the systematic use of data and information for cycles of improvement. In other words, the approaches are consistent over time, build in learning and evaluation, and show maturity. Scores above 50 percent rely on clear evidence that approaches are systematic.
Show Deployment	Ensure that the response gives clear and sufficient information on deployment. For cxample, one must be able to distinguish from a response whether an approach described is used in one, some, most, or all parts of the organization.
	Deployment can be shown compactly by using summary tables that outline what is done in different parts of the organization. This is particularly effective if the basic approach is described in a narrative.
Show Focus, Consistency, and Integration	The response demonstrates that the organization is focused on key processes and on improvements that offer the greatest potential to improve business performance and accomplish organization action plans.
	There are four important factors to consider regarding focus and consistency: (1) the Business Overview should make clear what is important; (2) the Strategic Planning category, including the strategy and action plans, should highlight areas of greatest focus and describe how deployment is accomplished; (3) descriptions of organization-level analysis (Item 4.3) should show how the organization analyzes performance information to set priorities; and (4) the Process Management category should highlight product, service, support, and supplier processes that are key to overall business performance. The role of senior leaders in aligning the work of the organization (Item 1.1) should show how performance information is tracked and used by leaders. Focus and consistency in the Approach-Deployment items should yield corresponding results reported in Category 7.
Respond Fully to Item Requirements	Ensure that the response fully addresses all important parts of each item and each Area to Address. Missing information will be interpreted by examiners as a gap in approach and/or deployment. All areas should be addressed and checked in final review. Individual components of an Area to Address may be addressed individually or together.

Cross-Reference When Appropriate

Applicants should try to make each item response self-contained. However, some responses to different items might be mutually reinforcing. It is then appropriate to reference responses to other items, rather than to repeat information. In such cases, applicants should use Area designators (for example, "see Area 3.2a(1)").

Use a Compact Format

Applicants should make the best use of the 50 application pages permitted. Applicants are encouraged to use flow charts, tables, and "bulletized" presentation of information.

Refer to the Scoring Guidelines

The evaluation of item responses is accomplished by consideration of the criteria item requirements and the maturity of the organization's approaches, breadth of deployment, and strength of the improvement process relative to the scoring guidelines. Therefore, applicants need to consider both the criteria and the scoring guidelines in preparing responses.

Guidelines for Responding to Results Items

The Baldrige criteria place great emphasis on results. All results items remain in Category 7 for 1998. Items 7.1, 7.2, 7.3, 7.4, and 7.5 call for results related to all key requirements, stakeholders, and goals.

Focus on Reporting Critical Results

Results reported should cover the most important requirements for business success, highlighted in the Business Overview, and the Strategic Planning and Process Management categories, and included in responses to other items, such as Human Resource Focus (Category 5) and Process Management (Category 6).

Four key requirements for effective presentation of results data include the following:
- Trends show directions of results and rates of change
- Performance levels show performance on some meaningful measurement scale
- Comparisons show how trends or levels compare with those of other, appropriately selected organizations
- Breadth of results shows completeness of deployment of improvement activities

No Minimum Time

No minimum period of time is required for trend data. However, results data might span five years or more for some results. Trends might be much shorter for some of the organization's improvement activities. Because of the importance of showing deployment and focus, new data should be included even if trends and comparisons are not yet well established.

Compact Presentation

Presenting many results can be done compactly by using graphs and tables. Graphs and tables should be labeled for easy interpretation. Results compared with others should be "normalized"—presented in a way (such as use of ratios) that takes into account various size or inflation factors. For example, if the organization's work force has been growing, reporting safety results in terms of accidents per 100 employees would permit more meaningful trend data than in terms of the total number of accidents.

**Link Results
with Text**

Descriptions of results and the results themselves should be close together in the application. Use figure numbers that correspond to items. For example, the third figure for Item 7.5 should be 7.5-3. (See the example below.)

The following graph illustrates data an applicant might present as part of a response to Item 7.5, Company-Specific Results. In the Business Overview and in Item 3.1, the applicant has indicated on-time delivery as a key customer requirement and critical performance goal.

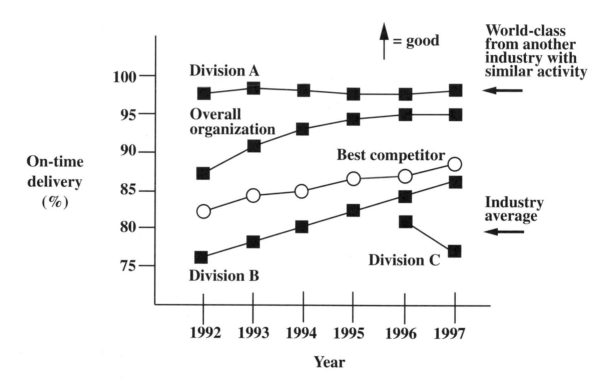

Figure 7.5-3   On-Time Delivery Performance

Using the graph, the following characteristics of clear and effective data presentation are illustrated.
- A figure number is provided for reference to the graph in the text.
- Both axes and units of measure are clearly labeled.
- Trend lines report data for a key business requirement—on-time delivery.
- Results are presented for several years.
- Appropriate comparisons are clearly shown.
- The organization shows, using a single graph, that its three divisions separately track on-time delivery.
- An upward-pointing arrow appears on the graph, indicating that

increasing values are "good." (A downward-pointing arrow would indicate that decreasing values are "good.")

To help interpret the scoring guidelines, the following comments on the graphed results would be appropriate.

- The current overall organization performance level is excellent. This conclusion is supported by the comparison with competitors and with a world-class level.
- The organization exhibits an overall excellent improvement record.
- Division A is the current performance leader—showing sustained high performance and a slightly positive trend. Division B shows rapid improvement. Its current performance is near that of the best industry competitor, but trails the world-class level.
- Division C—a new division—is having early problems with on-time delivery. The applicant has analyzed and explained the early problems in the application text. Its current performance is not yet at the level of the best industry competitor.

Complete Data Be sure that results data are displayed for all relevant customer, financial, market, human resource, operational performance, and supplier performance characteristics. If you identify relevant performance measures and goals in other parts of the analysis, (for example, Items 1.2, 2.1, 2.2, 3.1, 3.2, 4.1, 4.2, 4.3, 5.1, 5.2, 5.3, 6.1, 6.2, and 6.3), be sure to include the results of these performance characteristics in Category 7. As each relevant performance measure is identified in the assessment process, create a blank chart and label the axes. Define all units of measure, especially if they are industry-specific or unique to the applicant. As data are collected, populate the charts. If expected data are not provided in the application, examiners may assume that the trends or levels are not good. Missing data drive the score down in the same way that poor trends do.

Break Out Data   Avoid aggregating the data. Where appropriate, break data into meaningful components. If you serve several different customer groups, display performance and satisfaction data for each group. As the following graph demonstrates, only one of the three trends is positive, although the average is positive. Examiners will seek component data when aggregate data are reported. Only presenting aggregate data instead of meaningful component data could reduce the score.

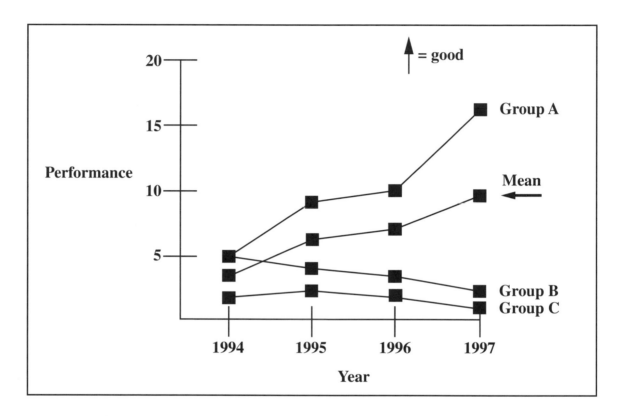

The Importance of Criteria Notes   Several items are followed by one or more notes that offer some insight and explanation about the item. Often these notes suggest activities or measures that other organizations have used to meet the requirements of the item. There are many ways to manage a high-performance system that are not included in the notes. Notes should be considered suggestions and *not* requirements.

Data and Measures

Comparison data are required for all items in Category 7. These data are designed to demonstrate how well the organization is performing. To judge performance excellence, one must possess comparison data. In the following chart, performance is represented by the line connecting the squares. Clearly the organization is improving, but how "good" is it? Without comparison data, answering that question is difficult.

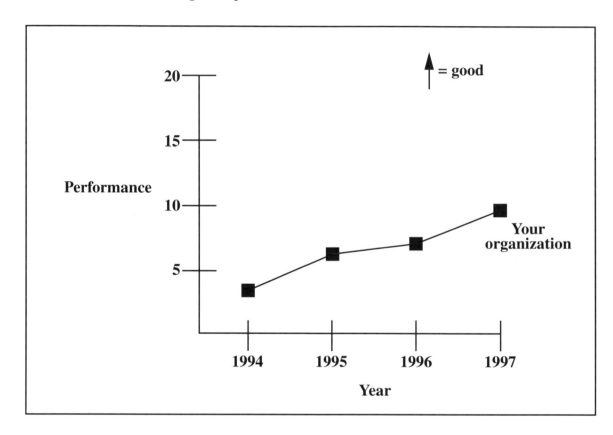

Now consider the chart with comparison data added.

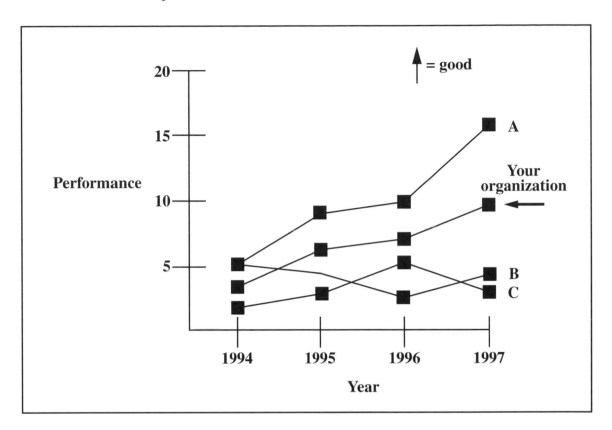

Note the position of three hypothetical comparisons, represented by the letters A, B, and C. Consider the following two scenarios.

- If **A** represents the industry average and both **B** and **C** represent area competitors, examiners would conclude that the organization's performance was substandard, even though it is improving.

- If **A** represents a best-in-class (benchmark) organization and **B** represents the industry average, examiners would conclude that organizational performance is very good.

In both scenarios, the organizational performance remained the same but the examiner's perception of it changed.

Measures

Agreeing on relevant measures is a difficult task for organizations in the early phases of quality and performance improvement. The task is easier if the following guidelines are considered.

- Clearly define customer requirements. Clear customer requirements are easier to measure. Clearly defined customer requirements require probing and suggesting. For example, the customer of a new computer wants the equipment to be reliable. After probing to find what "reliable" means, we discover that (1) the customer expects it to work all of the time. If it does stop working, the customer expects fast service—(2) prompt appearance at the site, (3) immediate access to parts, and (4) the ability to fix it right the first time.

- For each of the four requirements defined, identify a measure. For example, mean time between failures is one indicator of reliability, but it does not account for all of the variation. Since the customer is concerned with run time, we must assess how long it took the repair technician to arrive at the site, diagnose the problem, and fix it. Measures include *time in hours, days, weeks* between failures, *time in minutes* between the service call and the computer regaining capability (time to fix), *time in minutes* waiting for parts, and the associated costs in terms of cash and worker effort.

- Collect and report data. Several charts might be required to display these factors.

Scoring System

The scoring of applicant responses to criteria items (Items) and feedback are based on three evaluation dimensions: (1) Approach; (2) Deployment; and (3) Results. Applicants need to furnish information relating to these dimensions. Specific factors for these dimensions are described as follows:

Approach

Approach refers to how the applicant addresses the item requirements—the method(s) used. The factors used to evaluate approaches include the following:
- Appropriateness of the methods to the requirements
- Effectiveness of use of the methods—degree to which the approach
  - Is systematic, integrated, and consistently applied
  - Embodies evaluation/improvement/learning cycles
  - Is based on reliable information and data
- Evidence of innovation and/or significant and effective adaptations of approaches used in other types of applications or businesses

Deployment

Deployment refers to the extent to which the applicant's approach is applied to all requirements of the item. The factors used to evaluate deployment include the following:
- Use of the approach in addressing business and item requirements
- Use of the approach by all appropriate work units

Results

Results refers to outcomes in achieving the purposes given in the item. The factors used to evaluate results include the following:
- Current performance
- Performance relative to appropriate comparisons and/or benchmarks
- Rate, breadth, and importance of performance improvements
- Demonstration of sustained improvement and/or sustained high-level performance
- Linkage of results measures to key performance measures identified in the Business Overview and in approach/deployment items

Item Classification and Scoring Dimensions

Items are classified according to the kinds of information or data applicants are expected to furnish relative to the three evaluation dimensions. The two types of items and their designations are

1. Approach/deployment (for all items in Categories 1–6)
2. Results (for all items in Category 7)

Approach and deployment are linked to emphasize that descriptions of Approach should always indicate the Deployment—consistent with the specific requirements of the item. Although Approach and Deployment dimensions are linked, feedback to the applicant reflects strengths and/or areas for improvement in either or both dimensions.

Results items call for data showing performance levels and trends on key measures and/or indicators of organization performance. However, the evaluation factor, "breadth" of performance improvements, is concerned with how widespread an applicant's improvement results are. This is directly related to the Deployment dimension. That is, if improvement processes are widely deployed, there should be corresponding results. A score for a results item is thus a composite based upon overall performance, taking into account the breadth of improvements and their importance.

Importance as a Scoring Factor

The three evaluation dimensions described above are all critical to evaluation and feedback. However, evaluation and feedback must also consider the importance of improvements in Approach, Deployment, and Results to the applicant's business. The areas of greatest importance should be identified in the Business Overview, and in items such as 2.1 (strategic planning), 2.2 (company strategy), 3.1 (customer and market knowledge), 6.1 (management of product and service processes), and Category 7. Of particular importance are the key customer requirements and key strategies and action plans.

Assignment of Scores to Applicants' Responses

Baldrige Award examiners observe the following guidelines in assignment of scores to applicants' responses.

- All relevant areas to address should be included in the item response. Also, responses should reflect what is important to the applicant's business.
- In assigning a score to an item, an examiner first decides which scoring range (such as 40 percent to 60 percent) best fits the overall item response. Overall "best fit" does not require total agreement with each of the statements for that scoring range. Actual score within the range depends on an examiner's judgment of the closeness of the item

response in relation to the statements in the next higher and next lower scoring ranges.

- An approach/deployment item score of 50 percent represents an approach that meets the basic objectives of the item and that is deployed to the principal activities covered in the item. Higher scores reflect maturity (cycles of improvement), integration, and broader deployment.

- A results item score of 50 percent represents clear indication of improvement trends and/or good levels of performance in the principal results areas covered in the item. Higher scores reflect better improvement rates and better comparative performance, as well as broader coverage.

Approach/Deployment	
0%	• No systematic approach evident; anecdotal information
10% to 30%	• **Beginning** of a systematic approach, responsive to the primary purposes of the item • **Early** stages of a transition from reacting to problems to a general improvement orientation • **Major gaps exist** in deployment that would inhibit progress in achieving the primary purposes of the item
40% to 60%	• A **sound, systematic approach, responsive to the primary purposes of the item** • A **fact-based improvement process** in place in key areas; more emphasis is placed on improvement than on reaction to problems • **No major gaps** in deployment, though some areas or work units may be in very **early stages of deployment**
70% to 90%	• A **sound, systematic approach, responsive to the overall purposes of the item** • A fact-based improvement process and organizational learning/sharing are key management tools; **clear evidence of refinement** and **improved integration** as a result of improvement cycles and analysis • Approach is well-deployed, **with no major gaps**; deployment may vary in some areas or work units
100%	• A **sound, systematic approach, fully responsive to all the requirements of the item** • A very strong, fact-based improvement process and extensive organizational learning/sharing are key management tools; **strong refinement and integration**—backed by excellent analysis • Approach is **fully deployed without any significant weaknesses or gaps** in any areas or work units
Results	
0%	• **No results or poor results** in areas reported
10% to 30%	• Early stages of developing trends; some improvement and/or early **good performance levels in a few areas** • **Results not reported for many to most areas** of importance to the applicant's key business requirements
40% to 60%	• Improvement trends and/or good performance levels **reported for many to most areas** of importance to the applicant's key business requirements • **No pattern of adverse trends and/or poor performance levels in areas of importance to the applicant's key business requirements** • **Some** trends and/or current performance levels—**evaluated against relevant comparisons** and/or benchmarks—show areas of strength and/or **good to very good relative performance levels**
70% to 90%	• Current performance is **good to excellent in most areas of importance** to the applicant's key business requirements • **Most** improvement trends and/or **current performance levels are sustained** • **Many** to most trends and/or current performance levels—**evaluated against relevant comparisons** and/or benchmarks—**show areas of leadership** and very good relative performance levels
100%	• Current performance is **excellent** in most areas of importance to the applicant's key business requirements • **Excellent** improvement trends and/or sustained excellent performance levels in most areas • Strong evidence of **industry and benchmark leadership demonstrated** in many areas

Supplementary Scoring Guidelines

> *Author's note: Many examiners and organizations have found the official scoring guidelines to be vague, increasing the difficulty of reaching consensus on a score and increasing scoring variation. To resolve this problem, I developed the following supplemental scoring guidelines. Many state award programs have used these guidelines for several years and found that they make the consensus process easier and produce comparable scores.*

Approach/ Deployment

1. For each approach/deployment item, first determine the appropriate level on the approach scale. This sets the upper possible score the applicant may receive on the item.
2. Then read the corresponding level on the deployment scale. For example, if the approach level is 40 percent, read the 40 percent standard on the deployment scale where one would expect "a few minor gaps in deployment exist" and "many work units are in the early stages of deployment." If that is the case, the final score is 40 percent.
3. However, if the deployment score is lower than the approach score then it establishes the lower range of possible final scores for the item. The actual final score will be between the low and high scores. For example, if only "isolated units are using quality practices; most are not," the lowest possible score would be 10 percent. This final score must be between 40 and 10 percent (e.g., 10, 20, 30, or 40 percent).
4. Never increase a poor approach score based on good deployment.
5. See pages 188-189 for terms key to scoring approach/deployment items.

Results

1. For results items, base your assessment only on the standards described on the results scale. *Do not consider approach or deployment standards at all.*
2. Determine the extent to which performance results are positive, complete, and at high levels relative to competitors or similar providers or an industry standard.
3. To determine the extent to which all important results are reported, examiners should develop a list of the key measures the applicant indicates are important. Start with the measures listed in the overview section. Then add to the key measures list based on key data reported in Item 2.1 and the goals in 2.2, as well as measures that may be mentioned in Categories 5 and 6. Key measures can be reported anywhere in an application.

Score	Approach	Deployment
0%	Anecdotal, no systematic approach evident.	Anecdotal, undocumented.
10%	Beginning of systematic approach is evident. **Several key** requirements of the item not addressed. Generally reactive to problems.	**Isolated units** are using the required practices. Progress in achieving primary purposes of item is significantly inhibited.
20%	A **partially systematic approach** is evident to a limited extent. Some key requirements of the item not addressed. Generally reactive approach to problems.	**Some units** are using the required practices. Progress in achieving primary purposes of item is noticeably inhibited.
30%	A systematic approach is evident and clearly evolving. A **few key** requirements of the item not addressed. Transitioning from reactive to proactive problem solving (prevention).	**Several units** are using the required practices. **Some major gaps** in deployment exist. Progress in achieving primary purposes of item is somewhat inhibited.
40%	Systematic approach is fully developed. Emphasis on prevention. **Several minor** requirements of the item not addressed. **No systematic evaluation** or improvement system is in place. Some fact-based decision processes are evident. Random improvements may have been made.	**Many work units** in the **very early stages** of deployment. **No major gaps** in deployment exist that inhibit progress in achieving primary purposes of item.
50%	Systematic approach is fully developed. **Some** minor requirements of the item not addressed. Fact-based improvement system includes process evaluation in key areas (**but no refinements are in place**). **Random improvements** may have been made.	**Some work units** may still be in the **early** stages of deployment. No major gaps in deployment exist that inhibit progress in achieving primary purposes of item.
60%	Systematic approach is fully developed. **A few** minor requirements of the item not addressed. Fact-based improvement system includes **at least one evaluation** and improvement cycle completed, including **some systematic refinement** based on the evaluation in key areas.	A **few work units** may still be in the early stages of deployment. No major gaps in deployment exist that inhibit progress in achieving primary purposes of item.
70%	**Fact-based, integrated** improvement system is fully developed. Overall requirements of the item are addressed. **Some systematic** evaluation and improvement cycles and refinements with some improved integration are evident.	**Approach is well deployed** with **some work units** in the middle to advanced stages. No major gaps exist that inhibit progress in achieving primary purposes of item.
80%	Fact-based, integrated improvement system is fully developed. Overall requirements of the item are addressed. **Several systematic** evaluation and improvement cycles and refinements with substantially improved integration are evident.	Approach is well deployed with **many work units** in the advanced stages. No major gaps exist that inhibit progress in achieving primary purposes of item.
90%	Fact-based, integrated improvement system is fully developed. Overall requirements of the item are addressed. **Many systematic** evaluation and improvement cycles and refinements with substantially improved integration are evident. **Some innovative** refinements are evident.	Approach is well deployed with **most work units** in the advanced stages. No major gaps exist that inhibit progress in achieving primary purposes of item.
100%	Fact-based, integrated improvement system is fully developed. **All requirements** of the item are fully addressed. **Excellent analysis with many systematic** evaluation and improvement cycles and refinements and extensive organizational learning and sharing evident. **Substantial innovative** refinements are evident.	Approach is **fully deployed to all areas and work units** with no significant gaps or weaknesses in deployment.

Score	Scoring Results
0%	**No results** or poor results in areas reported.
10%	Results **not reported for most areas** of importance to the applicant's key business requirements. **Limited positive results** and trends are evident for the results that are reported.
20%	Results not reported for **many to most areas** of importance to the applicant's key business requirements. **Some positive results** and a **few trends** are evident for the results that are reported.
30%	Results not reported for **many areas** of importance to the applicant's key business requirements. Some positive results and **improvement trends are evident** for the results that are reported.
40%	Results **are reported for many key areas** of importance to the applicant's key business requirements. Positive trends are reported for **many areas** of importance to the applicant's key business requirements. **No pattern of adverse trends** and/or poor performance exists in areas important to business success. **Some** trends and/or performance levels, **evaluated against relevant comparisons** and/or benchmarks, show **good relative performance** levels.
50%	Results are reported for **many to most key areas** of importance to the applicant's business requirements with positive trends in **many to most key areas** important to the item and key business factors. No pattern of adverse trends and/or poor performance exists in areas important to business success. Some trends and/or performance levels, evaluated against relevant comparisons and/or benchmarks, show good to **very good relative performance** levels.
60%	Results are reported for **most key areas** of importance to the applicant's business requirements with positive trends in many to most key areas important to the item and key business factors. No pattern of adverse trends and/or poor performance exists in areas important to business success. Some trends and/or performance levels, evaluated against relevant comparisons and/or benchmarks, show **very good relative performance** levels.
70%	Results are reported for most key areas of importance to the applicant's business requirements **with sustained** positive trends in many to most key areas important to the item and key business factors. No pattern of adverse trends and/or poor performance exists in areas important to business success. Many trends and/or performance levels, evaluated against relevant comparisons and/or benchmarks, show **very good relative performance** levels.
80%	Results are reported for **most to all key areas** of importance to the applicant's business requirements **with sustained** positive trends in most key areas important to the item and key business factors. No pattern of adverse trends and/or poor performance exists in areas important to business success. **Many to most** trends and/or performance levels, evaluated against relevant comparisons and/or benchmarks, **show very good relative performance** levels.
90%	Results are reported **for all key areas** of importance to the applicant's business requirements with sustained positive trends in most key areas important to the item and key business factors. No pattern of adverse trends and/or poor performance exists in areas important to business success. **Most trends** and/or performance levels, evaluated against relevant comparisons and/or benchmarks, **show excellent relative performance** levels.
100%	**Excellent** (world-class) results and **strong sustained trends** in **all areas important** to the item and key business factors. **Strong evidence** of industry and benchmark **leadership in many areas.**

Approach/Deployment Terms

Systematic Look for evidence of a system—a repeatable, predictable process that is used to fulfill the requirements of the item. Briefly describe the system. Be sure to explain *how* the system works. You must communicate the nature of the system to people who are not familiar with it. This is essential to achieve the 30 percent scoring threshold.

Integrated Determine the extent to which the system is integrated or linked with other elements of the overall management system. Show the linkages across categories for key themes such as those displayed earlier for each item.

Consider the extent to which the work of senior leader is integrated. For example,

1. Senior executives (Item 1.1) are responsible for shaping and communicating the organization's vision, values, and expectations throughout the leadership system and work force.

2. They develop relationships with key customers (Item 3.2) and monitor customer satisfaction (Item 7.1) and organization performance (Items 7.2, 7.3, 7.4, and 7.5).

3. This information, when properly analyzed (Item 4.3), helps them set priorities and allocate resources to optimize customer satisfaction and operational and financial performance.

4. With this in mind, senior executives participate in strategy development (Item 2.1) and ensure the alignment of the workplace to achieve organizational goals (Item 2.2).

5. Senior executives may also become involved in supporting new structures to improve employee performance [Item 5.1], training effectiveness (Item 5.2), and employee well-being and satisfaction (Item 5.3).

Similar relationships (linkages) exist between other items. Highlight these linkages to demonstrate integration.

Prevention-Based Prevention-based systems are characterized by actions to minimize or prevent the recurrence of problems. In an ideal world, all systems would produce perfect products and flawless service. Since that rarely happens, high performing organizations are able to act quickly to recover from a problem (fight the fire) and then take action to identify the root cause of the problem and prevent it from surfacing again. The nature of the problem, its root cause, and appropriate corrective action is communicated to all relevant employees so that they can implement the corrective action in their area before the problem arises.

Continuous Improvement

Continuous improvement is a bedrock theme. It is the method that helps organizations keep their competitive edge. Continuous improvement involves evaluation and improvement of processes crucial to organizational success. Evaluation and improvement completes the high-performance management cycle. Continuous improvement evaluations can be complex, data-driven, statistical processes, or as simple as a focus group discussing what went right, what went wrong, and how it can be done better. The key to optimum performance lies in the pervasive evaluation and improvement of all processes. By practicing systematic, pervasive, continuous improvement, time becomes the organization's ally. Consistent evaluation and refinement practices can drive the score to 60 percent or 70 percent, and higher.

Complete

Each item contains one or more areas to address. Many areas to address contain several parts. Failure to address all areas and parts can push the score lower. If an area to address or part of an area does not apply to your organization, it is important to explain why. Otherwise, examiners may conclude that the system is incomplete.

Innovative

The highest-scoring organization is able to demonstrate that its process is innovative, unique, world-class, and a trendsetter. When the process is so good that it becomes the benchmark for others (and is deployed throughout the organization), the score moves to the 90 percent to 100 percent range.

Anecdotal

If your assessment describes a process that is essentially anecdotal and does not systematically address the criteria, it is worth very little (0 to 10 points).

Deployment

The extent to which processes are widely used by organization units affects scoring. For example, a systematic approach that is well integrated, evaluated consistently, and refined routinely may be worth 70 percent to 90 percent. However, if that process is not in place in all key parts of the organization, the 70 percent to 90 percent score will be reduced, perhaps significantly, depending on the nature and extent of the gap.

Major gaps are expected to exist at the 0 to 30 percent level. At the 40 percent to 60 percent level, no major gaps exist, although some units may still be at the early stages of development. At the 70 percent to 90 percent level, no major gaps exist and many to most units are in the advanced stages of development in the area called for in the criteria.

Summary

For each item examined, the process is rated as follows:

- Anecdotal: 0 to 10 percent
- Systematic: 10 percent to 30 percent
- Fully developed: 40 percent
- Prevention-based and evaluated: 50 percent
- Integrated: 50 percent to 100 percent
- Refined: 60 percent to 80 percent
- Widely used, with no gaps in deployment: 70+ percent

Systematic, integrated, prevention-based, and continuously improved systems that are widely used are generally easier to describe than undeveloped systems. Moreover, describing numerous activities or anecdotes does not convince examiners that an integrated, prevention-based system is in place. In fact, simply describing numerous activities and anecdotes suggests that a system does not exist. However, by tracing critical success threads through the relevant items in the criteria, the organization demonstrates that its system is integrated and fully deployed.

To demonstrate system integration, pick several critical success factors and show how the organization manages them. For example, trace the leadership focus on performance.
- Identify performance-related data that are collected to indicate progress against goals (Item 4.1).
- Show how performance data are used to set work priorities (Item 4.3).
- Show how performance effectiveness is considered in the planning process (Item 2.1) and how work at all levels is aligned to increase performance (Item 2.2).
- Demonstrate the impact of human resource management (Item 5.1) and training (Item 5.2) on performance.
- Show how design, development, production, delivery, and support processes (Items 6.1 and 6.2) are enhanced to improve results.
- Report the results of improved performance (7.2, 7.3, 7.4, and 7.5).
- Determine how improved performance affects customer satisfaction levels (Item 7.1).
- Show how customer concerns (Item 3.1 and 3.2) are used to drive the selection of key measures (4.1) and impact design and delivery processes (6.1).

Note that the application is limited to 50 pages, **not including the 5 page Business Overview.** This may not be sufficient to describe in great detail the approach, deployment, results, and systematic integration of all of your critical success factors, goals, or key processes. Thus, you must pick the most important few, indicate them as such, then thoroughly describe the threads and linkages throughout the application.

Award Criteria Goals and Values

Award Criteria Purposes

The Malcolm Baldrige Criteria for Performance Excellence are the basis for making awards and for giving feedback to applicants. In addition, the criteria have three other important roles in strengthening competitiveness of U.S. organizations.
- To help improve performance practices and capabilities
- To facilitate communication and sharing of best practices information among and within organizations of all types
- To serve as a working tool for understanding and managing performance, planning, training, and assessment

Award Criteria Goals

The criteria are designed to help organizations enhance their competitiveness through focus on dual, results-oriented goals.
- Delivery of ever-improving value to customers, resulting in marketplace success
- Improvement of overall organization performance and capabilities

Core Values and Concepts

The award criteria are built on a set of core values and concepts. These values and concepts are the foundation for integrating key business requirements within a results-oriented framework. Core values and concepts are summarized on pages 5 through 8. The text of the Baldrige Performance Excellence Criteria core values and concepts follows:

Customer-Driven Quality

Quality is judged by customers. Thus, quality must take into account all product and service features and characteristics that contribute value to customers and lead to customer satisfaction, preference, and retention.

Value and satisfaction may be influenced by many factors throughout the customer's overall purchase, ownership, and service experiences. These factors include the organization's relationship with customers that helps build trust, confidence, and loyalty.

Customer-driven quality addresses not only the product and service characteristics that meet basic customer requirements. It also includes those features and characteristics that differentiate them from competing offerings. Such differentiation may be based upon new or modified offerings, combinations of product and service offerings, customization of offerings, rapid response, or special relationships.

Customer-driven quality is thus a strategic concept. It is directed toward customer retention, market share gain, and growth. It demands constant sensitivity to changing and emerging customer and market requirements, and the factors that drive customer satisfaction and retention.

It also demands awareness of developments in technology and of competitors' offerings, and rapid and flexible response to customer and market requirements.

Customer-driven quality means much more than defect and error reduction, merely meeting specifications, or reducing complaints. Nevertheless, defect and error reduction and elimination of causes of dissatisfaction contribute to the customers' view of quality and are thus also important parts of customer-driven quality. In addition, the organization's success in recovering from defects and mistakes ("making things right for the customer") is crucial to building customer relationships and to customer retention.

Leadership

An organization's senior leaders need to set directions and create a customer orientation, clear and visible values, and high expectations. The values, directions, and expectations need to address all stakeholders. The leaders need to ensure the creation of strategies, systems, and methods for achieving excellence and building knowledge and capabilities. The strategies and values should help guide all activities and decisions of the organization. The senior leaders need to commit to the development of the entire work force and should encourage participation, learning, innovation, and creativity by all employees. Through their personal roles in planning, communications, review of organization performance, and employee recognition, the senior leaders serve as role models, reinforcing the values and expectations and building leadership and initiative throughout the organization.

Continuous Improvement and Learning

Achieving the highest levels of performance requires a well-executed approach to continuous improvement and learning. The term "continuous improvement" refers to both incremental and "breakthrough" improvement. The term "learning" refers to adaptation to change, leading to new goals and/or approaches. Improvement and learning need to be "embedded" in the way the organization operates. Embedded means improvement and learning: (1) are a regular part of daily work; (2) seek to eliminate problems at their source; and (3) are driven by opportunities to do better, as well as by problems that must be corrected. Sources of improvement and learning include: employee ideas; R&D; customer input; best practice sharing; and benchmarking.

Improvement and learning include: (1) enhancing value to customers through new and improved products and services; (2) developing new business opportunities; (3) reducing errors, defects, waste, and related costs; (4) responsiveness and cycle time performance; (5) productivity and effectiveness in the use of all resources; and (6) the organization's performance in fulfilling its public responsibilities and service as a good citizen. Thus, improvement and learning are directed not only toward better products and services but also toward being more responsive, adaptive, and efficient—giving the organization additional marketplace and performance advantages.

Valuing Employees
An organization's success depends increasingly on the knowledge, skills, and motivation of its work force. Employee success depends increasingly on having opportunities to learn and to practice new skills. Organizations need to invest in the development of the work force through education, training, and opportunities for continuing growth. Opportunities might include classroom and on-the-job training, job rotation, and pay for demonstrated knowledge and skills. On-the-job training offers a cost effective way to train and to better link training to work processes. Work force education and training programs may need to utilize advanced technologies, such as computer-based learning and satellite broadcasts. Increasingly, training, development, and work units need to be tailored to a diverse work force and to more flexible, high-performance work practices.

Major challenges in the area of valuing employees include: (1) integration of human resource practices—selection, performance, recognition, training, and career advancement; and (2) alignment of human resource management with strategic change processes. Addressing these challenges requires use of employee-related data on knowledge, skills, satisfaction, motivation, safety, and well-being. Such data need to be tied to indicators of organization or unit performance, such as customer satisfaction, customer retention, and productivity. Through this approach, human resource contributions may be better integrated and aligned with business directions.

Fast Response
Success in competitive markets demands ever-shorter cycles for new or improved product and service introduction. Also, faster and more flexible response to customers is now a more critical requirement. Major improvement in response time often requires simplification of work units and processes. To accomplish this, the time performance of work processes should be among the key process measures. There are other important benefits derived from this time focus: time improvements often drive simultaneous improvements in organization, quality, and productivity. Hence it is beneficial to integrate response time, quality, and productivity objectives.

Design Quality and Prevention

Organizations need to emphasize design quality—problem and waste prevention achieved through building quality into products and services and efficiency into production and delivery processes. Costs of preventing problems at the design stage are lower than costs of correcting problems that occur "downstream." Design quality includes the creation of fault-tolerant (robust) or failure-resistant processes and products.

A major success factor in competition is the design-to-introduction ("product generation") cycle time. To meet the demands of rapidly changing markets, organizations need to carry out stage-to-stage integration ("concurrent engineering") of activities from basic research to commercialization. Increasingly, design quality also depends upon the ability to use information from diverse sources and data bases, that combine customer preference, competitive offerings, price, marketplace changes, and external research findings. Emphasis should also be placed on capturing learning from other design projects.

From the point of view of public responsibility, the design stage is critical. In manufacturing, design decisions determine process wastes and the content of municipal and industrial wastes. The growing environmental demands mean that design strategies need to anticipate environmental factors.

Consistent with the theme of design quality and prevention, improvement needs to emphasize interventions "upstream"—at early stages in processes. This approach yields the maximum cost and other benefits of improvements and corrections. Such upstream intervention also needs to take into account the organization's suppliers.

Long-Range View of the Future

Pursuit of market leadership requires a strong future orientation and a willingness to make long-term commitments to key stakeholders—customers, employees, suppliers, stockholders, the public, and the community. Planning needs to anticipate many changes, such as customers' expectations, new business opportunities, technological developments, new customer and market segments, evolving regulatory requirements, community/societal expectations, and thrusts by competitors. Plans, strategies, and resource allocations need to reflect these commitments and changes. Major parts of the long-term commitment are developing employees and suppliers and fulfilling public responsibilities.

Management by Fact

Modern businesses depend upon measurement and analysis of performance. Measurements must derive from the organization's strategy and provide critical data and information about key processes, outputs, and results. Data and information needed for performance measurement and improvement are of many types, including: customer, product and service performance, operations, market, competitive comparisons, supplier, employee-related, and cost and financial. Analysis refers to extracting larger meaning from data and information to support evaluation and decision making at all levels within the organization. Analysis entails using data to determine trends, projections, and cause and effect—that might not be evident without analysis. Data and analysis support a variety of organization purposes, such as planning, reviewing organization performance, improving operations, and comparing organization performance with competitors' or with "best practices" benchmarks.

A major consideration in performance improvement involves the creation and use of performance measures or indicators. Performance measures or indicators are measurable characteristics of products, services, processes, and operations the organization uses to track and improve performance. *The measures or indicators should be selected to best represent the factors that lead to improved customer, operational, and financial performance. The measures or indicators tied to customer and organization performance requirements should provide a clear basis for aligning all activities with the organization's goals and action plans.* Through the analysis of data from the tracking processes, the measures or indicators themselves may be evaluated and changed to better support such goals.

Partnership Development
Organizations need to build internal and external partnerships to better accomplish their overall goals.

Internal partnerships might include labor-management cooperation, such as agreements with unions. Agreements might entail employee development, cross-training, or new work organizations, such as high performance work teams. Internal partnerships might also involve creating network relationships among organization units to improve flexibility, responsiveness, and knowledge sharing.

External partnerships might be with customers, suppliers, and education organizations for a variety of purposes, including education and training. An increasingly important kind of external partnership is the strategic partnership or alliance. Such partnerships might offer a company entry into new markets or a basis for new products or services. A partnership might also permit the blending of a company's core competencies or leadership capabilities with complementary strengths and capabilities of partners, thereby enhancing overall capability, including speed and flexibility. Internal and external partnerships should develop longer-term objectives, thereby creating a basis for mutual investments. Partners should address the key requirements for success, means of regular communication, approaches to evaluating progress, and means for adapting to changing conditions. In some cases, joint education and training could offer a cost-effective means to develop employees and carry out other beneficial activities to ensure success.

Company Responsibility and Citizenship

An organization's leadership needs to stress its responsibilities to the public and needs to practice good citizenship. This responsibility refers to basic expectations of the organization—business ethics and protection of public health, safety, and the environment. Health, safety, and the environment include the organization's operations as well as the life cycles of its products and services. Organizations need to emphasize resource conservation and waste reduction at their source. Organization planning should anticipate adverse impacts from facilities, production, distribution, transportation, use, and disposal of products. Plans should seek to prevent problems, to provide a forthright organization response if problems occur, and to make available information and support needed to maintain public awareness, safety, and confidence. Organizations should not only meet all local, state, and federal laws and regulatory requirements. They should treat these and related requirements as areas for continuous improvement "beyond mere compliance." This requires use of appropriate measures in managing performance.

Practicing good citizenship refers to leadership and support—within limits of an organization's resources—of publicly important purposes, including areas of public responsibility. Such purposes might include education improvement, improving health care in the community, environmental excellence, resource conservation, community services, improving industry and business practices, and sharing of nonproprietary information. Organization leadership as a corporate citizen also entails influencing other organizations, private and public, to partner for these purposes. For example, individual organizations could lead efforts to help define the obligations of their industry to its communities.

Results Focus

An organization's performance measurements need to focus on key results. Results should be guided by and balanced by the interests of all stakeholders—customers, employees, stockholders, suppliers and partners, the public, and the community. To meet the sometimes conflicting and changing aims that balance implies, organization strategy needs to explicitly include all stakeholder requirements. This will help to ensure that actions and plans meet differing stakeholder needs and avoid adverse impact on any stakeholders. The use of a balanced composite of performance measures offers an effective means to communicate short- and longer-term priorities, to monitor actual performance, and to marshal support for improving results.

Changes from the 1997 Award Criteria

The Baldrige performance excellence criteria continue to evolve toward comprehensive coverage of strategy-driven performance, addressing the needs of all stakeholders—customers, employees, stockholders, suppliers and partners, and the public. The criteria for 1998 place a greater emphasis on the alignment of organization strategy, customer and market knowledge, a high performance work force, key organization processes, and business results through a focus on aligning action plans throughout the organization. Increased focus has been given to all aspects of organizational and employee learning. *Although the number of Areas to Address has been reduced by one (from 30 to 29), the requirements contained in the criteria are essentially the same.*

The most significant changes made in the criteria and the criteria booklet are summarized as follows:

- The number of Areas to Address was reduced from 30 to 29 with a reduction of two Areas in Category 2 and the addition of one Area in Category 3. No requirements from 1997 were eliminated or reduced as a result of these changes.
- The number of item notes was increased from 45 to 51 to provide additional guidance, particularly in Categories 2 and 6. *Notes are intended to clarify the requirements of the criteria. They do not impose additional requirements that applicant organizations must meet.*

All users of the 1998 Criteria for Performance Excellence are cautioned to note that some changes in wording have been made in all items, many item notes, and the scoring guidelines.

Noteworthy Changes by Category

Leadership

Item 1.1 was reformatted to clarify: (1) the organization's overall leadership system and (2) the senior leaders' roles in providing effective leadership. Senior leaders and the leadership systems are expected to promote innovation. In addition, a requirement was added that asks leaders to use employee feedback in the evaluation of the effectiveness of the leadership system.

Strategic Planning	Areas 2.1b, 2.2a, and 2.2b from 1997 were combined into one Area, 2.2a, for 1998. This change is intended to strengthen the systems perspective of performance planning, plan implementation, and plan deployment. It also seeks to eliminate some of the confusion over the requirements of 2.1b and 2.2a in 1997. Both seemed to be asking for similar information about the deployment of strategy through the creation and deployment of action plans. In 1998, the planning process is covered in Item 2.1 and the process of converting the plan to action and deploying action plans throughout the organization is covered in Item 2.2.

Customer and Market Focus

In Item 3.1, organizations are now required to determine customer expectations, requirements, and preferences based on information from *former* customers as well as current and potential customers and markets.

A new Area 3.2c, Relationship Building, was added. Sub Area, 3.2c(1) focuses attention on the need for proactive organization processes to build longer-term relationships with customers. In addition, Sub Area 3.2c(2) adds an explicit requirement to evaluate, improve, and keep current the processes used by the organization to provide access, determine customer satisfaction, and build relationships.

Information and Analysis

Selection, use, and analysis of organization and comparative information and data were more closely aligned with key organization processes, *action plans,* and opportunities for improvement. This change is intended to strengthen the systems perspective of performance management. This enhanced focus on action plans applies to all three items in the Information and Analysis category.

In Item 4.3, Analysis and Review of Company Performance, organizations must show how human resource performance is considered as a part of operational performance analyses [4.3a(2)]. In Area 4.3b(1) a new requirement has been added asking for a description of the performance measures regularly reviewed by senior leaders to assess progress relative to action plans, goals, and changing business needs.

Human Resource Focus

The category title was changed to reflect a focus on employees as internal customers, and to prevent the misperception that Category 5 focuses on the organization's human resource department.

Area 5.1b was expanded to ensure that compensation and recognition approaches were designed to apply to all individuals and groups (including managers and *supervisors*), and reinforce overall organizational objectives for *customer satisfaction*, performance *improvement*, and *employee and organization* learning.

Area 5.2a(1) was changed to ensure education and training support action plans and address organization needs including *leadership development of employees*.

Area 5.3b was strengthened to place an emphasis on how the organization encourages and motivates employees to *develop and utilize their full potential*.

Process Management

Area 6.1a(4) was added to make it clear that design processes should be evaluated and improved to achieve better performance including improvements to products and services, transfer of learning to other parts of the organization, and reduced cycle time. Expected improvements in cycle time is also required in Area 6.1b(3).

Item 6.3 was expanded to enhance the focus on preferred and key supplier relationships and partnering processes including examining how the organization helps its key suppliers meet performance requirements [6.3a(1)], how their performance is evaluated, and what incentives are provided by the organization to increase supplier performance [6.3a(2)].

Business Results

Item 7.1 was expanded to encourage reporting results by customer groups and market segments, as appropriate rather than aggregating these results into one set of numbers.

Human Resource Results point values, Item 7.3, were increased by 15 points to reflect the importance of employees as internal customers. Points in Items 7.1, 7.2, and 7.5 were each reduced by 5 points, keeping the Category 7 total the same at 450 points.

Self-Assessments of Organizations and Management Systems

Baldrige-based self-assessments of organizational performance and management systems take several forms, ranging from rigorous and time intensive to simple and somewhat superficial. This section discusses the various approaches to organizational self-assessment and the pros and cons of each. Curt Reimann, the first director of the Malcolm Baldrige National Quality Award Office and the closing speaker for the 10th Quest for Excellence Conference, spoke of the need to streamline assessments to get a good sense of strengths, areas for improvement, and the vital few areas to focus leadership and drive organizational change. Three distinct types of self-assessment will be examined: the written narrative, the Likert scale survey, and the behaviorally anchored survey.

Full-Length Written Narrative

The Baldrige application development process is the most time-consuming yet detailed organizational self-assessment process. To apply for the Baldrige award, applicants must prepare a 50 page written narrative to address the requirements of the performance excellence criteria. In the written self-assessment, the applicant is expected to describe the processes and programs it has in place to drive performance excellence. The Baldrige application process serves as the vehicle for self-assessment in most state- and company-level quality awards. The process has not changed since the national quality award program was created in 1987 (except for reducing the maximum page limit from 85 to 50 pages).

Over the years, three methods have been used to prepare the full-length, comprehensive written narrative self-assessment.

- The most widely used technique involves gathering a team of people to prepare the application. The team members are usually assigned one of the seven categories and asked to develop a narrative to address the criteria requirements of that category. The category writing teams are frequently subdivided to prepare responses item by item. After the initial draft is complete, an oversight team consolidates the narrative and tries to ensure processes are linked and integrated throughout. Finally, top leaders review and scrub the written narrative to put the best spin on the systems, processes, and results reported.
- Another technique is similar to that described above. However, instead of subdividing the writing team according to the Baldrige categories, the team remains together to write the entire application. In this way,

the application may be more coherent and the linkages between business processes are easier to understand. This approach also helps to ensure consistency and integrity of the review processes. However, with fewer people involved, the natural "blind spots" of the team may prevent a full and accurate analysis of the management system. Finally, as with the method described above, top leaders review and scrub the written narrative.

- The third method of preparing the written narrative is the least common and involves one person writing for several days to produce the application. Considering the immense amount of knowledge and work involved, it is easy to understand why the third method is used so rarely.

With all three methods, external experts are usually involved. All four 1997 Baldrige Award recipients reported they hired consultants to help them finalize their application by sharpening its focus and clarifying linkages. In fact, the author of this book worked with two of them to do this.

Pros:

- All of the Baldrige-winning organizations in 1997 reported, during the 10th Quest for Excellence Conference, that the discipline of producing a full-length written self-assessment (Baldrige application) helped them learn about their organization and identify areas for improvement before the site visit team arrived. The written narrative self-assessment process clearly helped focus leaders on their organization's strengths and areas for improvement—provided that a complete and honest assessment was made.
- All of the winners plan to use the self-assessment processes repeatedly to guide future improvement strategies.
- The written narrative self-assessment also provides rich information to help examiners conduct a site visit (the purpose of which is to verify and clarify the information contained in the written self-assessment).

Cons:

- The written narrative self-assessment is extremely time- and labor-intensive. Organizations that use this approach for Baldrige or state applications or for internal organizational review, report that it requires between 1,000 and 4,000 person-hours of effort—sometimes more but rarely less. People working on the self-assessment are diverted from other tasks during this period.
- Because the application is usually closely scrutinized and carefully scrubbed, and because of page limits it may not fully and accurately describe the actual management processes and systems of the organization.

Decisions based on misleading or incomplete information may take the organization down the wrong path.

- Although the written self-assessment provides information to help guide a site visit, examiners cannot determine the depth of deployment because only a few points of view are represented in the narrative.
- Finally, and perhaps most importantly, the discipline and knowledge required to write a meaningful narrative self-assessment is usually far greater than that possessed within the vast majority of organizations. Remember, even the four current (1997) Baldrige winners hired expert consultants to help them prepare and refine their written narrative.

Short Written Narrative

Two of the most significant obstacles to writing a useful full-length written narrative self-assessment are poor knowledge of the performance excellence criteria and the time required to produce a meaningful assessment. If people do not understand the criteria, it takes significantly longer to prepare a written self-assessment. In fact, the amount of time required to write an application/assessment is inversely related to the knowledge of the criteria possessed by the writers. The difficulty associated with writing a full-length narrative has prevented many organizations from participating in state, local, or company award programs.

To encourage more organizations to begin the performance improvement journey, many state award programs developed progressively higher levels of recognition, ranging from "commitment" at the low-end, through "demonstrated progress," to "achieving excellence" of the top of the range. However, even with progressive levels of recognition, the obstacle of preparing a 50 page written narrative prevented many from engaging in the process. To help resolve this problem, several state programs permit applicants who seek recognition at the lower levels to submit a 7 to 20 page "short" written narrative self-assessment. (Most states still require applicants for the top level award to complete a full-length written self-assessment.) The short form ranges from requiring a one page description per category to one page per item (hence the 7 to 20 page range in length).

Pros:
- It clearly takes less time to prepare the short form.
- Because of the reduced effort required to complete the self-assessment, states find more organizations are beginning the process of assessing and improving their performance.

Cons:
- The short form provides significantly less information to help examiners prepare for the site visit. Although it does take less time to

prepare than the full-length version, the short form still requires several hundred hours of team preparation.

- The short form is usually closely scrutinized and carefully scrubbed just as its full-length cousin. This reduces accuracy and value to both the organization and examiners.
- The knowledge required to write even a short narrative prevents organizations in the beginning stages from preparing an accurate and meaningful assessment
- Finally, there is not enough information presented in the short form to understand the extent of deployment of the systems and processes covered by the criteria.

The Likert Scale Survey

Just about everyone is familiar with a Likert scale survey. These surveys typically ask respondents to rate, on scale 1 to 5, the extent to which they strongly disagree or strongly agree with a comment.

The following is an example of a simple Likert scale survey item:

Senior leaders effectively communicate values and customer focus.				
1	2	3	4	5
Strongly Disagree				**Strongly Agree**

A variation on the simple Likert scale survey item has been developed in an attempt to improve consistency among respondents. Brief descriptors have been added at each level as shown below in the Descriptive Likert scale survey item:

1	2	3	4	5
No	Few	Some	Many	Most...
Senior leaders effectively communicate values and customer focus.				

Pros:
- The Likert scale survey is quick and easy to administer. People from all functions and levels within the organization can provide input.

Cons:
- Both the simple and the descriptive Likert scale survey items are subject to wide ranges of interpretation. One person's rating of "2" and another person's rating of "4" may actually describe the same systems or behaviors. This problem of scoring reliability raises questions about the accuracy and usefulness of both the simple and the descriptive survey techniques for conducting organizational self-assessments. After all, a

quick and easy survey that produces inaccurate data still has low value. That is the main reason why states have not adopted the Likert scale survey as a tool for conducting the self-assessments, even for organizations in the beginning stages of the quality journey.

The Behaviorally Anchored Survey

A behaviorally anchored survey contains elements of a written narrative and a survey approach to conducting a self-assessment. The method is simple. Instead of brief descriptors such as "strongly agree/strongly disagree" or "no-few-some-many-most," a more complete behavioral description is presented for each level of the survey scale. Respondents simply identify the behavioral description that most closely fits the activities in the organization. A sample is presented below:

	1	2	3	4	5
Reviewing Organization Performance [1.1a(2.3)]					
1F	The organization's leaders and managers evaluate the organization's performance against goals. This review process is not systematic and results in minimal or random adjustments.	Some of the organization's leaders and managers review the organization's performance against goals but do not systematically use the review process to reinforce directions or drive improvements.	Many of the organization's leaders and managers review the organization's performance against goals and systematically use the review process to reinforce directions and drive improvements.	Most of the organization's leaders and managers review the organization's performance against goals and systematically use the review process to reinforce directions and drive improvements.	All of the organization's leaders and managers review the organization's performance against goals and systematically use the review process to reinforce directions and drive improvements.
How is this done? (Approach) How widely is process used? (Deployment)					
How should it be improved?					

	1	2	3	4	5	
Leadership System Performance and Accountability [1.1a(2-4)]						Level
1G	*Performance* evaluations of a few leaders consider quality objectives but they have not been incorporated into the formal review *process.*	*Performance* evaluations of the *leadership system* look at the effectiveness of how some leaders review organization performance but do not consider employee feedback in the evaluation.	*Performance* evaluations of the *leadership system* look at the effectiveness of how most leaders review organization performance and include employee feedback (such as upward evaluation or 360 degree feedback).	*Performance* evaluations of the *leadership system* look at the effectiveness of how all leaders review organization performance and include employee feedback (such as upward evaluation or 360 degree feedback). A few improvements in leader performance have been made as a result.	*Performance* evaluations of the *leadership system* look at the effectiveness of how all leaders review organization performance and include employee feedback (such as upward evaluation or 360 degree feedback). Continuous improvements in leader performance are being made as a result.	

How is this done? (Approach) How widely is process used? (Deployment)

Suggested action steps to improve, if needed:

Since the behavioral descriptions in the survey combine the requirements of the criteria with the standards from the scoring guidelines, it is possible to produce accurate Baldrige-based scores for items and categories for the entire organization and for any subgroup or division. The following tables provide sample scores (item scores are also available) for the entire organization and for three job classifications:

1998 Baldrige Criteria	Total Points	% of Total Pts	Points Scored
Leadership	110	34.5	38
Strategic Planning	80	25	20
Customer & Market Focus	80	26.3	21
Information & Analysis	80	23.8	19
Human Resource Focus	100	34	34
Process Management	100	29	29
Business Results	450	22.7	102.2
Totals	1000	26.3	263

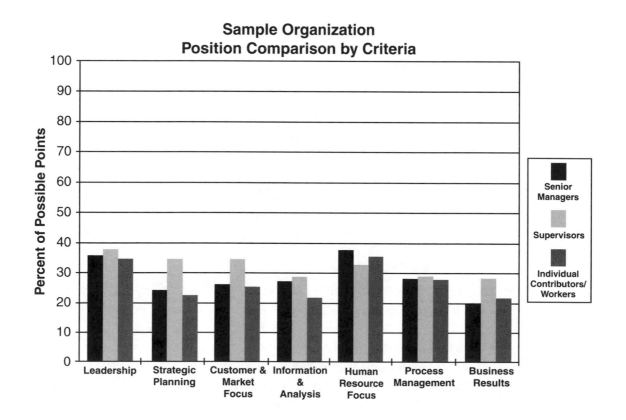

Sample Organization
Position Comparison by Criteria

The behaviorally anchored survey also asks respondents to identify one or two critical areas for improvement for each category. The analyses of these data are reported in the form of Pareto charts for each of the seven categories of the Malcolm Baldrige Criteria for Performance Excellence. These reference each of the seven sections of the Organization Assessment Workbook to help focus attention on the vital few. A sample follows:

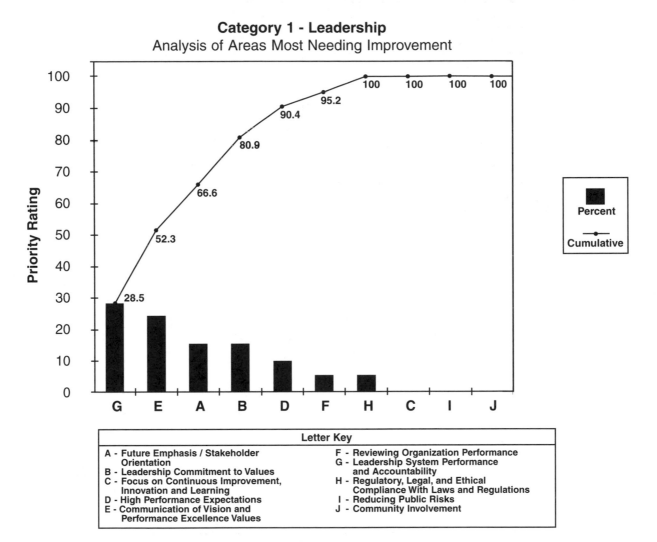

Category 1 - Leadership
Analysis of Areas Most Needing Improvement

Each chart displays the letters that correspond to the key requirements from each of the seven categories along the horizontal axis. Percentages are charted along the vertical axis. The percentage of employee votes for each area are represented as bars on the graph. The chart is arranged with the largest bar on the left of the graph, indicating the area selected by employees that they feel is most in need of improvement. The line charted above the bars represents the cumulative percentages of each bar, beginning on the left of the chart.

For example, in the Category 1 - Leadership chart, the letters G, E, and A relate to survey themes and represent an opportunity to address 67% of the key issues in 30% of the areas (3 of 10) for the identified category (Leadership). In this example, the letters C, I, and J did not receive any votes. No respondent believed these areas were high priorities for improvement.

Finally, a complete report of the comments and explanations of the respondents can be prepared and used by examiners and organization leaders for improvement planning.

Pros:

- Properly written behavioral anchors increase the consistency of rating. That is, one respondent's rating of "2" is likely to be the same as another respondent's rating of "2".
- Although completing a behaviorally anchored survey requires more reading than a Likert scale survey, the amount of time and cost required to complete it is still significantly less than the time and cost required to prepare even a short written narrative.
- Because it is easy and simple to use, the behaviorally anchored survey does not impose a barrier to participation as does the written narrative. States and companies who use surveys with properly written behavioral anchors find the accuracy of the assessment to be as good and in many cases better than that achieved by the narrative self-assessment, and significantly better than Likert scale assessments. By obtaining input from a cross-section of functions and levels throughout the organization, a performance profile can be developed which not only identifies strengths and areas for improvement, but deployment gaps as well—something the written narrative assessments do not effectively provide.
- For organizations doing business throughout the world, the behaviorally anchored survey—translated into the native language of respondents—permits far greater input than the written narrative.
- Finally, accurate survey data, based on behavioral anchors, can be used to compare or benchmark organizations within and among industries, and can also support longitudinal performance studies.

Cons:

- Organizations with highly developed performance management systems that seek to apply for top state or national recognition may prefer to practice developing the full-length narrative self-assessment because it is usually required.

- Examiners who are comfortable with the Baldrige application review process, which requires 25 or more hours to conduct an individual review of a full-length narrative self-assessment, may initially find it disconcerting to develop comments and plan a site visit based on data gathered from a survey. Additional training of examiners is required to develop skills at using survey data to prepare feedback and plan site visits.

NOTE: The preceding sample of a behaviorally anchored self-assessment survey is administered by the National Council for Performance Excellence, Winooski, Vermont, and used with their permission. Readers may contact them by calling Wendy Staeger at (802) 655-1922 or by writing to NCPE, One Main Street, Winooski, VT 05404. The Vermont Council for Quality and its board of examiners use this survey technique to assess Vermont schools, government agencies, and businesses. The behaviorally anchored survey has completely replaced the written narrative self-assessment as the application for the Vermont Quality Award as well as the Aruba National Quality Award. Examiners successfully use survey data to plan and conduct site visits. At the same time, organization leaders use survey data for improvement planning. The Florida Sterling Award is also using the behaviorally anchored survey approach for organizations in the early stages of developing performance excellence systems.

In conclusion:
- The full-length written narrative self-assessment is costly. It provides useful information both to examiners and the organizations completing it. The process of completing the written self-assessment can help more advanced organizations to focus and work together as a team.
- The usefulness of the short form written self-assessment is marginal especially for beginning organizations; little useful information is provided to examiners and managers/employees of the organization. However, because it takes less time to complete, one of the barriers to participation is lowered.
- Concerns over the accuracy and inter-rater reliability of the simple and descriptive Likert scales make their use in conducting effective organizational assessments of management systems questionable.
- The behaviorally anchored survey combines the benefits of survey speed with the accuracy and completeness of a well-developed written narrative self-assessment. In addition, the behaviorally anchored survey can identify gaps in deployment unlike the written narrative self-assessment.

A complete copy of the self-assessment survey can be obtained from the National Council for Performance Excellence, One Main Street, Winooski, Vermont 05404.

The Site Visit

Introduction

Many people and organizations have asked about how to prepare for site visits. This section is intended to help answer those questions and prepare the organization for an on-site examination. It includes rules of the game for examiners and what they are taught to look for. As we all know, the best preparation for this type of examination is to see things through the eyes of the trained examiner.

Before an organization can be recommended to receive the Malcolm Baldrige National Quality Award, it must receive a visit from a team of business assessment experts from the National Board of Examiners. Approximately 25 percent to 30 percent of organizations applying for the Baldrige Award in recent years have received these site visits.

The Baldrige Award site visit team usually includes two senior examiners—one of whom is designated as team leader—and four to seven other examiners. In addition, the team is accompanied by a representative of the National Quality Award Office and a representative of ASQ—which provides administrative services to the Baldrige Award office under contract.

The site visit team usually gathers at a hotel near the organization's headquarters on the Sunday morning immediately preceding the site visit. During the day, the team makes final preparations and plans for the visit.

Each team member is assigned lead responsibility for one or more categories of the award criteria. Each examiner is usually teamed with one other examiner during the site visit. These examiners usually conduct the visit in pairs to ensure the accurate recording of information.

Site visits usually begin on a Monday morning and last one week. By Wednesday or Thursday most site visit teams will have completed their on-site review. They retire to the nearby hotel to confer and write their reports. By the end of the week, the team must reach consensus on the findings and prepare a final report for the panel of judges.

**Purpose of
Site Visits**

Site visits help clarify uncertain points and verify self-assessment (that is, application) accuracy. During the site visit, examiners investigate areas most difficult to understand from self-assessments, such as the following:

- Deployment—how widely a process is used throughout the organization
- Integration—whether processes fit together to support performance excellence
- Process ownership—whether processes are broadly owned, simply directed, or micromanaged
- Employee involvement—whether the extent to which employees' participation in managing processes of all types is optimized
- Continuous improvement maturity—the number and extent of improvement cycles and resulting refinements in all areas of the organization and at all levels

**Characteristics
of Site Visit
Issues**

Examiners look at issues that are an essential component of scoring and role model determination. They have a responsibility to

- Clarify information that is missing or vague.
- Verify significant strengths identified from the self-assessment.
- Verify deployment of the practices described in the self-assessment.

Examiners will

- Concentrate on cross-cutting issues
- Examine data, reports, and documents
- Interview individuals and teams
- Receive presentations from the applicant organization

Examiners are not permitted to conduct their own focus groups or surveys with customers, suppliers, or dealers or disrupt work processes. Conducting focus groups or surveys would violate the confidentiality agreements as well as be statistically unsound.

Typically Important Site Visit Issues

- Role of senior management in leading and serving as a role model
- Degree of involvement and self-direction of employees below upper management
- Comprehensiveness and accessibility of the information system
- Utility and validity of available data
- Extent that facts and data are used in decision making
- Degree of emphasis on customer satisfaction
- Extent of systematic approaches to work processes
- Deployment and integration of quality principles and processes
- Training effectiveness
- Use of compensation, recognition, and rewards to promote key values
- Extent that strategic plans align organizational work
- Extent of the use of measurable goals at all levels in the organization
- Evidence of evaluation and improvement cycles in all work processes and in system effectiveness
- Improvement levels in cycle times and other operating processes
- Extent of integration of all processes—operational and support
- Level of maturity of improvement initiatives
- Extent of benchmarking effort
- Level of supplier involvement in performance improvement activities
- Uncovering improvements since the submission of the application (self-assessment) and receiving up-to-date business results

Discussions with the Applicant Prior to the Site Visit

Prior to the site visit, all communication between the applicant organization and its team must be routed through their respective single points of contact. Only the team leader may contact the applicant on behalf of the site visit team prior to the site visit. This helps ensure consistency of message and communication for both parties. It prevents confusion and misunderstandings.

The team leader should provide the applicant organization with basic information about the process. This includes schedules, arrival times, and equipment and meeting room needs.

Applicant organizations usually provide the following information prior to the site visit team's final site visit planning meeting at the hotel on the day before the site visit starts:
- List of key contacts
- Organization chart
- Facility layout
- Performance data requested by examiners

The team leader, on behalf of team members, will ask for supplementary documentation to be compiled (such as results data brought up to date) to avoid placing an undue burden on the organization at the time of the site visit.

The site visit team will select sites that allow them to examine key issues and check deployment in key areas. This information may or may not be discussed with the applicant prior to the site visit. Examiners will need access to all areas of the organization.

Conduct of Site Visit Team Members (Examiners)

Examiners are not allowed to discuss findings with anyone but team members. Examiners may not disclose the following to the applicant:
- Personal or team observations and findings
- Conclusions and decisions
- Observations about the applicant's performance systems, whether in a complimentary or critical way

Examiners may not discuss the following with anyone:
- Observations about other applicants
- Names of other award program applicants

Examiners may not accept trinkets, gifts, or gratuities of any kind (coffee, cookies, rolls, breakfast, and lunch are okay), so applicant organizations should not offer them. At the conclusion of the site visit, examiners are not permitted to leave with any of the applicant's materials including logo items or catalogs—not even items usually given to visitors.

Examiners will dress in appropriate business attire unless instructed otherwise by the applicant organization.

Opening Meeting

An opening meeting will be scheduled to introduce all parties and set the structure for the site visit. The meeting is usually attended by senior executives and the self-assessment writing team. The opening meeting usually is scheduled first on the initial day of the site visit (8:30 or 9:00 A.M.). The team leader generally starts the meeting, introduces the team, and opens the site visit. Overhead slides and formal presentations are usually unnecessary.

The applicant organization usually has one hour to present any information it believes important for the examiners to know. This includes time for a tour, if necessary.

Immediately after the meeting, examiners are likely to want to meet with senior leaders and those responsible for preparing sections of the self-assessment (application).

Conducting the Site Visit

The team will follow the site visit plan, subject to periodic adjustments according to its findings.

The site visit team will need a private room to conduct frequent caucuses. Applicant representatives are not present at these caucuses. The team will also conduct evening meetings at the hotel to review the findings of the day, reach consensus, write comments, and revise the site visit report.

If, during the course of the site visit, someone from the applicant organization believes the team or any of its members are missing the point, the designated point of contact should inform the team leader or the Baldrige Award office monitor. Also, someone who believes an examiner behaved inappropriately should inform the designated point of contact, who will inform the team leader or the award office monitor.

Employees should be instructed to mark every document given to examiners with the name and work location of the person providing the document. This will ensure that it is returned to the proper person. Records should be made of all material given to team members.

Organizational personnel may not ask examiners for opinions and advice. Examiners are not permitted to provide any information of this type during the site visit.

Team Leader's Site Visit Checklist

This checklist provides a summary of activities required of site visit team leaders.

Preparation

- Size of team and length of visit determined, with starting and ending date and time selected
- All team members receive copies of consensus report
- Team notified of starting/ending times and locations
- Background information on new team members (if any) received
- Category lead and team pairing assignments made for each team member
- New team members complete review of narrative
- Site visit notebooks prepared
- Individual team members prepare assigned site visit issues
- Subteam members exchange site visit issues for comments
- Revised site visit issues received from subteams
- Site visit issues reviewed by Team Leader and comments sent to subteams
- Team asked to revise site visit themes or issues (as appropriate)

Previsit Meeting

- Examiner introductions/reintroductions
- Site visit issues and themes reviewed and approaches outlined
- Sites selected to visit and logistics reviewed
- Specific requests for first day listed (interviews and data)
- Caucus plans established

Continued on next page

Team Leader's Site Visit Checklist—continued

Conduct of Visit

- Opening presentation conducted
- Followed site visit plan
- Revised plan as required
- Caucused frequently
- Maintained records of findings
- Maintained records of applicant documents received
- Answered all selected site issues; developed information on site visit themes
- Closing meeting conducted

Site Visit Report

- Team completed site visit issues
- Team completed item and category summary forms
- Completed overall summary form
- Team initiated report
- Report copied; original given to award office representative before leaving site
- Leader kept copy, narrative, and other notes (or a back-up person has material)
- Collected and returned all applicant material prior to leaving site
- Collected all narratives, materials, and notes; sent or given to award office

Feedback Report

- Senior examiner/feedback author collected feedback points during site visit
- Senior examiner/feedback author reviewed feedback points with team during site visit report writing session
- Reviewed feedback report completed before leaving site and sent to award office

Generic Site Visit Questions

Examiners must verify or clarify the information contained in an application, whether or not the examiners have determined a process to be a strength or an area for improvement. Examiners must verify the existence of strengths as well as clarify the nature of each significant area for improvement.

Before and during the site visit review process, examiners formulate a series of questions based on the Baldrige performance excellence criteria. Because the site visit must verify or clarify all significant aspects of the organization's performance management systems against the criteria, it is possible to identify a series of generic questions that examiners are likely to ask during the site visit process. These questions are presented in the following section to help prepare applicants for the assessment process.

Category 1—Leadership

1. Describe the process your organization used in developing your mission, vision, and values. To top leaders: Who was involved with that process? How do you create future opportunities for the organization?
   - Please share with us the mission, vision, and values of this organization.
   - What are your organization's top priorities?
   - How do you ensure that all your employees know this?
   - How do you know how effective you are at communicating your commitment to the vision and values?
2. How do you, as a leader, see your role in supporting processes to ensure performance excellence?
   - How do you role model the behaviors you want your managers and other employees to emulate (follow)?
   - What do the leaders personally do to lead this organization? What do you do that visibly displays to employees throughout the organization your personal involvement and commitment to the vision and values? How do you promote innovation?
   - What percentage of your time is spent on quality and performance review and improvement activities?
   - What is your process for evaluating the effectiveness of the leadership system? How do you include or use employee feedback in the evaluation?
   - Please identify specific examples where the senior leadership improved the leadership system as a result of these evaluations. How do managers evaluate and improve their own personal leadership effectiveness? How is employee feedback used here?

3. What are the criteria for promoting managers within the organization?
    - How are you making managers accountable for performance improvement, employee involvement, and customer satisfaction objectives?
    - What measures do you personally use to track progress toward achieving the organization's key business drivers? How often do you monitor these measures?
    - Can we see a copy of a manager's evaluation form?
    - How have you improved the process over the years of evaluating managers?
4. Share with us what you feel are the most important requirements of your key customers.
    - (Pick one of the requirements.) Which department is responsible for delivering this?
    - Please show us evidence of continuous improvement within that department.
5. What is the process used to monitor the performance of your organization? How does it relate to the organization's strategic business plan?
    - Do measurable goals exist?
    - How were the goals established?
    - How are they monitored? How often?
    - How are they key to your stakeholders primary needs and expectations?
    - What are the key success factors (or key result areas, critical success factors, key business drivers) for your organization, and how do you use them to drive performance excellence?
6. As a corporate citizen, what is your process for contributing to and improving the environment and society?
    - What do you do to anticipate public concerns over the possible impact of your organization? What are some examples? How do you measure progress?
    - What are some ways your organization ensures that employees act in an ethical manner in all business transactions? How is this monitored to ensure compliance?
    - Do you have any plans or processes for systematic evaluation and improvement in place?

Category 2—Strategic Planning

1. When was the last time the strategic plan was updated? How recent is it? Can we review a copy?
2. How did you develop this plan? What factors did you consider in the development of your strategic plan?
    - How does your strategic plan address supplier capabilities?

- What role do your stakeholders play in the development of the strategic plan?
- How do you identify resources needed to prepare for new opportunities and requirements?
- Are the objectives for your organization derived from this plan? If not, from where do they come?

3. How do you plan for development, education and training needs of the organization? What are the organization's human resource plans (long/short term)?
   - Summarize the organization's plans related to work design, innovation, rapid response, compensation and recognition, employee development and training, health, safety, ergonomics, special services and employee satisfaction.
   - How do these plans optimize the use of human resources?
   - How do these plans align to the strategic plan?
   - What are examples of changes to the human resource plans based on inputs from the strategic planning in the following areas: recruitment, training, compensation, rewards, incentives, fringe benefits, programs?

4. How do you deploy these goals, objectives, and action plans throughout the organization to ensure that work is aligned and action is taken to achieve the plan?
   - How do you ensure that organizational, work unit, and individual goals and plans are aligned?
   - How do you ensure that supplier and partner goals are aligned with your strategic plan?

5. What is (summarize) your process for evaluation and improvement of the strategic planning and plan deployment process, including the human resource planning process?
   - What are examples of improvements made as a result of this evaluation process?

6. How has your performance relative to plan been tracked?

7. Who do you consider to be your top competitors, and how does your planned performance compare to theirs?
   - How do you determine who your top competitors are?

8. What are your specific goals and objectives? Please provide a copy of your long-range performance projections. How did you go about establishing these projections? How do these projections compare with your competitors' projections for the same time period?

Category 3—Customer and Market Focus

1. How do you know what your former, current and potential customers expect of you? How does your organization determine short- and long-term customer requirements?
   - How do you differentiate key requirements from less important requirements?
   - How do you anticipate requirements and prepare to meet them?
   - How do you evaluate and improve processes for determining customer requirements?
2. How do you provide easy access for your customers to obtain information and assistance or complain? What do you expect to learn from customer complaints?
   - What is your process of handling customer complaints? Do you monitor or track complaint data? What do you do with the information?
   - What percent of complaints are resolved at first contact? Describe the training you provide to customer-contact employees.
   - Describe your process for follow-up with customers. What do you do with feedback from customers regarding products and services? What triggers action?
   - What are the customer contact requirements or service standards? How were they determined? How do you know if standards are being met?
   - How do you evaluate and improve the customer relationship process?
   - What are some improvements you've made to the way you determine customer requirements? How did you decide they were important to make, and when were they made?
3. How often do senior managers talk to customers?
   - What do they do with this information?
4. What are your key measures for customer satisfaction and dissatisfaction? How do these measures provide information on likely future market behavior (loyalty, repurchase, referrals)?
   - How do you measure customer satisfaction and dissatisfaction? Do you measure satisfaction/dissatisfaction for all key customer groups/segments? What are your customer groups or segments? How do you determine them? How do you differentiate them in regard to products and services you offer? What process do you use to ensure the objectivity and validity of customer satisfaction data?
   - What do you do with the information?
   - How do you disseminate satisfaction/dissatisfaction information to your employees? What action do they take as a result?
   - How do you know appropriate action is taken?

- How do you go about improving the way you determine customer satisfaction? Please provide some examples of how you have improved it over the past several years? When were the requirements made?

5. What processes do you use to build loyalty, positive referral, and lasting relationships with customers?
    - How do you differentiate these process according to customer group?

6. How do you evaluate the effectiveness of processes for customer satisfaction determination and relationship enhancement? What requirements have resulted from this evaluation?

Category 4—Information and Analysis

1. What are the major performance indicators critical to running your organization?

2. How do you determine whether the information you collect and use for decision making is complete, timely, reliable, accessible and accurate? What is the process you use to determine the relevance of the information to organizational goals and action plans?
    - What criteria do you use for data selection? How do you ensure that all data collected meet these criteria?
    - Describe how you obtain feedback from the users of the information. How is this feedback used to make improvements?

3. You have told us what your top priorities are. How do you benchmark against these? Please describe how needs and priorities for selecting comparisons and benchmarking are determined. Share an example of the process of prioritization.
    - How do you use competitive or comparative performance data generally?
    - How are the results of your benchmarking efforts used to set stretch targets?
    - How are the results of your benchmarking efforts used to improve work processes?
    - How do you evaluate and improve your benchmarking processes?
    - Show us samples of comparative studies. Picking some at random, determine: Why was the area selected? How were comparison data selected and obtained? How were data in the example used?

4. Please share with us an example of analysis of information important to your customers and your own organization's success.
    - How are data analyzed to determine relationships between customer information and financial performance; operational data and financial performance; or operational data and human resource

performance? What data and analyses do you use to understand your people, your customers, and your market?

- How widely are these analyses used for decision making? What actions are you taking to extend the analysis across all parts of the organization?
- What are you doing to improve the analysis process?

Category 5—Human Resource Focus

1. Do employees know and understand organization/work unit priorities? How do you determine this?
   - What do you do to ensure effective communication among employees and work units?
   - What do you do to encourage initiative and self-directed responsibility? What authority do employees have to direct their own actions and make business decisions?
   - (To employees.) What authority do you have to make decisions about resolving problems, changing process steps, and communications across departments?
   - What is the process you have used to evaluate and enhance opportunities for employees to take individual initiative and demonstrate self-directed responsibility in designing and managing their work? Show examples of actions taken and improvements made. When were they made?

2. How does the organization link recognition, reward, and compensation to customer satisfaction, performance improvement, and organization learning? Describe your approach to employee recognition and compensation. How does your approach reinforce achievement of goals and objectives?
   - (General question for employees.) Do you feel that your contributions to the organization are recognized? How have you been recognized for contributing to achieving organization action plans?
   - What specific reward and recognition programs are utilized?

3. What ongoing training is provided for your employees?
   - How is your training curriculum designed and delivered? How do you integrate employee, supervisor, and manager feedback into the design of your training program? What methods are used?
   - How does your training program impact operational performance goals? How do you know your training improves your business results? Show examples.
   - What training and education do you provide to ensure that you meet the needs of all categories of employees? What training does a new employee receive to obtain the knowledge and skills necessary for success and high performance including leadership development of employees?

- If applicable, how do employees in remote locations participate in training programs?
- What is your system for improving training? Please give us some examples of improvements made and when they were made?

4. What are your standards for employee health and safety? Does your approach to health and safety address the needs of all employee groups?
    - How do you determine that you have a safe and healthy work environment? How do you measure this?
    - How are you performing against those standards? How were they derived?
    - What are your procedures for systematic evaluation and improvement?

5. How do your senior leaders, managers, and supervisors encourage employees to develop and put to use their full potential?

6. How is employee satisfaction measured? What do you do with the information?
    - What are the key areas of concern? To employees, ask: What does the organization do to enhance your career development?
    - What special services, facilities, activities, and opportunities does your organization provide employees?
    - What do you do to improve employee satisfaction systematically? Please give us some examples of improvements.

Category 6—Process Management

1. What is your process for designing new or revised products and services to ensure that customer requirements are met?
    - How do suppliers, partners, customers, and support organizations participate in the design process?
    - How are design changes handled and methods used to ensure that all changes are included?
    - How do you test new products or services before they are introduced to be sure they perform as expected?
    - How do you evaluate and improve the process for designing new products/services, including reductions in cycle time? Please provide some examples of improvements and when they were made.

2. What are your key production and delivery processes and their requirements, including quality indicators and performance?
    - What steps have you taken to improve the effectiveness/efficiency of key work processes, including cycle time?
    - What are the processes by which you deliver these products and services to ensure that customer expectations will be met or exceeded?

- Once you determine that a process may not be meeting measurement goals or performing according to expectations, what process do you use to determine root cause and to bring about process improvement?

3. Please give an example of how a customer request or complaint resulted in an improvement of a current process or the establishment of a new process?

4. Please share with us your list of key support processes, requirements, and associated process measures, including in-process measures.
   - How is performance of support services systematically evaluated and refined? Please provide some examples.
   - What are the steps you have taken to design your key support processes? How do you determine the types of services needed? How do your support services interact with and add value to your operational processes?
   - How does your organization maintain the performance of key support services? Share some examples of processes used to determine root causes of support problems and how you prevent recurrence of problems.

5. Who are your most important (key) suppliers?
   - How do you determine critical characteristics your key suppliers must meet so that your needs are met? What are the key performance requirements? What type of assistance do you provide your suppliers to help them meet your requirements? Please explain how you measure your supplier's performance and provide feedback.
   - Show how you systematically help your key suppliers improve their performance and deliver better products and services to you at a lower cost. Please provide some examples.
   - What are your supplier management or procurement department goals and objectives? How do you measure and improve their performance? Please share with us some examples.

Category 7—Business Results

1. What are the customer satisfaction trends and performance levels at this time? [Links to Item 3.2]
   - Please show a breakout of data by customer group or segment.
   - How do these customer satisfaction trends and levels compare with those of your competitors or similar providers?

2. What are the current levels and trends showing financial or marketplace performance or economic value?
   - Please provide data on key financial measures such as return on investment (ROI), operating profits (or budget reductions as appropriate), or economic value added.

- Please provide data on market share or business growth, as appropriate. Identify new markets entered and the level of performance in those markets.
- How do these trends compare with those of your competitors or similar providers?

3. What are the current levels and trends showing the effectiveness of your human resource practices? [Links to Category 5]
   - Please provide data on key indicators such as safety/accident record, absenteeism, turnover by category and type of employee/manager, grievances, and related litigation.
   - How do these trends compare with those of your competitors or similar providers?

4. Please show us your supplier/partner performance data trends and current levels for each key indicator such as on-time delivery, error rate, and reducing costs. [Links to Item 6.3]
   - How does your performance on these key indicators compare to your competitors, other providers, or benchmarks?

5. How do you measure the quality of your products and services?
   - Please show us your performance data.
   - How do you know which factors are most important to your customers? [Links to Item 3.1]
   - How does your performance on these key indicators compare to your competitors, other providers, or benchmarks? [Links to Item 6.2]

6. How do you measure support service effectiveness and efficiency?
   - Please show us your performance data.
   - How do you know what the key performance indicators should be?
   - How does your performance on these key indicators compare to your competitors, other providers, or benchmarks?

7. How do you measure operating effectiveness and efficiency?
   - Please show us your performance data.
   - How do you know what the key performance indicators should be? [Links to Item 6.1 and 6.2]
   - How does your performance on these key indicators compare to your competitors, other providers, or benchmarks?

General Cross-Cutting Questions Examiners Are Likely To Ask Employees

- Who are your customers?

- What are the organization's mission, vision, and quality values? What are your goals?

- What is the strategic plan for the organization? What are the organization's goals, and what role do you play in helping to achieve the goals?

- What kind of training do you receive? Was it useful?

- How are you involved in the work and decision making of the organization?

- Is this a good place to work? Why (or why not)?

- What activities are recognized or rewarded?

Summary of Eligibility Categories and Restrictions

Basic Eligibility Public Law 100-107 establishes the three business eligibility categories of the Award: Manufacturing, Service, and Small Business. Any for-profit business or subunit headquartered in the United States or its territories, including U.S. subunits of foreign companies, may apply for the Award. Eligibility is intended to be as open as possible. For example, publicly or privately owned, domestic or foreign owned companies, joint ventures, corporations, sole proprietorships, and holding companies may apply. Not eligible are: local, state, and national government agencies; not-for-profit organizations; trade associations; and professional societies.

Award Eligibility Categories and Terms

Manufacturing Companies or subunits that produce and sell manufactured products or manufacturing processes, and producers of agricultural, mining, or construction products.

Service Companies or subunits that sell services.

Small Business Businesses with not more than 500 employees engaged in manufacturing and/or the provision of services.

Subunits

A subunit is a unit or division of a larger (parent) company. Subunits of companies in the manufacturing and service eligibility categories might be eligible. The subunit must have more than 500 employees, or have more than 25 percent of the employees of the parent, or, if owned by a holding company, have been independent prior to being acquired.

Further, the subunit must be largely self-sufficient so that it can be examined in all seven criteria categories and it must be a discrete business entity that is readily distinguishable from other parts of the parent organization. It cannot be primarily an internal supplier to other units in the parent organization or a business support function (sales, distribution, legal services, etc.).

NOTE: Subunits of "chain" organizations (where each unit performs a similar function or manufactures a similar product) are no longer categorically ineligible. Their eligibility is now determined by the same rules as other subunits.

Other Restrictions on Eligibility

Location

Although an applicant may have facilities outside the United States or its territories, in the event of a site visit, the applicant must ensure that the appropriate people and materials are available for examination in the United States to document the operational practices associated with all major business functions of the applicant. In the event that the applicant wins the Award, it must be able to share information on the seven criteria categories at the Quest for Excellence Conference and at its U.S. facilities.

Multiple-

Application Restrictions

A subunit and its parent may not both apply for Awards in the same year; and, only one subunit of a company may apply for an Award in the same year in the same business eligibility category.

Future Eligibility Restrictions

If an organization or a subunit that has more than 50 percent of the total employees of the parent receives an Award, the organization and all its subunits are ineligible to apply for another Award for a period of five years. If a subunit receives an Award, that subunit and all its subunits are ineligible to apply for another Award for a period of five years. After five years Award winners are eligible to reapply for the Award or to reapply "for feedback only."

Eligibility Determination

To ensure that Award recipients meet all reasonable requirements and expectations in representing the Award throughout the United States, potential applicants must have their eligibility approved prior to applying for the Award. Potential applicants for the 1998 Award are encouraged to submit their Eligibility Determination Form as early as possible after they are available, but not later than April 15, 1998.

Fees for the 1998 Award Cycle

Eligibility Determination Fees

The eligibility determination fee is $100 for all potential applicants. This fee is nonrefundable.

Application Fees

Manufacturing company category—$4500
Service company category—$4500
Small business category—$1500
Supplemental sections—$1500 (NOTE: Supplemental sections fees are charges to companies that want a business unit reviewed as part of the application process and that business unit falls under another eligibility sector. For example, assume that manufacturing is the core business of an automaker.

However, the automaker also operates a chain of service stations and a car rental system—both service sector companies. A supplemental section fee could be charged for this review.)

These fees cover all expenses associated with distribution and review of applications and development of feedback reports.

Site Visit

Review Fees

Site visit review fees will be set when the visits are scheduled. Fees depend upon the number of examiners assigned and the duration of the visit. Site visit review fees for applicants in the Small Business category will be charged at one-half of the rate charged for companies in the Manufacturing and Service categories.

Site visit fees cover all expenses and travel costs associated with site visit participation and development of site visit reports. These fees are paid only by those applicants reaching the site visit stage.

Feedback

All applicants receive a feedback report. The feedback report—a tool for continuous improvement—is
* An assessment written by a team of leading U.S. quality and performance experts
* An applicant-specific listing of strengths and areas for improvement based on the Baldrige Award criteria
* Used by organizations as part of their strategic planning processes to focus on their customers and to improve productivity

The report does not provide suggestions or ideas on how to improve.

The feedback report contains the Baldrige Award evaluation team's response to the written application. Length varies according to the detail presented in the written responses to the Baldrige Award criteria. The report includes the following components:
* Background
* Application review process
* Scoring
* Distribution of numerical scores for all applicants
* Overall scoring summary of applicant
* Criteria category scoring summary of applicant
* Details of the applicant's strengths and areas for improvement (feedback reports often contain more than 150 strengths and areas for improvement)

Strict confidentiality is observed at all times and in every aspect of application review and feedback.

A survey of 1993 and 1994 Baldrige Award applicants conducted by the National Quality Award Office showed that more than 90 percent of respondents used the feedback report in their strategic and business planning processes.

Information about current and past winners and their achievements was drawn from the award office web page. General information on the National Institute of Standards and Technology is available on the World Wide Web at http://www.nist.gov and on the Baldrige Award program at http://www.quality.nist.gov.

Malcolm Baldrige National Quality Award Winners

1997 Winners

- 3M Dental Products Division, St. Paul, Minnesota (Manufacturing)
- Merrill Lynch Credit Corporation, Jacksonville, Florida (Service)
- Solectron Corporation, Milpitas, California (Manufacturing)
- Xerox Business Services, Rochester, New York (Service)

3M Dental Products Division. Established in 1964 and competing in a $4 billion global market, 3M DPD manufactures and markets more than 1,300 dental products, including restorative materials, crown and bridge materials, dental adhesives, and infection control products. Over the last 10 years, the division has doubled global sales and market share, and, from 1991 to 1996, it doubled its rate of profit. Most of its 700 employees are based at its St. Paul, Minnesota, headquarters and at its manufacturing and distribution facility in Irvine, California.

Merrill Lynch Credit Corporation. A wholly owned subsidiary of Merrill Lynch & Company, MLCC offers real estate and securities-based consumer credit product—including home financing, personal credit, investment financing, and commercial real-estate financing. About 90 percent of its approximately 830 employees, known as partners, are located in MLCC's Jacksonville, Florida, headquarters. The company's field representatives, the Mortgage & Credit Specialists, are MLCC's primary sales force. These partners market all MLCC products through the nationwide network of over 14,000 Merrill Lynch Financial Consultants. MLCC will originate over $4 billion in loans for 1997 and has a servicing portfolio of nearly $10 billion.

Solectron Corporation. Solectron Corporation is a worldwide provider of electronics design, manufacturing, and support services to leading original equipment manufacturers. It offers a broad range of pre-manufacturing, manufacturing, and post-manufacturing solutions. It also oversees materials logistics, managing customers' supply chains to meet product schedules. Founded in 1977, Solectron is a publicly held company with revenues of $3.7 billion in fiscal year 1997. Dr. Ko Nishimura is chairman, president, and chief executive officer of the company, which employs more than 18,000 employees at 17 sites around the world. Headquartered in Milpitas, California, Solectron has doubled its market share since 1992 and achieved a compound annual sales growth rate of 47 percent. Careful execution of this commitment on a global scale also has earned the rapidly expanding company its second Baldrige Award.

Xerox Business Services. Xerox Business Services, a 14,000-person division of Xerox Corporation, is headquartered in Rochester, New York. It has grown into a $2 billion business in less than 5 years. Revenues and profits have increased by more than 30 percent annually, and XBS's share of the U.S. document-outsourcing market has grown to 40 percent, nearly 3 times the share of its nearest competitor. The company has 4,300 customers and is adding several hundred new accounts each year. XBS has five regional offices located in Des Plaines, Illinois; Rochester and New York, New York; Irving, Texas; and Denver, Colorado. The U.S. operation also includes 14 Document Technology Centers and 38 field operations offices.

1988–1997 Baldrige Award Winners and Contact Information

This section contains a list of Baldrige Award winners and key contact personnel from 1988 to 1997 as reported by NIST and the Office of Quality Programs. First the 1997 winners are presented, then the others in alphabetical order.

3M DENTAL PRODUCTS DIVISION—1997 (Manufacturing)
Jim Wilson, Quality Specialist
3M Center; Building 260-2A-11
St. Paul, MN 55144
Telephone: 1-800-634-2249/612-737-1164; Fax: 612-737-6049
www.mmm.com/dental/baldrige
Karyn Pierce, Communications Supervisor
3M Center, Building 275-2E-03
St. Paul, MN 55144
Telephone:1-800-634-2249/ 612-733-2138; Fax: 612-733-2481

MERRILL LYNCH CREDIT CORPORATION—1997 (Service)
Lee Lomax, Director of Quality & Business Improvement
4802 Deer Lake Drive East
Jacksonville, FL 32246
Telephone: 904-218-6242; Fax: 904-218-6124
Wendell Collins, Vice President-Publicity
800 Scudders Mill Road
Plainsboro, NJ 08536
Telephone: 609-282-3121; Fax: 609-282-1295

SOLECTRON CORPORATION—1997 (Manufacturing)
Denise Co, Quality Assurance Associate
847 Gilbraltar Drive
Milpitas, CA 95035
Telephone: 408-956-6963: Fax: 408-957-2645
www.solectron.com/about-quality.html
Michael Donner, Director, Corporate Communications
847 Gilbraltar Drive
Milpitas, CA 95035
Telephone: 408-956-6688; Fax: 408-956-7699

XEROX BUSINESS SERVICES—1997 (Service)
John Lawrence, Partner
70 Linden Oaks Parkway
Rochester, NY 14625
Telephone: 888-927-9467; Fax: 716-264-5701
www.xerox.com/xbs/baldrige/
David Galante, Manager, Worldwide Marketing Communications
70 Linden Oaks Parkway
Rochester, NY 14625
Telephone: 888-927-9467; Fax: 716-383-7813

ADAC LABORATORIES—1996 (Manufacturing)
Doug Keare, Vice President of Quality
540 Alder Drive
Milpitas, CA 95035
Telephone: 408-321-9100; Fax: 408-321-9686

AMES RUBBER CORPORATION—1993 (Small Business)
Charles A. Roberts, Vice President, Total Quality
23-47 Ames Boulevard
Hamburg, NJ 07419
Telephone: 201-209-3200; Fax: 201-827-8893

ARMSTRONG WORLD INDUSTRIES, INC. BUILDING PRODUCTS
OPERATIONS—1995 (Manufacturing)
Robert Knezovich, Manager, Quality Management
Armstrong Building Products Operations
2500 Columbia Avenue
Lancaster, PA 17604
Telephone: 717-396-2540; Fax: 717-396-6330

AT&T CONSUMER COMMUNICATIONS SERVICES—1994
(Service)
AT&T Quality Office
900 Route 202/206, Room 4A100Y
Bedminster, NJ 07921
Telephone: 800-473-5047; Fax: 908-234-5680
As of 1/1/97, AT&T Consumer Communications Services became part of the new Consumer & Small Business Division of AT&T.

AT&T NETWORK SYSTEMS GROUP TRANSMISSION SYSTEMS
BUSINESS UNIT—1992 (Manufacturing)
Louis E. Monteforte, Quality Director, North America
Lucent Technologies, Inc. (including what was formerly TSBU)
283 King George Road, Room C4D22
Warren, NJ 07059
Telephone: 908-559-3041; Fax: 908-559-2125

AT&T UNIVERSAL CARD SERVICES—1992 (Service)
Mitch Montagna, Senior Manager, External Communications
8787 Baypine Road
Jacksonville, FL 32256
Telephone: 904-954-8896; Fax: 904-954-8720

CADILLAC MOTOR CAR COMPANY—1990 (Manufacturing)
Joseph R. Bransky, Director; Quality and Reliability
General Motors Corporation
30007 Van Dyke Ave., Room 142-37
Warren, MI 48090
Telephone: 810-492-7704; Fax: 810-492-7943
Tom Klipstine, Communications Staff
NAO Headquarters, Building 1-8
30400 Mound Road
Warren, MI 48090
Telephone: 810-986-6132; Fax: 810-986-9253

CORNING INCORPORATED TELECOMMUNICATIONS PRODUCTS
DIVISION—1995 (Manufacturing)
Wendell P. Weeks, Division Vice President
Telecommunications Products Division
MP-RO-04
Corning, NY 14831
Telephone: 800-525-2524 x. 30; Fax: 607-754-7517
Catherine Shaw, Communications Coordinator
Telecommunications Products Division
MP-RO-04
Corning, NY 14831
Telephone: 607-974-7268; Fax: 607-974-4829

CUSTOM RESEARCH INC.—1996 (Small Business)
Beth Rounds, Senior Vice President
10301 Wayzata Boulevard
Minneapolis, MN 55426
Telephone: 612-542-0882; Fax: 612-542-0835

DANA COMMERCIAL CREDIT CORPORATION—1996 (Service)
Jim Beckham, Director of Quality
P.O. Box 906
Toledo, OH 43697-0906
Telephone: 419-322-7460; Fax: 419-322-7580
Tricia Akins, Director, Corporate Communications
201 W. Big Beaver Road, Suite 800
Troy, MI 48084
Telephone: 810-680-4341; Fax: 810-680-4262

EASTMAN CHEMICAL COMPANY—1993 (Manufacturing)
Katherine Watkins, Coordinator, Corporate Information Center
P.O. Box 511
Kingsport, TN 37662
Telephone: 1-800-695-4322 x. 1150 or x. 3078; Fax: 423-229-1525
Nancy Ledford, Advanced Corporate Relations Representative
Building 75
Kingsport, TN 37662
Telephone: 423-229-5264; Fax: 423-229-8280
www.eastman.com

FEDERAL EXPRESS CORPORATION—1990 (Service)
Quality Questions and Information
Glenn Pearson, Manager, Quality and Process Improvement
1980 Nonconnah Boulevard
Memphis, TN 38132
Telephone: 901-395-4562; Fax: 901-395-4511
Forum and Speaker Bureau
Myron Lowery, Manager, Corporate Relations
2005 Corporate Avenue
Memphis, TN 38132
Telephone: 901-395-3472; Fax: 901-395-4928
Reporters and Editors Only
Melanye Lunsford, Assoc. Specialist Media Relations
2005 Corporate Avenue
Memphis, TN 38132
Telephone: 901-395-4768; Fax: 901-395-4928

GLOBE METALLURGICAL, INC.—1988 (Small Business)
Norman Jennings, Quality Director
P.O. Box 157
Beverly, OH 45715
Telephone: 614-984-2361; Fax: 614-984-8635
Marcia Taylor, Public Relations
6450 Rockside Woods Boulevard South, Suite 390
Cleveland, OH 44131
Telephone: 216-328-0145; Fax: 216-328-1644

GRANITE ROCK COMPANY—1992 (Small Business)
Dave Franceschi, Quality Services Manager
P.O. Box 50001
Watsonville, CA 95077-5001
Telephone: 408-724-5611; Fax: 408-724-3484

GTE DIRECTORIES CORPORATION—1994 (Service)
Michael English, Director, Quality and Customer Services
GTE Place, West Airfield Drive
P.O. Box 619810
D/FW Airport, TX 75261-9810
Telephone: 972-453-7988; Fax: 972-453-6758
Heidi Jaquish, Executive & External Communications Manager
GTE Place, West Airfield Drive
P.O. Box 619810
D/FW Airport, TX 75261-9810
Telephone: 972-453-6473; Fax: 972-453-7231

IBM ROCHESTER—1990 (Manufacturing)
IBM Rochester, Center for Excellence
3605 Highway 52 North
Rochester, MN 55901-7829
Telephone: 507-253-9000; Fax: 507-253-4461

MARLOW INDUSTRIES—1991 (Small Business)
Ms. Tiki Miller, Baldrige Award Coordinator
10451 Vista Park Road
Dallas, TX 75238-1645
Fax: 214-341-5212

MILLIKEN & COMPANY—1989 (Manufacturing)
Craig Long, Director of Quality
P.O. Box 1926, M-186
Spartanburg, SC 29304
Telephone: 864-503-2003; Fax: 864-503-2505
Richard Dillard, Director of Public Affairs
P.O. Box 1926, M-285
Spartanburg, SC 29304
Telephone: 864-503-2546; Fax: 864-503-2100

MOTOROLA, INC.—1988 (Manufacturing)
Richard Buetow, Senior Vice President and Director of Quality
1303 East Algonquin Road
Schaumburg, IL 60196
Telephone: 847-576-5516; Fax: 847-538-2663
Margot Brown, Director, Media Relations, Corporate Communications
1303 East Algonquin Road, 7th Floor
Schaumburg, IL 60196
Telephone: 847-576-5304; Fax: 847-576-7653
www.mot.com

SOLECTRON CORPORATION—1991 and 1997 (Manufacturing)
Denise Co, Quality Assurance Associate
847 Gilbraltar Drive
Milpitas, CA 95035
Telephone: 408-956-6963: Fax: 408-957-2645
www.solectron.com/about-quality.html
Michael Donner, Director, Corporate Communications
847 Gilbraltar Drive
Milpitas, CA 95035
Telephone: 408-956-6688; Fax: 408-956-7699

TEXAS INSTRUMENTS INCORPORATED DEFENSE SYSTEMS &
ELECTRONICS GROUP—1992 (Manufacturing)
Karen Hollingsworth, Director of Total Quality
Texas Instruments Incorporated Systems Group
P.O. Box 405, Mail Station 3461
Lewisville, TX 75067
Telephone: 972-462-3222; Fax: 972-462-5155

THE RITZ-CARLTON HOTEL COMPANY—1992 (Service)
Patrick Mene, Vice President of Quality
3414 Peachtree Road., N.E., Suite 300
Atlanta, GA 30326
Telephone: 404-237-5500; Fax: 404-261-0119
Karon Cullen, Corporate Director of Public Relations
3414 Peachtree Road., N.E., Suite 300
Atlanta, GA 30326
Telephone: 404-237-5500; Fax: 404-365-9643

TRIDENT PRECISION MANUFACTURING INC.—1996 (Small Business)
Joe Conchelos, Vice President of Quality
734 Salt Road
Webster, NY 14580-9796
Telephone: 716-265-1009; Fax: 716-265-0126

WAINWRIGHT INDUSTRIES, INC.—1994 (Small Business)
Chuck Donaldson, Plant Manager
P.O. Box 640
St. Peters, MO 63376
Telephone: 314-278-5850; Fax: 314-278-8806
David A. Robbins, Vice President
P.O. Box 640
St. Peters, MO 63376
Telephone: 314-278-5850; Fax: 314-278-8806

WALLACE COMPANY—1990 (Small Business)
Assets of the Wallace Company have been acquired by Wilson Industries.

WESTINGHOUSE ELECTRIC CORP. COMMERCIAL NUCLEAR FUEL
DIVISION—1988 (Manufacturing)
Adrianne Tomasic
Westinghouse Science & Technology Ctr.
1310 Beulah Road.
Pittsburgh, PA 15235
Telephone: 412-256-2802; Fax: 412-256-1310

XEROX CORPORATION BUSINESS PRODUCTS & SYSTEMS—1989
(Manufacturing)
Maurina Boughton or Donna Bislow
Xerox Corporation
Xerox Square—18B
100 Clinton Avenue South
Rochester, NY 14644
Telephone: 716-423-6487; Fax: 716-423-6041
Samuel M. Malone, Jr., Director Quality Services
Xerox Square—18B
100 Clinton Avenue South
Rochester, NY 14644
Telephone: 716-423-9190; Fax: 716-423-6041
sam_malone@mc.xerox.com

ZYTEC CORPORATION—1991 (Manufacturing)
Karen Scheldroup, Baldrige Office
7575 Market Place Drive
Eden Prairie, MN 55344
Telephone: 612-941-1100 x. 104; Fax: 612-903-9688

Innovative State Quality Award Practices

The Baldrige evaluation process has served for many years as *the* way to conduct quality and performance excellence reviews. However, in the past few years, several state award programs—not encumbered by statutory restrictions—have created new processes to deliver products that respond to changing business needs and meet their customer requirements better.

The Feedback Report

The feedback report is the key deliverable of the award process. Customers of the process—the applicants—want the report quickly and want the report to be accurate and actionable.

One of the more innovative approaches has been taken by Minnesota and Florida and involves site visiting every applicant/participant. This ensures that the feedback report is more accurate for everyone because it is based on expert inspection rather than self-assessment narrative. In addition, scores are provided at the item level, not just at the category level, to help applicants pinpoint areas of concern.

Another innovative approach involves providing an immediate oral feedback report following the site visit. The oral feedback covers the key points at the category level.

The national quality award office has consistently ensured that feedback comments are nonprescriptive. This means that examiners may not offer suggestions about how to improve processes identified as needing improvement. However, most state-level applicants not only want immediate feedback, they also want some suggestions as to how to make some of the needed improvements.

The Florida Sterling Council provides applicants who are scoring in the lower ranges with a separate section of improvement suggestions on request. This helps these applicants focus on the vital few improvement practices that will help them on their quality journey. The Florida Sterling Council also trains examiners to become mentors who assist organizations in the early stages of quality and performance improvement systems development.

Broad Eligibility

Most states have expanded eligibility for their award process to all sectors of their economy—not just the business sector. These states recognized that other sectors impact heavily on the success of the private sector. Education, health care, and government can help, or significantly hurt, the state's economy and private sector business within the state. Accordingly, schools, government agencies at all levels, health care institutions, public utilities, and not-for-profit organizations have begun to benefit from quality assessments at the state level.

Although the national quality award office is interested in expanding eligibility to education and health care sectors, Congress has refused to permit the expansion. It is long overdue.

Progressive Recognition

Under the enabling legislation for the Malcolm Baldrige National Quality Improvement Act of 1987 (Public Law 100-107) the U.S. Department of Commerce, National Institute of Standards and Technology (then National Bureau of Standards) was authorized to provide up to two awards in only three categories: manufacturing, service, and small business. If three equally qualified applicants presented themselves in one year and all were role models of excellence, one had to be eliminated. The level of competition is intense, and many decide not to apply because they have determined themselves to not be "good enough."

This problem led to three innovations at the state level.

- First, many states, such as New York, Illinois, Minnesota, Florida, and others, decided that no artificial limit should be imposed on the number of awards that may be given in a year. All applicants determined by the panel of judges to be role models of performance excellence would be eligible to receive the quality award. The award moved from competition to qualification.

- Second, many states recognized that a primary purpose of the assessment and review process was to encourage development and improvement at all performance levels, not merely to recognize those organizations that made it to the top. Accordingly, several states such as Tennessee, Minnesota, Illinois, and New Mexico offer levels of awards to recognize and encourage progress.

- Third, states such as New York, Minnesota, and Florida, offer special recognition for exemplary practices of organizations that have not reached full role model status, but can offer excellent examples to others for some of their activities.

All of these innovations represent significant steps forward in our nationwide effort to restore global competitiveness in all sectors of our economy.

Glossary

Action Plans

Action plans (*key business drivers* in the 1996 criteria) refer to principal organization-level drivers, derived from short- and long-term strategic planning. In simplest terms, action plans are set to accomplish those things the organization must do well for its strategy to succeed. Action plan development represents the critical stage in planning when general strategies and goals are made specific so that effective organizationwide understanding and deployment are possible. Deployment of action plans requires analysis of overall resource needs and creation of aligned measures for all work units. Deployment might also require specialized training for some employees or recruitment of personnel.

An example of an action plan element for a supplier in a highly competitive industry might be to develop and maintain a price leadership position. Deployment should entail design of efficient processes, analysis of resource and asset use, and creation of related measures of resource and asset productivity, aligned for the organization as a whole. It might also involve use of a cost-accounting system that provides activity-level cost information to support day-to-day work. Unit and/or team training should include priority setting based on costs and benefits. Organization-level analysis and review should emphasize overall productivity growth. Ongoing competitive analysis and planning should remain sensitive to technological and other changes that might greatly reduce operating costs for the organization or its competitors.

Alignment

Alignment refers to consistency of processes, actions, information, and decisions among organization units in support of key organizationwide goals.

Effective alignment requires common understanding of purposes and goals and use of complementary measures and information to enable planning, tracking, analysis, and improvement at three levels: the organization level, the key process level, and the work unit level.

Asset Productivity

The productive use that is made of an organization's assets. An overall measure of asset productivity could be made by dividing the total sales/revenue/budget by total asset value. In addition, specific asset productivity can be determined by making similar calculations against a specific asset or set of assets, such as a specific plant, production line, or even the productivity of land assets (acreage).

Benchmarking

The part of an improvement process in which an organization compares its performance against that of other organizations, determines how those organizations achieved higher performance levels, and uses the information to improve its own performance. Although it is difficult to benchmark some processes directly in some businesses, many of the things one organization does are very similar to things that others do. For example, most organizations move information and tangible products, pay people, train them, appraise their performance, and more. A key to successful benchmarking is to identify the process elements of work and find others who are the best at that process.

Continuous Improvement

The ongoing improvement of products, programs, services, or processes by small increments or major breakthroughs.

Customer

An organization or person who receives or uses a product or service. The customer may be a member or part of another organization or the same organization, or an end user.

Cycle Time

Cycle time refers to time performance—the time required to fulfill commitments or to complete tasks.

Time measurements play a major role in the criteria because of the great importance of time performance to improving competitiveness. Cycle time is used in the criteria booklet to refer to all aspects of time performance. Other time-related terms in common use are setup time, lead time, changeover time, delivery time, and time to market.

Data

Numerical information used as a basis for reasoning, discussion, determining status, decision making, and analysis.

Effectiveness	The extent to which a work process produces intended results.
Efficiency	The effort or resources required to produce desired results. More efficient processes require fewer resources than do less efficient processes.
Employee Involvement	A practice within an organization whereby employees regularly participate in making decisions on how their work is done, including making suggestions for improvement, planning, goal setting, and monitoring performance.
High-Performance Work	*High-performance work,* a term used in the item descriptions and comments, refers to work approaches systematically pursuing ever-higher levels of overall performance, including quality and productivity.
	Approaches to high-performance work vary in form, function, and incentive systems. Effective approaches generally include cooperation between management and the work force, including work force bargaining units; cooperation among work units, often involving teams; self-directed responsibility (sometimes called empowerment); individual and organizational skill building and learning; flexibility in job design and work assignments; an organizational structure with minimum layering (flattened), where decision making is decentralized and decisions are made closest to the front line; and effective use of performance measures, including comparisons. Some high-performance work systems use monetary and nonmonetary incentives based on factors such as organization performance, team and/or individual contributions, and skill building. Also, some high-performance work approaches attempt to align the design of organizations, work, jobs, and incentives.
Indicator	When two or more measurements are required to provide a more complete picture of performance, the measurements are called *indicators*. For example, the number of complaints is an indicator of dissatisfaction, not an exclusive measure of it. Cycle time is a discrete measure of the time it takes to complete a process. However, it is only one indicator of process effectiveness. Other indicators may include measures of rework, waste, and defects.

Integrated	Refers to the interconnections between the processes of a management system. For example, to satisfy customers an organization must understand their needs, convert those needs into designs, produce the product or service required, deliver it, assess ongoing satisfaction, and adjust the processes accordingly. People need to be trained or hired to do the work, and data must be collected to monitor progress. Performing only a part of the required activities is disjointed and not integrated.
Inter-rater reliability	The degree to which multiple raters, observing the same phenomenon, will give it the same rating. If they do, it has high inter-rate reliability; if not, it has low inter-rate reliability.
Leadership System	*Leadership system* refers to how leadership is exercised throughout the organization—the bases for and the way that key decisions are made, communicated, and carried out at all levels. It is based on shared values, expectations, and purposes; communicated and reinforced via interactions among leaders and managers; reflected in the decisions the leaders make; and evident in the actions of the organization. It includes the formal and informal mechanisms for leadership development used to select leaders and managers, to develop their leadership skills, and to provide guidance and examples regarding behaviors and practices.
	An effective leadership system creates clear values respecting the requirements of organization stakeholders and sets high expectations for performance and performance improvement. It builds loyalties and teamwork based on the values and the pursuit of shared purposes. It encourages and supports initiative and risk-taking; focuses on simplicity of organization, purpose, and function; and avoids chains of command requiring long decision paths. An effective leadership system includes mechanisms for the leaders' self-examination and improvement.
Measures	*Measures* refer to numerical information that quantifies (measures) input, output, and performance dimensions of processes, products, services, and the overall organization.
Performance	*Performance* refers to output results information obtained from processes, products, and services that permits evaluation and comparison relative to goals, standards, past results, and to others. Performance might be expressed in nonfinancial and financial terms.

Operational performance refers to performance relative to effectiveness and efficiency measures and indicators. Examples include cycle time, productivity, and waste reduction. Operational performance might be measured at the work unit level, the key process level, and the organization level.

Product and service quality refers to operational performance relative to measures and indicators of product and service requirements, derived from customer preference information. Product and service quality measures should correlate with, and allow the organization to predict, customer satisfaction. Examples of product and service quality include reliability, on-time delivery, defect levels, and service response time. For example, consider a coffee shop that serves breakfast coffee. Product and service quality indicators and measures may include time to serve; time to process payment; freshness (time between brewing and serving); bitterness (acidity measured by pH level); hot (temperature); and strong (ratio of coffee to water and grind coarseness). Taken together, these measures can predict customer satisfaction.

Customer-related performance refers to performance relative to measures and indicators of customers' perceptions, reactions, and behaviors. Examples include customer retention, complaints, and customer survey results. Customer-related performance generally relates to the organization as a whole.

Financial and marketplace performance refers to performance using measures of cost and revenue, including asset utilization, asset growth, and market share. Financial measures are generally tracked throughout the organization.

Supplier and partner performance refers to performance relative to processes and requirements of Item 6.3. The performance of suppliers and partners usually includes factors such as cost reduction, on-time delivery, error or defect rates, and specialized measures important to the customer.

Human resource performance relates to the activities in Category 5. Human resource performance measures usually include absenteeism, employee satisfaction ratings, safety incidents, turnover rates, strikes, worker grievances, and compensation claims.

Prevention-Based

Seeking the root cause of a problem and preventing its recurrence rather than merely solving the problem and waiting for it to happen again (a reactive posture).

Process

Process refers to linked activities with the purpose of producing a product or service for a customer (user) within or outside the organization. Generally, processes involve combinations of people, machines, tools, techniques, and materials in a systematic series of steps or actions. In some situations, processes might require adherence to a specific sequence of steps, with documentation (sometimes formal) of procedures and requirements, including well-defined measurement and control steps.

In many service situations, particularly when customers are directly involved in the service, process is used in a more general way—to spell out what must be done, possibly including a preferred or expected sequence. If a sequence is critical, the service needs to include information for customers to help them understand and follow the sequence. Service processes involving customers also require guidance to the providers on handling contingencies related to customers' likely or possible actions or behaviors.

Some organizations do not recognize the importance of the services they provide. Consider the coffee shop again. If the focus is only on making the best coffee and the service is poor—making customers wait too long—the coffee shop will lose customers. Delivery service value must be considered as important to success as delivering product value.

In knowledge work such as strategic planning, research, and analysis, process does not necessarily imply formal sequences of steps. Rather, the process implies general under-standings regarding competent performance such as timing, options to be included, evaluation, and reporting. Sequences might arise as part of these understandings.

Productivity

Productivity refers to measures of efficiency of the use of resources. Although the term is often applied to single factors such as staffing (labor productivity), machines, materials, energy, and capital, the productivity concept applies as well to total resources used in producing outputs. Overall productivity—sometimes called *total factor productivity*—is determined by combining the productivities of the different resources used for an output. The combination usually requires taking a weighted average of the different single factor productivity measures, where the weights typically reflect costs of the resources. The use of an aggregate measure of overall productivity allows a determination of whether or not the net effect of overall changes in a process—possibly involving resource trade-offs—is beneficial.

Effective approaches to performance management require understanding and measuring single factor and overall productivity, particularly in complex cases with a variety of costs and potential benefits.

Refinement	The result of a systematic process to analyze performance or a system and improve it.
Root Cause	The original cause or reason for a condition. The root cause of a condition is that cause which, if eliminated, guarantees that the condition will not recur.
Service Standard (Customer Contact Requirements)	A set, measurable level of performance. For example, an objective of an organization might be "prompt customer service." A customer contact requirement or service standard would stipulate how prompt the service should be—"Equipment will be repaired within 24 hours," or "The phone will be answered by a person on or before the second ring."
System	A set of well-defined and well-designed processes for meeting the organization's quality and performance requirements.
Systematic Approach	A process that is repeatable and predictable, rather than anecdotal and episodic.
Values	The principles and beliefs that guide an organization and its people toward the accomplishment of its mission and vision.
Waste Reduction	Obtained from redesigning a product to require less material or from recycling waste to produce useful products.

Clarifying Confusing Terms

Comparative Information vs. Benchmarking

Comparative information includes benchmarking and competitive comparisons. *Benchmarking* refers to collecting information and data about processes and performance results that represent the best practices and performance for similar activities inside or outside the organization's business or industry. Competitive comparisons refer to collecting information and data on performance relative to direct competitors or similar providers.

For example, a personal computer manufacturer, ABC Micro, must store, retrieve, pack, and ship computers and replacement parts. ABC Micro is concerned about shipping response time, errors in shipping, and damage during shipping. To determine the level of performance of its competitors in these areas, and to set reasonable improvement goals, ABC Micro would gather competitive comparison data from similar providers (competitors). However, these performance levels may not reflect best practices for storage, retrieval, packing, and shipping.

Benchmarking would require ABC Micro to find organizations who carry out these processes better than anyone else and examine both their processes and performance levels—such as the catalog company L.L. Bean.

Benchmarking seeks best-practices information. Competitive comparisons look at competitors, whether or not they are the best.

Customer-Contact Employees

Customer-contact employees are any employees who are in direct contact with customers. They may be direct service providers or answer complaint calls. Whenever a customer makes contact with an organization, either in person or by phone or other electronic means, that customer forms an opinion about the organization and its employees. Employees who come in contact with customers are in a critical position to influence customers for the good of the organization, or to its detriment.

Customer Satisfaction vs. Customer Dissatisfaction

One is not the inverse of the other. The lack of complaints does not indicate satisfaction although the presence of complaints can be a partial indicator of dissatisfaction. Measures of customer dissatisfaction can include direct measures through surveys as well as complaints, product returns, and warranty claims.

Customer satisfaction and dissatisfaction are complex to assess. Customers are rarely "thoroughly" dissatisfied, although they may dislike a feature of a product or an aspect of service. There are usually degrees of satisfaction and dissatisfaction.

Data vs. Information

Information can be qualitative and quantitative. *Data* are information that lend themselves to quantification and statistical analysis. For example, an incoming inspection might produce a count of the number of units accepted, rejected, and total shipped. This count is considered *data*. These counts add to the base of *information* about supplier quality.

Education vs. Training

Training refers to learning about and acquiring job-specific skills and knowledge. *Education* refers to the general development of individuals. An organization might provide training in equipment maintenance for its workers, as well as support the education of workers through an associate degree program at a local community college.

Empowerment and Involvement

Empowerment generally refers to processes and procedures designed to provide individuals and teams the employee tools, skills, and authority to make decisions that affect their work—decisions traditionally reserved for managers and supervisors.

Empowerment as a concept has been misused in many organizations. For example, managers may pretend to extend decision authority under the guise of chartering teams and individuals to make recommendations about their work, while continuing to reserve decision-making authority to themselves.

This practice has given rise to another term—*involvement*—which describes the role of employees who are asked to become involved in decision making, without necessarily making decisions. Involvement is a practice that many agree is better than not involving them at all, but still does not serve to optimize their contribution to initiative, flexibility, and fast response.

Measures and Indicators

The award criteria do not make a distinction between measures and indicators. However, some users of these terms prefer the term indicator (1) when the measurement relates to performance, but is not a direct or exclusive measure of such performance—for example, the number of complaints is an indicator of dissatisfaction, but not a direct or exclusive measure of it; and (2) when the measurement is a predictor (leading indicator) of some more significant performance, for example, gain in customer satisfaction might be a leading indicator of market share gain.

Operational Performance and Predictors of Customer Satisfaction

Operational performance processes and predictors of customer satisfaction are related but not always the same. Operational performance measures can reflect issues that concern customers as well as those that do not. Operational performance measures are used by the organization to assess effectiveness and efficiency, as well as predict customer satisfaction.

In the example of the coffee shop, freshness is a key customer requirement. One predictor of customer satisfaction might be the length of time, in minutes, between brewing and serving. The standard might be 10 minutes or less to ensure satisfaction. Coffee more than 10 minutes old would be discarded.

A measure of operational effectiveness might be how many cups were discarded (waste) because the coffee was too old. The customer does not care if the coffee shop pours out stale coffee and, therefore, that measure is not a predictor of satisfaction. However, pouring out coffee does affect profitability and should be measured and minimized.

Ideally, an organization should be able to identify enough measures of product and service quality to predict customer satisfaction accurately and monitor operating effectiveness and efficiency.

Performance Requirements vs. Performance Measures

Performance requirements are an expression of customer requirements and expectations. Sometimes performance requirements are expressed as design requirements or engineering requirements. They are viewed as a basis for developing measures to enable the organization to determine, generally without asking the customer, whether the customer is likely to be satisfied.

Performance measures can also be used to assess efficiency, effectiveness, and productivity of a work process. Process performance measures might include cycle time, error rate, or throughput.

Support Services

Support services are those services that support the organization's product and service delivery core operating processes. Support services might include finance and accounting, management information services, software support, marketing, public relations, personnel administration (job posting, recruitment, payroll), facilities maintenance and management, research and development, secretarial support, and other administration services.

Of course, if an organization is in business to provide a traditional support service such as accounting, then accounting services provided to its external customers become its core work/operating process and are no longer considered a support service. Internal accounting services would continue to be considered a support service.

In the human resources area (Category 5), the criteria require organizations to manage their human resource assets to optimize performance. However, many human resources support services might also exist such as payroll, travel, position control, recruitment, and employee services. These processes must be designed, delivered, and refined systematically according to the requirements of Item 6.2.

A similar relationship exists in the supplier area. Item 6.3 requires an organization to strengthen supplier and partner performance. This may take place through several measures including training suppliers and/or building partnerships between operating units in the organization and suppliers.

However, the details of developing work specifications, requests for quotations, and other aspects of procurement process might be assigned to a procurement department. That department would be considered a support service that must design its own products and services to meet the requirements of its internal customer and would be received as a support structure (6.2).

Activity	Where covered or described
Filling a job vacancy	6.2
Designing training to meet the overall requirements of the human resource plan	5.2
Systematically improving supplier performance	6.3
Procuring needed supplies for the computer assembly line on time	6.2

Nature of Business: ABC Micro—Building and Selling Personal Computers

Teams and Natural Work Units

Natural work units reflect the people that normally work together because they are a part of a formal work unit. For example, on an assembly line, three or four people naturally work together to install a motor in a new car. Hotel employees who prepare food in the kitchen might constitute another natural work unit.

Teams may be formed of people within a natural work unit or may cross existing (natural) organization boundaries. To improve room service in a hotel, for example, some members of several natural work units such as the switchboard, kitchen workers, and waiters may form a special team. This team would not be considered a natural work team. It might be called a *cross-functional* work team because its members come from different functions within the organization.

Appendix: Comparing Baldrige with the European Quality Model

The European Quality Award criteria were derived from the Malcolm Baldrige Criteria for Performance Excellence. Although there are differences in structure, both criteria contain essentially the same requirements. The European model is organized into nine groupings called criteria, each with parts and areas to address. The Baldrige model is organized into seven groupings called categories each with items and areas to address. The Baldrige requirements tend to be more detailed and specific than a comparable European Quality Award criterion. Both models have a heavy emphasis on achieving performance results that are important to business success.

The European Quality Model, as does the Baldrige Model, tells us that "customer satisfaction", "people (employee) satisfaction" and 'impact on society" are achieved through "leadership" which drives the "policy and strategy," "people management," "resources," and "processes," leading to excellence in "business results." Each of the nine elements, therefore, is a criterion that can be used to assess the organization's progress along the path to excellence. The "results" indicate what the company has achieved and is achieving; the "enablers" indicate how those results are being achieved. The table below provides a top-level comparison of the EFQM Model requirements with those of the Baldrige criteria. To receive a copy of the European Quality Award Self-Assessment 1997 Guidelines for Companies or the Self-Assessment Guidelines for the Public Sector contact European Quality Award Foundation at www.efqm.org. The e-mail address is info@efqm.org.

Comparing the European Quality Award Model with the Baldrige Criteria

European Quality Award Requirements	1.1	1.2	2.1	2.2	3.1	3.2	4.1	4.2	4.3	5.1	5.2	5.3	6.1	6.2	6.3	7.1	7.2	7.3	7.4	7.5
Leadership: How the behavior and actions of the executive team and all other leaders inspire, support, and promote a culture of Total Quality Management. Leaders:																				
1a. visibly demonstrate their commitment to a culture of Total Quality Management	●																			
1b. support improvement and involvement by providing appropriate resources and assistance	●							●												
1c. are involved with customers, suppliers and other external organizations	●																			
1d. recognize and appreciate people's efforts and achievements	●									●										
Policy and Strategy: How the organization formulates, deploys, reviews its policy and strategy, and turns it into plans and actions. Policy and strategy are:																				
2a. based on information which is relevant and comprehensive			●			●		●												
2b. developed			●																	
2c. communicated and implemented	●			●																
2d. regularly updated and improved			●	●																
People Management: How the organization releases the full potential of its people. People:																				
3a. resources are planned and improved					●															
3b. capabilities are sustained and developed										●	●	●								
3c. agree on targets and continuously review performance	●		●							●		●						●		
3d. are involved, empowered, and recognized										●										
3e. and the organization have an effective dialogue	●									●										
3f. are cared for											●									
Resources: How the organization manages resources effectively and efficiently. How:																				
4a. financial resources are managed	●							●					●							
4b. information resources are managed				●										●						
4c. supplier relationships and materials arc managed				●										●	●				●	
4d. buildings, equipment, and other assets are managed				●									●	●						
4e. technology and intellectual property are managed				●									●	●						
Processes: How the organization identifies, manages, reviews, and improves its processes. Processes:																				
5a. key to the success of the business are identified	●		●			●		●					●							
5b. are systematically managed	●												●	●	●					
5c. are reviewed and targets are set for improvement				●				●					●	●	●					
5d. are improved using innovation and creativity										●			●	●						
5e. are changed and the benefits evaluated										●			●	●						
Customer Satisfaction: What the organization is achieving in relation to the satisfaction of its external customers.																				
6a. the customers' perception of the organization's products, services, and customer relationships				●	●	●		●									●			
6b. additional measurements relating to the satisfaction of the organization's customers				●	●	●	●	●									●			
People Satisfaction: What the organization is achieving in relation to the satisfaction of its people.																				
7a. the people's perception of the organization							●		●			●						●		
7b. additional measurements relating to people satisfaction				●			●		●			●								
Impact on Society: What the organization is achieving in satisfying the needs and the expectations of the local, national, and international community at large (as appropriate). This includes the perception of the organization's approach to quality of life, the environment, the preservation of global resources, and the organization's own internal measures of effectiveness. It will include its relations with authorities and bodies which affect and regulate its business.																				
8a. society's perception of the organization		●																		
8b. additional measurements of the organization's impact on society		●					●													●
Business Result: What the organization is achieving in relation to its planned business objectives and in satisfying the needs and expectations of everyone with a financial interest or stake in the organization.																				
9a. financial measurements of the organization's performance																		●		
9b. additional measurements of the organization's performance																				●

Additional correlations between the Baldrige and European Quality Award criteria might exist, depending on the interpretation of where results of some support areas are reported.

Index

Comments and Areas for Improvement:
Insights to Performance Excellence 1998

Please give us your comments, feedback, and suggestions for making this book more useful. We believe in the importance of continuous improvement and in meeting your needs. Your comments will help determine what improvements can be made in all ASQ Quality Press books.

Please share your opinion by circling the number below:

Ratings of the book	Needs Work		Satisfactory		Excellent	Comments
Structure, flow, and logic	1	2	3	4	5	
Content, ideas, and information	1	2	3	4	5	
Style, clarity, ease of reading	1	2	3	4	5	
Held my interest	1	2	3	4	5	
Met my overall expectations	1	2	3	4	5	

I read the book because:

The best part of the book was:

The least satisfactory part of the book was:

Other suggestions for improvement:

General comments:

Name/Address: (optional)

Thank you for your feedback. If you do not have access to a fax machine, please mail this form to:
ASQ Quality Press, 611 East Wisconsin Avenue, P.O. Box 3005, Milwaukee, WI 53201-3005   Phone: 414-272-8575